COMPROMISED

The Affordable Care Act and Politics of Defeat

BRENDAN W. WILLIAMS

Cover photo courtesy of White House Photo Office

ISBN: 1503319172
ISBN 13: 9781503319172
Library of Congress Control Number: 2014921065
CreateSpace Independent Publishing Platform
North Charleston, South Carolina

PRAISE FOR COMPROMISED

"AN INSIDER'S ACCOUNT of the historic passage of Obamacare. . . . Williams walks readers through the labyrinth of political compromises that ultimately diluted the original reformist spirit of the ACA and, in his view, rendered it a dubious achievement. His analysis is consistently rigorous, and it's particularly strong when it turns to complex issues such as state-run health insurance exchanges . . . . A fair, rigorous take on health reform in the United States." – *Kirkus Reviews*

"This book recounts many sordid examples of how politicians in both parties have sold out along the way to corporate stakeholders promoting expanded markets and profits for their shareholders over service to patients and families." – John Geyman, M.D., Professor Emeritus of Family Medicine, University of Washington School of Medicine, author of *Health Care Wars: How Market Ideology and Corporate Power Are Killing Americans*

CONTENTS

1

INTRODUCTION

It SEEMED SO promising.

After eight years of the Bush, Jr. Administration — a tenure culminating in an apocalyptic economic meltdown — the nation had elected a charismatic young Democratic senator as its president in 2008.

America turned decisively against the Republican Party. Barack Obama beat the former Vietnam prisoner of war John McCain, winning even "red states" like Indiana and North Carolina.

After an interminable recount in Minnesota resulted in comedian Al Franken, author of "Rush Limbaugh is a Big Fat Idiot," beating incumbent Republican Senator Norm Coleman, Democrats, with two independents caucusing with them, had a dominating 59-seat majority in the United States Senate. In April 2009 longtime Republican Senator Arlen Specter of Pennsylvania switched parties, giving Democrats 60 seats.

Mild-mannered Harry Reid of Nevada was the leader of a Senate Democratic majority big enough to withstand the Senate's self-imposed filibuster rule.

Meanwhile, the House of Representatives was even more firmly under the control of San Francisco's Nancy Pelosi, the first woman speaker, with Democrats holding a 257-178 advantage.

How could the stars align more perfectly for progressives?

Surely their moment had arrived. The Democratic mandate exceeded that enjoyed by President Bill Clinton upon his 1992 election. Democrats had not held so many Senate seats since 1979.

Where to begin? Hanging over everything was the rotten economy and jobless-ness that eventually peaked at 10 percent. Obviously the economy would have to be put back on track and the Wall Street banks that caused the economic collapse brought to heel. But addressing climate change and health care reform were also long-frustrated Democratic ideals.

By February 17, 2009 the American Recovery and Reinvestment Act of 2009 had been signed into law to jump start the economy with $787 billion in stimulus spending. Reasonable economists continue to debate as to whether this amount was enough given the severity of the economic crisis.

On May 15, 2009 the American Clean Energy and Security Act of 2009 was introduced by Congressman Henry Waxman of California, while the first major health care reform bill, America's Affordable Health Choices Act of 2009, was intro-duced by Congressman John Dingell of Michigan on July 14, 2009.

The first bill would die, after Obama and Reid sacrificed the House Democrats who had voted to address climate change in a 219-215 arm-twister – a futile vote featured in many of their 2010 defeats. The second bill, however, would be the gen-esis of the Patient Protection and Affordable Care Act (ACA) that eventually passed.

Health care reform was an ideal pursued since Franklin Roosevelt was president. The ACA represented the most substantive change to the American health care sys-tem since 1965, when President Lyndon Johnson signed Medicaid and Medicare into law in President Harry Truman's Missouri presidential library.

Yet the ACA would be as different from those programs, and the era of Democratic liberalism that inspired them, as could be imagined. It would also be a long distance from the ideal Obama touted when, as an obscure U.S. Senate candidate needing labor support, he addressed the Illinois AFL-CIO in June 2003: "I happen to be a proponent of a single-payer universal health care program."[1]

The ACA would, instead, resemble the Republican alternative to President Clinton's proposed Health Security Act in 1993, and even be less liberal than a pro-posal President Richard Nixon outlined in 1974. The story of how it got that way tells you everything you need to know about Washington, D.C.

No reasonable person could deny the U.S. health care system was broken.

The 2010 Census found that 82.6% of all Americans had some type of health insurance. Of those, 65.7% had private insurance. The rest were covered through public plans like Medicare and Medicaid. If family income was over twice the federal poverty level, odds of coverage were greater – 89.6% of this population had insur-ance, of which 82.9% was private.

Those 65-and-older have Medicare coverage.

Yet these numbers do not tell the whole story.

A Commonwealth Fund survey found 84 million Americans in 2012 – "nearly half of all working-age U.S. adults" – had either gone without health insurance for a period "or had out-of-pocket costs that were so high relative to their income they were considered underinsured."[2]

Nor are those on Medicare, Americans 65-and-older, immune from financial worry. Medicare generally does not cover long-term care. Although long-term care is a huge issue in an aging society, the only ACA provision addressing it – a defined benefit through a voluntary payroll deduction – was abandoned by the Obama Administration as impractical and repealed by Congress. Long-term care insurance is an unreliable, consumer-chiseling product if even available.

The United States health care system is spectacularly expensive and inefficient. Its results belie its costs. For example, the United States has trailed industrialized nations like Great Britain, France and Germany in preventable deaths.[3] It has the highest first-day infant mortality rate in the industrialized world – more than the 27 European Union countries combined.[4] It even trails Cuba in that regard.[5]

The forces of the status quo are powerful, however. President Dwight Eisenhower famously warned of a military-industrial complex. Yet money spent on health care lobbying of Congress from 1998 through 2012 was well over three times higher than that spent by defense interests.[6]

Call it the health care industrial complex. All of our health care system's financial incentives disfavor preventative care, having moved physicians away from general practice and into more remunerative specialty care. Health care costs – at $2.7 trillion annually, or almost one-fifth the nation's gross domestic product – threaten the U.S. economy.

Yet, despite the objective need for change, as 2014 approached, with its twin requirements of guaranteed issue of health insurance for consumers and guaranteed consumers for health insurers, the ACA was little understood by consumers; the object of active, or passive, noncompliance by most state governments; and at risk of collapse under the heavy weight of its own compromise-laden, outsourced magnificence.

I had a good vantage point to watch this unfold.

With my faith fading in politics, in 2007 I was one of the first three Democratic state legislators in Washington State to support a presidential candidate two years removed from being a state legislator himself. In 2008 our faith was vindicated when that longshot first-term U.S. senator, Barack Obama, won.

In November 2010, after three terms as a state representative, I had, out of disillusionment with legislative politics and some idealism about health care reform, become a deputy commissioner to Washington's elected insurance commissioner.

I went into this with my eyes wide open. Of the U.S. Senate vote in December 2009 to adopt what would become the ACA, I expressed concern, in a *Seattle Post-Intelligencer* column, about those "forced into the unloving embrace of a largely-unfettered insurance industry – with the government acting as industry leg-breaker and imposing fines if citizens do not pay the industry's inflated prices."[7]

Yet with the ACA, profoundly deferential to state regulation of insurance, the law of the land, there seemed to exist the unique opportunity to make it work for my state. I could not help but want to see the rest of the story. Generally what I saw wasn't pretty.

The 2010 election brought a backlash against the ACA nationwide that put conservative governors in power. Most insurance regulators are appointed by governors. Meanwhile, even those states moving ahead on the ACA were beset with delays in federal guidance, confusion about thousands of pages of federal regulations that were belatedly set forth, and their own state political complications in effectuating change.

Prior to the ACA, the last big change to health care was creation of the Medicare Part D prescription drug benefit, and Mike Leavitt, health and human services' secretary at that time for President George W. Bush, admitted later in the *New York Times* that "there were several times during the course of that implementation that the system nearly collapsed. We had lots of problems."[8]

The ACA is immeasurably more complex. Republicans in Congress succeeded in holding the Obama Administration to less money for ACA start-up than Republicans appropriated for Part D implementation. President Obama's health secretary was reduced to the compromising indignity of begging insurers for funding to promote the act.

Thus it was that, four years after the ACA became law, less than a third of states would operate their own ACA health insurance exchange marketplaces, and half were turning down free federal money for Medicaid expansion. Millions would still go uninsured. Because of the failure of so many states to expand Medicaid, as well as the ACA's discrimination against undocumented workers, 31 million uninsured were projected to still be "left behind" by 2025.

Whether the federal government, or states, operated new health insurance exchanges, state regulators are arbiters of health insurance rates. And most state insurance regulators lack the ability, or inclination, to challenge those rates. Where premiums were lower than expected, deductibles and other out-of-pocket costs had soared.

The one certainty for the future was that a mandate to buy, or provide, commercial insurance would exist. And that mandate existed only for individuals initially. The Obama Administration entirely exempted large corporations from a 2014 obligation to provide health insurance for employees. It also exempted them from enforcement of a provision prohibiting them from offering better coverage to top executives than their workers. For 2014, the Administration even allowed some insurers to ignore the ACA's out-of-pocket limits for the sick.

The ACA has not been subject to much focused progressive criticism, except as another example, in a long list, of moneyed influence over congressional policymaking. In part, it is because to criticize the ACA is to put oneself in the company of Tea Party cranks and obstreperous Republicans who refuse to even acknowledge the need to address health care problems in our country – and whose own critiques of the ACA can border on the lunatic.

Consider, for example, crazed Tea Party heroine Michelle Bachmann, a Minnesota congresswoman and failed 2012 presidential candidate, pumping up the volume in May 2013 comments on FOX News in the wake of a scandal involving the Internal Revenue Service investigating Tea Party groups:

> There's a huge national database that's being created right now. Your health care, my health care, all the Fox viewers' health care, their personal, intimate, most close-to-the-vest secrets will be in that database, and the IRS is in charge of that database? So the IRS will have the ability potentially . . . to deny health care, to deny access, to delay health care.[9]

Topping even herself, Bachmann coined the phrase "DeathCare" at the October 2013 Values Voters Summit.[10]

No matter the flaws of the ACA, one could fairly ask what the alternative was if criticism, or irrational conspiracy theories, were all Republicans had to offer. Yet that question ignores the fact that Democrats should measure themselves against their own ideals, not those of Republicans.

Although many labor unions – traditional Democratic allies – were expressing grave concerns about the ACA as early as late-2013, progressive criticism of the ACA fell outside media framing of an existential clash between Democrats and Republicans, with proxies for each side, not incidentally, expending vast resources on media advertising advancing their positions.

When, in October 2013, House Republicans closed the federal government in a budget battle over the ACA, it forced each side to double-down on its rhetoric. The ACA was either completely perfect or irredeemably awful.

Further curtailing criticism was the progressive impulse to be protective of a president who – however accommodating to Republicans – was the only hope in the face of the glowering antipathy of Senate Republican Leader Mitch McConnell of Kentucky and others. McConnell had flatly stated his objective was to see the president fail, and it was a sentiment common in Republican circles. Furthermore, this was a president subjected to vitriolic personal attacks that included the persistent assertion he was not even from this country – attacks at least somewhat related to the fact the president was African-American.

To question the ACA was to join such Republicans in diminishing Obama's signature policy accomplishment. Yet surely a progressive could acknowledge the ACA's shortcomings and not believe Obama was born in Kenya, nor regret he had beaten Republicans John McCain and Mitt Romney.

Academic criticism is muted by the fact that much of what passes for scholarship on the subject is either subsidized directly by health care interests or indirectly through foundations to which they contribute.

Yet the discomfiting fact is that to cheer for the ACA is to, at least incidentally, root for the unbridled excesses of the insurance and pharmaceutical industries. No greater giveaway of taxpayer resources in the name of a public good had occurred since the transcontinental railroads were beneficiaries during the Gilded Age. If the ACA is the best we can do, what is the future of the progressive movement and, indeed, our nation?

As former Montana Governor Brian Schweitzer, a single-payer advocate, told *MSNBC*: "I suppose I'm a Democrat and I ought to roll over like a fat dog and get scratched by the pharmaceutical and insurance companies because, gee, we have to apologize for so-called Obamacare."[11]

Progressives, inheritors of a movement based upon populism, also needed the humility to acknowledge it was at least possible the majority of Americans had some good reason to oppose the ACA. Doubts about it were widespread. Indeed, an April

2014 *Washington Post/ABC News* poll showed only 14% of liberals believed the ACA had lowered health care costs – a central claim of ACA proponents.[12]

Skepticism was not unforeseeable. In *The Price of Politics*, Bob Woodward recounts that Peter Orszag, the Obama Administration's first budget director, advised the Administration that "[y]ou can't hold this law out as perfect. It won't sell. People think it's a piece of crap."[13] In a 2014 *Washington Post* interview, Richard Kirsch, the head of Health Care for America Now, admitted "preemptive concessions to appease Republicans" put the ACA in a "much weaker position from a policy point of view and eventually from a political popularity point of view, as well."[14]

In implementing the ACA, the Obama Administration took the side, over consumers (including small businesses), of insurers at every turn. As Democrats sat mute, progressive aspects of the ACA, and there were not many, were largely eviscerated in the regulatory process. Health insurance is so complicated that one study showed a majority of those with insurance were not even "somewhat" confident they understood nine essential insurance terms – and fewer than one-quarter of the uninsured understood them. Less than one-third of the uninsured understood what "coinsurance" was.[15]

As health care consultant Jon Kingsdale, who ran the Massachusetts exchange that predated the ACA, was quoted saying in *Kaiser Health News:* "We took the most complex health care system on God's green earth, and made it 10 times more complex."[16]

In October 2013, upon enrollment beginning for the insurance in 2014, the ACA could hardly have had a rockier rollout. Millions received cancellation notices for plans in which they were enrolled prior to the ACA's passage – despite President Obama's frequent promises that those who liked their existing health plans could keep them. And malfunctioning plagued the federal government website that, in most states, acted as the only gateway through which insurance tax subsidies could be received. The Administration had outsourced even this essential portal's development to a health insurer's subsidiary.

Despite these formidable obstacles, the apparent enrollment of 6.7 million subsidy-receiving Americans in 2014 through health insurance exchanges suggested the question of whether there was a public appetite for health care coverage could no longer be debated. Yet, paradoxically, the ACA itself was as unpopular as ever. Democrats largely ran away from the ACA in the 2014 election, even as proxies for Democrats were forced to use the ACA as a motivating turnout tool. Some motivation: Polling showed only half of all *Democrats* stated ACA support would make them more likely to vote for a candidate; the same polling showed such ACA support would dissuade 8 out of 10 Republican voters.[17]

As October 2014 news of insurance cancellations sank his re-election campaign, for example, the campaign spokesperson for Democratic Senator Mark Udall of Colorado was reduced to stating, weakly, "There's nobody more upset about the bungled roll out of the health care law than Mark."[18] Voters could probably be forgiven for not feeling inspired.

One election-eve 2014 poll showed public approval of the Democratic Party had hit a 30-year-low, and only 35% of registered voters approved of the president's handling of ACA implementation.[19] The ACA had toppled a Democratic House majority in 2010, and a combination of Republican gerrymandering, and Democrats overloading safe districts with their own voters, made it likely Republicans would rule the House at least until 2022. In 2014 a lack of confidence in government, largely attributable to the ACA, brought down Senate Democrats. Republicans would hold their largest congressional majorities since 1929.

Even Democratic voters had not been fooled into thinking the ACA was a triumph. A telling sign came in May 2014 when Congresswoman Allyson Schwartz, using the claim of ACA co-authorship as her primary campaign issue, received less than 18% of the vote in Pennsylvania's Democratic gubernatorial primary. Greg Sargent, a *Washington Post* columnist, had heralded the one-time frontrunner for running "the most aggressively pro-Obamacare ad of the cycle."[20] Yet Pennsylvania liberals pointed out the "New Democrat" Schwartz was a reason why the ACA was so watered-down; one blog called her "an Obamacare frenemy."[21]

Following the 2014 election, with Democrats continuing to run away from what they had once characterized as their greatest accomplishment, Democratic Senator Charles Schumer of New York stated that "Democrats blew the opportunity the American people gave them. We took their mandate and put all of our focus on the wrong problem — health care reform."[22] Schumer's observations were all the more poignant given that he was the point person for Senate Democratic messaging, and was Reid's hand-picked successor as Democratic leader.

In an economy mired in an epic recession, policymakers had chosen to shore up the finances of insurance companies – not the insured. While ACA proponents trumpeted premium costs, out-of-pocket costs had soared. A deductible in 2014 might be the entire $6,350 out-of-pocket limit under the ACA; deductibles for the most common subsidized plans averaged $3,100.[23] Meanwhile a May 2014 report found that 49% of workers surveyed had less than $1,000 on hand for out-of-pocket medical expenses; 27% had less than $500.[24]

In a rare editorial criticism of the ACA, the *New York Times* admitted "low-income people who have enrolled in subsidized health plans may have trouble paying their cost-sharing" and suggested that "federal health officials need to review regularly whether health plan co-payments are actually affordable to those living on very modest incomes."[25]

When an October 2014 poll showed one-quarter of those with private insurance doubted they could pay for a major illness or injury, with over 45% complaining they were paying more under the ACA (only 29% reported paying less), the Obama Administration's indifferent response was that those avoiding care to save costs should simply understand their coverage better.[26] But how could they? For as 2015 enrollment opened, the *New York Times* reported the Administration "told insurance companies that it will delay requirements for them to disclose data on the number of people enrolled, the number of claims denied and the costs to consumers for specific services."[27]

Unquestionably, the act had proved to be a tremendous boon to the commercial insurance industry. From the time of the ACA's passage, the nation's largest health insurer, UnitedHealth Group, saw its stock rise 250% a share over a four-year period that ended with the March 31, 2014 close of open enrollment in the exchanges. Aetna shares soared 218% over that same period. One can compare those extraordinary gains to traditional blue-chip stocks like Coca-Cola (up 50%) or Microsoft (up 36%).

In a famous 1936 re-election speech, President Franklin D. Roosevelt rebuked moneyed interests that "had begun to think of the Government of the United States as a mere appendage to their own affairs. We know now that government by organized money is as dangerous as Government by organized mob."

Under the ACA, the federal government was now inextricably linked to, if not "a mere appendage" of, health insurers. Indeed, the revolving door between government and industry now spun so efficiently that when President Obama's Medicare director left to run the nation's health insurance lobby she was replaced by a former health insurance executive.

How did we get here?

2

THE COMPROMISER-IN-CHIEF

DURING THE 2008 presidential campaign, both Arizona Senator John McCain and Illinois Senator Barack Obama pledged to cover uninsured Americans and bar discrimination against preexisting conditions. Both supported re-importation of prescription drugs that are much cheaper in other countries, while Obama also spoke in favor of allowing Medicare to negotiate prices with drug manufacturers. Both paid homage to medical malpractice "reform."

To broaden health care coverage, McCain would have taxed employer-provided health care as income, with a tax credit to be used if employees dropped employer coverage to buy their own insurance. It was never exactly clear how this gambit could actually broaden coverage.

Obama favored a mandate for children to have insurance, and would otherwise have required employers to provide insurance or pay toward a new Medicare-like public option – which would also be available for individual enrollment with income-based subsidies.

Obama's campaign put out a manifesto entitled *The Blueprint for Change: Barack Obama's Plan for America*. Its section on health care was ambitious, and made big promises: "If you already have health insurance, the only thing that will change for you under this plan is the amount of money you will spend on premiums. That will be less." More specifically, it pledged: "Obama's plan will bring down the cost of health care and reduce a typical family's premiums by as much as $2,500 per year."

These cost-saving objectives would be driven at the national level, through creation of a new public option competing with private insurers: "The new public plan will be simple to enroll in and provide ready access to coverage." Separately, there would be "a National Health Insurance Exchange to help individuals who wish to purchase a private insurance plan. The Exchange will act as a watchdog group and help reform the private insurance market by creating rules and standards for participating insurance plans to ensure fairness and to make individual coverage more affordable and accessible."

In tackling health care reform, Obama would tread a path where his predecessors had failed.

Four previous presidents advocated universal health care.

In their conception of an economic security package, which would come to be referred to as Social Security, President Franklin Roosevelt and his labor secretary, Frances Perkins, had pushed in 1934 for legislation that would include health insurance for all. Opposing universal coverage, the reactionary American Medical Association (AMA), in misogynistic terms echoed in 1993, suggested Roosevelt was unduly influenced by his wife, Eleanor, at night and Perkins – the first woman cabinet secretary – during the day.

Perkins and Roosevelt abandoned their proposal. The insurance norm became relatively young and healthy workers insured by employers, which would assure AMA member prosperity and avoid the "socialized medicine" the AMA warned of. In signing the Social Security Act in 1935, Roosevelt admitted: "We can never insure one hundred percent of the population against one hundred percent of the hazards and vicissitudes of life[.]"[28]

But the dream would not die. Of Social Security, Roosevelt had stated: "This law . . . represents a cornerstone in a structure which is being built but is by no means complete." Perkins tried to get him to resurrect a universal health care proposal, but the policy window closed following Roosevelt's ill-fated "court packing" scheme in 1937. He would not obtain another major social policy legislative win in the run-up to American involvement in World War II.

Following Roosevelt's April 1945 death, his successor pursued the unaccomplished.

In a November 19, 1945 message to Congress, President Truman wrote, "Millions of our citizens do not now have a full measure of opportunity to achieve and enjoy good health. Millions do not now have protection or security against the economic effects of sickness. The time has arrived for action to help them attain that opportunity and that protection."[29]

This would be accomplished through expanding the existing Social Security system: "If instead of the costs of sickness being paid only by those who get sick, all the people – sick and well – were required to pay premiums into an insurance fund, the pool of funds thus created would enable all who do fall sick to be adequately served without overburdening anyone."

At that time, Truman reported, "Only about 3% or 4% of our population now have insurance providing comprehensive medical care."

Once again, the AMA sprang into action, screaming about socialized medicine and the specter of doctors as "slaves." The House refused to even hold hearings. Senator Robert Taft of Ohio, who walked out of a Senate hearing in protest, declared, "I consider it socialism. It is to my mind the most socialistic measure this Congress has ever had before it." The AMA assessed its members for what, at that time, was the biggest lobbying campaign in history. One AMA pamphlet asked: "Would socialized medicine lead to socialization of other phases of life? Lenin thought so. He declared socialized medicine is the keystone to the arch of the socialist state."[30]

Such reactionary obduracy persisted following Truman's surprise 1948 victory, and southern Democrats were as much an obstacle as Republicans.

No progress occurred until the 1965 enactment of Medicaid and Medicare under President Johnson, although both programs fell far short of universal health care ideals. Medicaid would serve the medically-indigent as a safety net while Medicare would be an entitlement for those 65-and-older.

With his resignation six months away, President Richard Nixon, in a February 6, 1974 message to Congress, cited "staggering bills" – such as the fact that "[t]he average cost of delivering a baby and providing postnatal care approaches $1,000" – in proposing a Comprehensive Health Insurance Plan under which "[n]o family would ever have annual out-of-pocket expenses for covered health services in excess of $1,500, and low-income families would face substantially smaller expenses."[31]

Nixon noted his "proposal would rely extensively on private insurers." There would be an employer mandate to provide insurance, where employers would pay 65 percent of the premium for the first three years, and 75 percent thereafter, with employees covering the balance. There would be no exclusion for pre-existing conditions.

Under Nixon's plan, "every American who participates in the program would receive a Health-card when the plan goes into effect in his State. This card, similar to a credit card, would be honored by hospitals, nursing homes, emergency rooms, doctors, and clinics across the country." Following care, "[b]ills for the services paid for with the Health-card would be sent to the insurance carrier who would reimburse the provider of the care for covered services, then bill the patient for his share, if any."

The enveloping cloud of Watergate made Nixon's plan a non-starter.

President Bill Clinton's 1993 health care reform plan, developed in heavy secrecy by then-First Lady Hillary Clinton as chair of a Task Force on National Health Care Reform, would also have created an employer mandate – requiring employers to provide coverage through health maintenance organizations. As Ira Magaziner, who worked with Hillary Clinton to spearhead reform efforts, stated in a March 1993 memo to both Hillary and President Clinton, "Health reform will never be politically simple, given the degree of change required and the political power of interests with a stake in the status quo."[32] That was an understatement.

Clinton's proposal was less federalized than those preceding it. According to *Health Security: The President's Report to the American People* – a 136-page book – the proposal allowed

> each state to tailor health reform to its unique needs and character-
> istics as long as it meets national guarantees and standards for qual-
> ity and access to care. Certain states, in fact, may choose to set up
> a single-payer system, where one agency collects and distributes all
> health care dollars for that state.

As President Clinton explained in a September 1993 speech to Congress:

> Under our plan, every American would receive a health care secu-
> rity card that will guarantee a comprehensive package of benefits
> over the course of an entire lifetime, roughly comparable to the
> benefit package offered by most Fortune 500 companies. This
> health care security card will offer this package of benefits in a way
> that can never be taken away.

The Clinton plan was famously defeated by a public relations campaign that included ads run by insurers depicting a middle-class couple, Harry and Louise, despairing over its costs. A June 2004 memorandum from Magaziner to the Clintons noted that "[m]uch of the criticism we have endured is unfair, but we must acknowl-edge that we have lost the communications battle on many fronts."[33] In his biography, *My Life*, Clinton would ruefully relate that "[t]he ads were completely misleading but clever and widely seen. In fact, the bureaucratic costs imposed by the insurance companies were a big reason Americans paid more for health care but still didn't have the universal coverage that citizens in every other prosperous country took for granted."[34]

The plan also received little help from Democrats in the Senate aristocracy. Senator Patrick Moynihan of New York, the Senate Finance Committee chairman, famously declared there was no health care crisis and pushed for welfare reform after making the health care reform bill untenable by larding it with New York pork.[35] Clinton's reform never received a House or Senate floor vote.

Despite the failure of the Clinton plan, the perception of governmental over-reach contributed to the 1994 takeover of the U.S. House by Republicans led by future Speaker Newt Gingrich of Georgia.

In their book, *The Liberal Hour:Washington and the Politics of Change in the 1960s*, authors G. Galvin Mackenzie and Robert Weisbrot noted that "[m]ost of the time, inertia is the most powerful force in government. Those who seek change have to succeed at dozens of potential veto points. Those who seek to prevent change usually have to succeed at only one."[36]

Yet Obama came into office determined to succeed where Democratic icons failed.

On December 11, 2008 Obama announced his friend and mentor Tom Daschle, the former Senate Democratic leader and South Dakota senator, would be his nominee to serve as secretary of Health & Human Services. Daschle withdrew in February 2009 over tax issues. He was replaced by Kansas Governor Kathleen Sebelius, who had also served two terms as an elected insurance commissioner. Sebelius was confirmed by the Senate in April 2009.

The difference was important. As problems plagued 2014 enrollment in health care plans, it was clear Sebelius had no real relationship with Obama.[37] Daschle, a known quantity in Washington, D.C. and confidante of the president, would have had a much greater portfolio to negotiate health care reform. When Obama had taken office as a U.S. senator he largely inherited Daschle's staff. Obama intended that Daschle serve both as health secretary and run a new White House Office of Health Reform. Daschle had even co-authored a book on health care reform. As Ron Suskind describes it in *Confidence Men:Wall Street,Washington, and the Education of a President*, Daschle might have steered Obama away from what Daschle regarded as the "false god" of bipartisanship preached by appeasers like Montana Senator Max Baucus, the Senate Finance Committee chair, and away from settling for "health *insurance* reform" instead of "health *care* reform."[38]

Many on the Obama team were very doubtful about the politics of health care reform. They thought the issue was a loser with a largely-insured middle class. Rahm Emmanuel, Obama's chief of staff, implored Obama not to pursue health care reform. Failing to persuade him, he then, joined by Vice President Joe Biden, tried to sell the president on a reform-lite plan for uninsured mothers and children. The so-called "Titanic" plan would cover perhaps 10 million.[39] As early as February 2009 Emmanuel was willing to discard a public option and any fight over health care costs.

By January 2010, the *Wall Street Journal* was reporting the disaffection of liberals with Emmanuel's deal-making on health care reform. The *Journal* related Emmanuel, in supporting "Congress dropping liberal ideas" (particularly a public option), was frequently communicating with the corporate-funded, now-defunct, Democratic Leadership Council on the issue. Emmanuel was long associated with the group.

With Daschle on the outside, and Emmanuel unconstructive, the key Administration player on health care reform was health care adviser Nancy-Ann DeParle, who moved the president away from substantive reform and toward commercial insurance. Fatefully, Obama, who had favored re-importation of prescription drugs, signaled to the pharmaceutical industry that he would reverse course in exchange for their support. DeParle e-mailed a drug lobbyist on June 3, 2009 to assure him of the Administration's "decision, based on how constructive you guys have been, to oppose importation on the bill."[40]

Savings to be extracted from the drug industry, in exchange for an exorbitant number of newly-insured customers, were dropped from $100 billion to $80 billion – and the industry funded front groups promoting reform like Healthy Economy Now. In a June 20, 2009 statement, Billy Tauzin, president and CEO of the Pharmaceutical Research and Manufacturers of America (PhRMA), praised "President Obama and Senate Finance Committee Chairman Baucus for their commitment to comprehensive health care reform – one of the most challenging issues of our lifetime."[41]

In what could only be regarded as a sign of the apocalypse, the couple that played Harry and Louise in 1993 in defeating President Clinton's plan was brought back to support Obama's health care reform efforts in a pharmaceutical industry ad – even appearing in a bizarre press conference with Democratic senators.

While Obama gave himself room to maneuver by not sending his own bill to Congress, he yielded control over the process. And after a furious public blowback against congressional efforts threatened to torpedo them, Obama, like Clinton before him, would give a speech on health care reform to a rare joint session of Congress. Expectations were high for Obama's September 2009 speech. Everything rode on it.

Moving away from previous generalities, the president prescribed some specifics, including an individual mandate to facilitate new protections like guaranteed issue of coverage: "[U]nless everybody does their part, many of the insurance reforms we seek – especially requiring insurance companies to cover pre-existing conditions – just can't be achieved."[42] He spoke in favor of limiting out-of-pocket expenses and requiring preventive care at no extra cost. He advocated tax credits for purchasing insurance through health benefit exchanges, which would be marketplaces "where individuals and small businesses will be able to shop for health insurance at competitive prices."

In a message to progressives dismayed over the quick demise of any single-payer system, Obama championed a public option to compete with commercial insurance: "[B]y avoiding some of the overhead that gets eaten up at private companies by profits, excessive administrative costs and executive salaries, it could provide a good deal for consumers. It would also keep pressure on private insurers to keep their policies affordable and treat their customers better[.]"

While Obama acknowledged that a public option's "impact shouldn't be exaggerated" he pledged he would "not back down on the basic principle that if Americans can't find affordable coverage, we will provide you with a choice."

In a sop to Republicans, Obama also embraced tort reform, stating, "I don't believe malpractice reform is a silver bullet, but I have talked to enough doctors to know that defensive medicine may be contributing to unnecessary costs."

In a truly bizarre moment that caught the temper of the times, Obama's health care address was interrupted by a shout of "You Lie!" from Congressman Joe Wilson, a South Carolina Republican.

Six months later Obama signed health care reform into law, having "back[ed] down on the basic principle that if Americans can't find affordable coverage, we will provide you with a choice." In *The Center Holds: Obama and his Enemies*, Jonathan Alter reports Obama's only lasting regret about health care reform was that he was not able to "put something in the bill reforming the medical malpractice system – something real that would hurt the trial lawyers who bolstered Democrats."[43]

3

THE DEAN OF THE HOUSE

EIGHTY-TWO-YEAR-OLD JOHN DINGELL of Michigan was entering his 28th term in the House of Representatives in 2009 when he received the task of spearheading President Obama's health care effort.

Dingell had served as a House page in 1937 when his father, John Dingell Sr., was in the House. He took the seat himself in 1955 two months after his father passed away. In 1957, just as his father had, Dingell introduced a national health insurance bill – he would continue to do so in every subsequent Congress. It was personal. His father survived near-death from tuberculosis in 1914 with union health care coverage rare at the time.[44]

Known as an ardent defender of the auto industry, Dingell was viewed as conservative on issues like the environment, and opposed gun control as a former National Rifle Association board member. Yet Dingell was pro-choice, voted against the 2002 Iraq War, and had a streak of economic populism. In 1999, he presciently warned Congress over repeal of the Glass-Steagall Act of 1933:

> [W]hat we are creating now is a group of institutions which are too
> big to fail. Not only are they going to be big banks, but they are
> going to be big everything, because they are going to be in secu-
> rities and insurance, in issuance of stocks and bonds and under-
> writing, and they are also going to be in banks. And under this
> legislation, the whole of the regulatory structure is so obfuscated
> and so confused that liability in one area is going to fall over into

liability in the next. Taxpayers are going to be called upon to cure the failures we are creating tonight, and it is going to cost a lot of money, and it is coming.[45]

In 2008 the more reliably-liberal Henry Waxman of California ended Dingell's 27-year interregnum as Democratic leader of the Committee on Energy and Commerce. To Waxman went the honor of sponsoring climate change legislation; Dingell received the consolation prize of health care reform. Yet it was the effort Dingell began that passed into law.

And Dingell was still idealistic. He wanted a single-payer system. In a 2009 interview with *Fortune*, Dingell stated: "I'm a peculiar fellow. I like to make progress. If I had my druthers I'd write a single payer bill like the British or the French or the Germans or the Japanese."[46]

Barring that, he would accept a public option. "The insurance regulators are not able to regulate insurance companies except regarding their solvency. But they can't do anything else, and the only way you can do this right is to give [insurance companies] competition. That's why we need the public option."[47]

Because so much attention focused upon the Senate, and its self-inflicted drama of obtaining 60 votes, the House's early role in shaping what became the ACA is mostly forgotten. Largely this is deserved, as the House abandoned its own position in the "reconciliation" process – limited to budget changes – that resulted in the final bill. In fact, the final ACA vehicle was an obscure House-passed bill, House Resolution (H.R.) 3590, originally addressing housing tax breaks for service members. Yet aspects of the House's early work are worth comment.

On July 24, Dingell introduced H.R. 3200, or America's Affordable Health Choices Act of 2009.

In legislation where you start out often shapes public perceptions more than where you end up. H.R. 3200 originated the great myth that health care reform allowed for "death panels." This was based upon an innocuous provision allowing Medicare payment for physicians counseling about end-of-life options such as advance directives. It fanned a firestorm of controversy among conservative pundits; Republican political figures happily added fuel.

In a Facebook post, failed vice presidential candidate Sarah Palin asserted, "The America I know and love is not one in which my parents or my baby with Down Syndrome will have to stand in front of Obama's 'death panel' so his bureaucrats can decide, based on a subjective judgment of their 'level of productivity in society,' whether they are worthy of health care."[48] Iowa Republican Senator Charles Grassley added to the demagoguery at a 2009 town hall meeting: "We should not have a government program that determines you're going to pull the plug on Grandma."[49]

TIME reported that "a single phrase — 'death panels' — nearly derailed health care reform, as town halls were flooded with angry voters who got their information online." As the *New Republic* would recount it, "Unemployment was on the march, and all this talk about preexisting conditions and insurance exchanges barely registered above the Fox News pundits screaming, 'Death panel!'"[50]

This bipartisan provision in an un-passed bill, allowing one Medicare-funded end-of-life consultation every five years to help prepare seniors for the inevitable, is a rhetorical gift that keeps on giving even though it was not put into the ACA itself given the volatility of the misinformation campaign. In one 2013 forum I addressed on the ACA a woman flatly stated her understanding that, as a diabetic, she would be denied access to insulin and forced to watch a video every five years about euthanasia.

By the summer of 2009, a nascent Tea Party movement was overwhelming congressional town halls with vitriol toward the Obama Administration and congressional Democrats.

In his book *Pity the Billionaire*, Thomas Frank amusingly recounts the example of a woman at a congressional town hall in Bremerton, Washington, who challenged her Democratic congressman – yet to be employed by a lobbying firm – to take $20 from her hand as "a down payment" on health care reform. Frank relates that "then she just stood there, staring at the congressman with those wild eyes, her arm in the air, immortalized in newspaper photographs like some kind of libertarian Norma Rae."[51] Yet, as Frank writes, the protests worked: "[A] populist outburst from the Right caused the inarticulate Democrats to abandon the most populist elements of their own plan and choose instead what we might call the elitist option, a crony-capitalist solution in which public choices would be diminished but corporate profits guaranteed."[52]

The House "markup" process on H.R. 3200 ran from July 16 to September 23. No serious move was made toward considering a single-payer system. When publicity-hungry Democratic Congressman Anthony Weiner of New York threatened to hold H.R. 3200 hostage in committee unless he was allowed to introduce a single-payer amendment, Pelosi bought him off with the promise of a prime speaking role during the floor debate on what, at that point, would be H.R. 3962 – even allowing him to preside over some of that debate – and gave him the floor vote's official tally sheet.[53] Weiner withdrew his amendment.

With six other sponsors, Weiner's amendment would have created a United States National Health Care program and provided that "[a]ll individuals residing in the United States (including any territory of the United States) are covered under the USNHC Program entitling them to a universal, best quality standard of care." Each would "receive a United States National Health Insurance Card in the mail, after filling out a United States National Health Insurance application form at a health care provider."[54] The program would be funded through an increase in income taxes on the top-5% of earners; "a modest and progressive excise tax on payroll and self-employment income"; and "a small tax on stock and bond transactions."

The amendment certainly had the benefit of simplicity compared to what followed.

Given the public blowback against it, H.R. 3200 was abandoned. Some of its ideas, sans death panels, were put forth in a new bill introduced by Dingell on October 29, 2009: H.R. 3962, or The Affordable Health Care for America Act.

The new bill contained revisions based upon Obama's September 2009 speech to Congress.

When H.R. 3962 was unveiled, the White House issued a strong statement of support, and accentuated the public option: "The Administration is pleased that the bill includes a public health insurance option offered in an exchange. As the President has said throughout this process, a public option that competes with private insurers is one of the best ways to ensure the choice and competition that are so badly needed in today's market."[55]

In his floor statement on the bill, Waxman, too, made that point: "There is a public health insurance option that will give Americans more choice and competition."[56]

H.R. 3962 was put on a track that seems unbelievably fast to anyone observing Congress in its partisan gridlock a few years later. Introduced October 29, it passed November 7 by a 220-215 vote. Only one Republican, one-term Congressman Anh "Joseph" Quang Cao of Louisiana, voted for it (Cao had beaten a New Orleans' Democratic congressman under indictment for 16 felony corruption charges), although he voted against the final act due to its alleged permissiveness on abortion.

The most lasting House contribution to health care reform proved to be the biggest setback to abortion rights since the landmark *Roe vs. Wade* decision in 1973 – and one administered by a Democratic Congress and president.

Before he retired, and inevitably worked for a health care lobbying firm, the tenure of Dingell's fellow Michigan Democrat, Congressman Bart Stupak, would have faded into obscurity had he not contributed an amendment that defines health care reform to this day.

Partnering with Republican Congressman Joe Pitts of Pennsylvania, Stupak offered a floor amendment to H.R. 3962 to prohibit using tax subsidies "to pay for any abortion or to cover any part of the costs of any health plan that includes coverage of abortion" except in cases of rape, incest, or where the mother's life was in danger.

In his floor remarks, Stupak stated that under his amendment "[h]ealth insurance companies can still offer policies in the exchange that cover abortion; they just can't sell those policies to individuals receiving affordability credits."[57]

"If enacted, this amendment will be the greatest restriction of a woman's right to choose to pass in our careers," argued Democratic Congresswoman Diana DeGette of Colorado.[58] Significantly, if the amendment passed, and there was a public option, it "cannot offer abortions to anyone, even those purchasing the policies with 100 percent private money." She dismissed as "offensive to women" the notion of "supplemental insurance for abortions."

Yet the amendment passed 240-194.

In a statement by its president, Cecile Richards, Planned Parenthood announced it had "no choice but to oppose HR 3962."[59] Richards argued the amendment "would leave women worse off after health care reform than they are today, violating President Obama's promise to the American people that no one would be forced to lose her or his present coverage under health reform." In contrast, National Right to Life exulted, "Today's bipartisan House vote is a sharp blow to the White House's pro-abortion smuggling operation."[60]

Upon reconciliation with the Senate in March 2010, Stupak settled for an executive order on top of language already inserted into the ACA by anti-choice Democratic Senator Ben Nelson of Nebraska. Even that agreement did not keep a Republican congressman from shouting "Baby Killer!" at Stupak during the final House floor debate.

In a *Washington Post* column, Stupak wrote of the executive order as "an 'ironclad' commitment from the president that no taxpayer dollars will be used to pay for abortions" and stated that "[t]o further protect against federal funding for abortion, during floor debate on the health-care reform bill I engaged in a colloquy with Rep. Henry Waxman to make clear congressional intent that the provisions in the bill, combined with the executive order, will ensure that outcome."[61]

Aside from kicking reproductive rights to the curb, health care reform had survived the House with some Democratic ideals reasonably intact – principally consumer protections and the public option. Now it headed to the Democratic supermajority in what is known as the "world's greatest deliberative body" (albeit one in which a senator was once caned into unconsciousness for opposing slavery) – the U.S. Senate.

We might have been better off with John Dingell. "The good ideas from the House never made it in," admitted Rahm Emmanuel's brother, Ezekiel Emmanuel, a medical doctor who advised the Obama Administration on health care reform.[62]

In a telling postscript that shows the contempt in which the more liberal House was held by the Obama Administration and Senate Democratic barons, an e-mail from the White House health reform director, DeParle, to the lead PhRMA negotiator, was later revealed in which DeParle commiserated about how unreasonably pro-consumer the House was in demanding more concessions, including re-importation, from PhRMA: "I think we should have included the House in the discussions, but maybe we never would have gotten anywhere if we had. I know this is tough for you guys, it is tough for us too. I am the one up there walking the halls in Longworth and Rayburn [House office buildings] and getting yelled at by members who don't like it."[63]

Disastrously, in the critical first year following the law's passage, DeParle would be tasked with implementing health care reform – despite the urging of a number of presidential advisers that an outside health reform "czar" be appointed who was knowledgeable, in particular, about the technological challenges that would come to plague implementation.[64]

4

SENATOR SELLOUT

CONVENING AS MEMBERS of the 111th Congress on January 6, 2009, the Democratic supermajority reenacted Rule 22 – the Senate rule whereby 41 members can stop all business on the Senate floor through threat of a filibuster. It was a fateful decision.

Democratic Senator Ted Kennedy of Massachusetts, the liberal icon, was dying of cancer when Democratic Senator Max Baucus of Montana visited him in 2008 to discuss health care reform. Kennedy chaired the Health, Education, Labor, and Pensions (HELP) Committee, which would seem paramount in the health care debate. However, it was the Finance Committee that Baucus chaired that had jurisdiction over revenue, Medicare and Medicaid. Kennedy and Baucus agreed to work together.

In contrast to the dynamic Kennedy, whose 2012 Democratic Convention speech for Obama electrified attendees waving "Kennedy" placards, Baucus was a mumbler and closed-door dealmaker. In social awkwardness, he was similar to his friend, and then-ranking Republican counterpart on Finance, Senator Grassley.

Yet, if the lobbyists in Washington, D.C. ever erect a statue (perhaps on K Street), Baucus would be the honoree. He churned committee and personal staff through the revolving door into the lobbying ranks. For health care reform, he brought back his former staffer, Elizabeth Fowler, from health insurance giant WellPoint. In December 2012 she would leave her role as an Obama health care adviser to lobby for pharmaceutical giant Johnson & Johnson. At the time of that departure, the *Huffington Post* reported 34 former Baucus staffers were lobbying – and Baucus was a leading recipient of health care contributions.[65]

The list of Baucus contributors told the story of how the ACA came to be the way it is. Just the top-5, from 2005-10, included names like pharmaceutical giant Schering-Plough, New York Life Insurance, biologic company Amgen, and Blue Cross-Blue Shield.[66] In contrast, during that same time, the top contributors for the Democratic seatmate of Baucus, Senator John Tester of Montana, were liberal MoveOn.org and the pacifist Council for a Livable World (for his 2012 re-election Tester held a sweepstakes for "Pearl Jam Premium Tickets").[67]

Obama's deputy chief of staff, Baucus alum Jim Messina, negotiated health care reform with his old boss, and then ran the president's 2012 re-election campaign. "He's like a son to me," Baucus told the *Washington Post*. "He's a father figure to me," gushed Messina.[68]

Messina's father figure went against Democrats in enacting the Medicare Part D drug benefit in 2003. Medicare, unlike Medicaid or the Department of Veteran Affairs, was prevented from using its purchasing power to lower pharmaceutical prices. And unlike the self-financed Part A, funded through dedicated payroll taxes upon employers and employees, Part D was funded almost entirely through general revenue, adding to the federal deficit.

One of only 11 Senate Democrats to support Part D, Baucus, as the then-ranking minority member on the Finance Committee, also broke ranks with Democrats to co-write the Bush tax breaks of 2001. Baucus had even tried to get his then-girlfriend (later wife) appointed as a United States attorney in Montana – he had lavished upon her, while she worked for his Senate office, a huge pay increase and international travel.[69]

Thus it was entirely logical a Democratic super-majority entrusted Baucus with health care reform.

In a joint letter to Obama dated April 20, 2009, Baucus and Kennedy wrote "[w]e must act swiftly, because the cost of inaction is too high for individuals, families, businesses, state and federal governments." They added:

> Since our committees share jurisdiction over health care reform legislation in the Senate, we have jointly laid out an aggressive schedule to accomplish our goal. Both committees plan to mark-up legislation in early June. Our intention is for that legislation to be very similar, and to reflect a shared approach to reform, so that the measures that our two committees report can be quickly merged into a single bill for consideration on the Senate floor.[70]

Only in Congress, where powerful egos must be massaged, would this duplication of effort make sense. At that time the *Washington Post*'s Ezra Klein reported it looked like Kennedy's committee was taking the lead in pushing

> the left edge of the possible. Huge Medicaid expansion, robust
> public plan, employer contribution, etc. And it is no accident that
> it's being released before the Finance Committee's bill: The hope
> is, in the first place, to push the Finance Committee's bill to the
> left, and in the second place, to push the merged bill to the left.[71]

Yet, with Kennedy absent due to cancer, his committee's work was completely overshadowed by the Finance Committee. By July 15, under an acting chair, future motion picture industry lobbyist Christopher Dodd, Democrat of Connecticut, the HELP Committee passed its version of health care reform, with a public option, by a party-line 13-10 vote – only to watch helplessly, along with House Democrats, as the real action took place in Finance.

On May 11 Baucus and Grassley had jointly released policy options for expanding health care coverage. Those ideas included establishment of a national Health Insurance Exchange and "a 'Medicare-like' public health insurance option" offered through a national Exchange.[72]

Conspicuously absent was even the discussion of a single-payer system, although, to be comprehensive, the 61-page document would have seemed to have room for such a possibility given its prominent disclaimer: "While these proposed options are jointly offered for discussion, not all the options in this document have the support of Chairman Baucus or Ranking Member Grassley."

Baucus refused to even allow advocates of a single-payer national health plan to testify in Finance hearings. In a June meeting with the California Nurses Association and Physicians for a National Health Program, Baucus admitted excluding that view was a mistake – but asserted it was too late to include it.[73]

Baucus was clear in laying out the ground rules: "Everything is on the table. Everything is on the table with the single exception of single pay. I do not think single pay is on the table. This country is not going to adopt single pay – at least not this time. I do not think. But everything else is clearly on the table."[74]

It was hard to claim with a straight face that "everything is on the table" if the model of health care embraced by most western democracies was not even to be openly discussed.

In fact the very idea of single-payer was treated as a joke, as the transcript of an exchange on May 12, 2009 between Baucus and Gerald Shea of the AFL-CIO reveals:

> Mr. SHEA. I cannot resist the opportunity to say, if we are going to do a radical change, I think single payor is really the way to go and we could cut out all of this——
> The CHAIRMAN. You have a lot of supportive demonstrators here.
> [Laughter.]
> Mr. SHEA. All of my members, yes.

Thus, for the record, the time allotted by the world's greatest deliberative body to consideration of a single-payer system can only be found in transcript descriptions of protests before the Finance Committee, such as this one:

> The CHAIRMAN. The committee will be in order. Comments from the audience are inappropriate and out of order. Any further disruption will cause the committee to recess until the police can restore order.
> [Interruption from the audience.]
> The CHAIRMAN. The committee will be in order. The committee will stand in recess until the police can restore order.
> [Interruption from the audience.]
> [Off the record.]
> Senator GRASSLEY. Mr. Chairman——
> [Interruption from the audience.]
> The CHAIRMAN. The committee will be in order.
> [Interruption from the audience.]
> The CHAIRMAN. The committee will stand in recess until the police can restore order.
> [Off the record.]
> The CHAIRMAN. Let me just speak a few minutes.
> [Interruption from the audience.]
> The CHAIRMAN. Sorry. The committee will be in order.
> [Interruption from the audience.]

The CHAIRMAN. The committee will recess until order can be restored. The committee will be recessed until the police can restore order. Will the police please come more expeditiously?

[Off the record.]

[Interruption from the audience.]

The CHAIRMAN. The committee will stand in recess until the police can restore order. I will say to everybody else out in the audience who may be similarly inclined, believe me, we hear you. We deeply respect the views of everyone here. We have got an extremely open process, and I just urge everyone to respect the views of others by not interrupting those who are speaking. There will be plenty of time to meet with everybody. This is a long, involved process.

While citizens were muzzled and arrested for protest, senators were free to speak. As Baucus noted, on another day opening with protest, "But of course, we never constrain Senators. Senators may want to speak on any subject that they might."

It is a testament to the status quo that no senators spoke up in favor of a single-payer system. It was also to the lasting shame of transactional participants from ostensibly-progressive groups that they did not condition their participation on the committee at least hearing from the significant progressive constituency championing the single-payer approach.

Baucus was at pains to court Republicans. In contrast to the speed with which the House acted, Senate Finance hearings extended for months while Baucus worked behind-the-scenes as part of a "Gang of Six" that included fellow conservative Democrats Jeff Bingaman of New Mexico and Kent Conrad of North Dakota, and Republicans Grassley, Olympia Snowe of Maine, and Mike Enzi of Wyoming.

This group met for more than sixty hours. Finance Committee records show 31 instances, between June 18 and September 14, of a "Bipartisan meeting to discuss health care reform" – including two meetings apiece on two days.[75] The meetings began well past the point Baucus had assured Obama he would report out a bill, and the glacial pace allowed Republicans to build grassroots opposition.

Democrats had acted with similar lassitude in pursuing reform under President Clinton, as Ira Magaziner recounted in a 1995 memorandum to Clinton: "Delay was fatal. Many interest groups were prepared to compromise with us on our terms in the winter and spring of 1993 when momentum was on our side. We lost momentum and gave them time to oppose us when we had to delay the bill[.]"[76]

Describing Baucus's efforts in 2009 to achieve consensus, Steven Pearlstein would write in the *Washington Post*:

> Max wasted four crucial months that summer in seemingly endless discussions with two Republican members of his committee who never could say what they wanted, were never going to bring other votes and, in the end, could not withstand pressure from their caucus to vote yes. Significantly, it was during those four months of rope-a-dope that the bill's opponents were able to undermine public support enough that it took heroic efforts by the White House to push it to final Senate passage.[77]

As Richard Kirsch, the chief executive of Health Care for America Now, related in 2014:

> You have to look at Baucus and Obama together on this. Jim Messina, who was one of the top people working for Obama and his deputy chief of staff, had been Baucus's chief of staff. They kept making concessions when it was clear the Republicans weren't going to support it. Even when it was crystal clear – and they gave up on getting Republican support – they didn't go back and present a better bill.[78]

Yet, in playing footsy with the likes of Grassley, Baucus was not alone in embracing delay. Snowe and five other senators signed a July 17 letter to Majority Leader Reid and Minority Leader McConnell urging "additional time to achieve a bipartisan result" and resisting "timelines which prevent us from achieving the best result."[79]

Those signing the letter were Democrats Ben Nelson of Nebraska, Mary Landrieu of Louisiana, and Ron Wyden of Oregon, Independent Joe Lieberman of Connecticut, and Republican Susan Collins of Maine. With Democrats' learned helplessness having given 41 senators the ability to hold up the progress of 59, every vote counted.

"You just watch as the bill diminishes in its scope and in its coverage and in its ferocity to try to attack the problem," said a dispirited Senator Jay Rockefeller, Democrat of West Virginia, in an August press briefing.[80] Rockefeller, a longtime health care proponent, was second to Baucus in Democratic seniority on Finance, yet entirely excluded from the negotiations. "Republicans won't be there to vote it out of committee when it comes right down to it, so that this all will have been a three-or-four-month delay game, which is exactly what the Republicans want," he forewarned.

During Baucus's extended courtship period, Ted Kennedy died August 25. On September 24, Massachusetts Governor Deval Patrick appointed Paul Kirk, a former Democratic National Committee chair, to Kennedy's seat. Kirk pledged not to seek election. It seemed impossible matters could drag out until the January 2010 special election, although it was safe to assume liberal Massachusetts would elect another Democrat to fill Kennedy's old seat.

As Baucus's September 15 deadline for his "Gang of Six" negotiations approached, it became obvious Republicans had played him for a fool. Only Snowe remained at the table. Snowe would vote for Baucus's bill in committee, but no Republican would vote for it on the floor. Yet the bill was rife with concessions to gain their votes.

On September 16, Baucus released his "Chairman's Mark" of the bill – re-releasing it September 22 with changes proposed by both Democratic and Republican members. At that point it was known as "The America's Healthy Future Act." A seven-day "Markup" – the longest held by the Finance Committee in 22 years – then began and not end until October 13.

On September 29, Baucus led the committee vote against two public option amendments from Senator Rockefeller and Senator Schumer. Baucus's reasoning proved ironic. Although he claimed to support a public option, he stated he didn't want to incur a Republican filibuster. His friend Grassley characterized a public option as a "slow walk toward government-controlled, single-payer health care."[81]

Rockefeller disagreed: "It is interesting about the public option because people assume that it is some kind of a Government takeover. Those are mostly people that have an ideological bent against it. And it is not. It is optional. It has been said before, you say again, people can get into it, can get out of it." He noted: "Seventy percent of the American people want this." And he did not spare insurance companies criticism: "The insurance companies in my judgment are determined to protect their profits and put their customers second. It is a harsh statement but a true statement." Under the Baucus approach, "nearly half a trillion dollars in premiums, I believe, would go directly to the pockets of insurance companies on Wall Street."

As Rockefeller related:

> In testimony before the House Democratic Steering and Policy Committee on September 16th, former CIGNA executive Wendell Potter, who had worked for CIGNA for 20 years as a top executive, warned that if Congress "fails to create a public insurance option to compete with the private insurers, the bill it sends to the President might as well be called" – and these are his words – "the Insurance Industry Profit Protection and Enhancement Act."

"The people that I represent need this," said Rockefeller. "They need this because they are helpless in front of the insurance companies."

Speaking in favor of Rockefeller's amendment, Schumer, who sought to catch Grassley in his contradiction of railing against government-run health care and yet supporting Medicare, said a public option would add "some real competition to the coagulated, ossified, and fundamentally anti-competitive insurance market."

Rockefeller's amendment fell 8-15. Next up was Schumer's.

Acknowledging he "might prefer Senator Rockefeller's" amendment to his own, Schumer touted his amendment as the product of "a realist." Yet he was no less critical of the insurance industry: "If the private insurance market is serving America so well, they have no public option to fear. If they are serving it poorly, the public option will force them to serve better." Of his amendment, he said, "Medicare has far more Government involvement than this public option, and yet most of the amendments from the other side and much of the rhetoric from the other side says keep Medicare the way it is, do not touch it."

Schumer noted Baucus had based his opposition on the assertion the public option could not muster 60 votes: "Mr. Chairman, with a great deal of respect for you and in a desire to help, we will work as hard as we can as the bill moves forward on to the Senate floor to show you we can get 60 votes."

Democratic Senator Maria Cantwell of Washington spoke in favor of Schumer's amendment: "This is about whether we are going to continue to do the same things that we are doing today or whether we are going to give the public a choice to do something differently. Without that choice to do something differently, we are going to see exorbitant rates."

Republican Senator Jon Kyl of Arizona defended the honesty of insurers absent a public option: "The State Insurance Commissioners are empowered to keep the insurance companies honest."

Schumer would retort:

> If the State Insurance Commissioners are doing such a good job, then why are the costs going through the roof? If the State Insurance Commissioners are doing such a good job, then why do we hear every day complaints from so many of our constituents who feel that they are not being treated well by their insurance companies even when their policy seems to say in black and white that they are entitled to something? The present system is broken. It is broken on the private side. Costs are going up everywhere.

"I do not see a bill out of this committee with public option getting 60 votes," reiterated Baucus. "I am going to vote against the amendment."

Schumer's amendment fell 10-13. The public option was dead.

The vigor with which Rockefeller and Schumer assailed health care reform without a public option was all the more remarkable given they knew their amendments were doomed. In other words, the dark future of insurance overlords they conjured was inevitable were they to vote for the Baucus bill without their amendments. It is hard to walk back such talk. Even candidates in bitter presidential primary races know there are certain lines not to cross if they are to leave the eventual nominee standing.

Nor had Rockefeller and Schumer backed away completely from the public option in voting for the bill in committee on October 13. Ingratiatingly, Schumer said to Baucus, "Your work here is a legislative tour de force the likes of which we have rarely seen in these halls."[82] Yet he insisted that "[t]o cut costs, we must have a public option in the final bill. It is the most effective way to cut insurance costs, period. The health insurance industry is one of the least competitive industries in the country."

Rockefeller maintained his reservations, asserting "the insurance industry gets too sweet a deal in this." He stressed the urgency of a public option, stating that "the insurance industry does not know how to stop itself. They are a train which just gathers speed, and with no impediments." Again defending a public option against big government charges, he noted, "I do not see it as a Government take-over. I see it as Government assistance to people who are getting killed by premium increases."

However, progressive Democrats folded their tents two months later. Their warnings about insurance industry avarice now stand as embarrassing artifacts given later efforts by those same Democrats to sell the ACA as a panacea.

On October 13, the day the Finance Committee reported out health care reform by a 14-9 vote, I happened to be in Washington, D.C. with a legal client, and was surprised at the ease with which we were admitted to the hearing on such a momentous occasion. At first, it seemed very impressive to be there. Yet, after about an hour of listening to committee members' speeches, we grew bored and left before the vote. So much for history.

On November 19 the Patient Protection and Affordable Care Act was released by Baucus, Reid, and Dodd – ostensibly merging the Finance Committee's bill with sparse remnants of that passed by the HELP Committee.

To provide a 60th vote in December 2009, Senator Ben Nelson extracted $100 million in extra Medicaid funding for Nebraska. Known as the "Cornhusker Kickback," the deal, undone in the House reconciliation, came to be seen as a symbol of the ACA's flaws. In addition to his $100 million, Nelson won language in the ACA that allowed states to bar insurance coverage of abortions. This language, as is detailed later, has proved quite fruitful in setting back women's reproductive rights as part of an unprecedented assault in state legislatures.

Unpopular in Nebraska, Nelson would not run for a third term in 2012. He left the Senate to lobby Congress for $950,000 a year as head of the predominantly-Republican, insurer-funded National Association of Insurance Commissioners. But his deal remained a symbol of the ACA. In oral argument on the ACA before the Supreme Court in 2012, Justice Antonin Scalia incoherently referenced the long-removed provision:

> [I]f we struck down nothing in this legislation but the – what you call the 'Cornhusker Kickback,' okay, we find that to violate the constitutional proscription of venality, okay? When we strike that down, it's clear that Congress would not have passed it without

that. It was the means of getting the last necessary vote in the Senate.

FOX News then dutifully reported the provision still existed.[83]

With Nelson's vote secure, the ACA passed the Senate December 24 by a 60-40 vote.

Fatefully, Congress then lapsed into its holiday torpor, which allowed the year to end, and the January 19, 2010, Massachusetts special election to occur, without an agreement with the House. In an upset, a state senator, Scott Brown, defeated lackluster Attorney General Martha Coakley and won Kennedy's old seat to become the first Republican U.S. senator from Massachusetts since 1972.

In the state credited as leading the way on health care reform, Brown had campaigned hard against it, which meant the normal process to compromise with the House could not occur. Any compromise, technically new legislation, would incur a Senate filibuster by 41 members. All of Baucus's concessions failed to avert this inevitability. Dealt out of health care reform, the House could only accept the Senate product through the budget reconciliation process — which it did March 21, 2010. With their votes no longer needed under the simple-majority approach, three Senate Democrats — including Ben Nelson — voted against the act. President Obama signed it into law March 23.

The blow Senate Republicans struck out of the gate would not be the final one, but it was heavy. Having bent the ACA in the compromised direction they favored, they undermined it structurally and with the public. Jacob Hacker and Paul Pierson detail the results of Republicans' tactics in *Winner-Take-All Politics: How Washington Made the Rich Richer — and Turned its Back on the Middle Class*: "Having slowed the bill's progress for months, they joined a relentless attack designed to erode public confidence in the health-care bill and the legislative process itself."[84] They noted that "[t]he prolonged stalemate had cost reformers a year and encouraged a dangerous souring of the public mood. . . . Why had Democrats spent so long in futile search for bipartisanship? They had the largest majorities in Congress in three decades."

On April 17, 2013 — with enrollment in exchanges just months away — Baucus hardly added to public confidence about his signature accomplishment when, in a public exchange with Secretary Sebelius about the ACA, he stated, "I just see a huge train wreck coming down."[85] Having laid the tracks, he knew better than anyone. A week later Baucus announced he would not seek a seventh term. He left office early in 2014 to become ambassador to China, selling his home in Washington, D.C. for a reputed $1.2 million.[86]

That month Rockefeller, who also decided not to run in 2014, described the ACA as "beyond comprehension" and "probably the most complex piece of legislation ever passed by the United States Congress."[87]

The Senate seats Baucus and Rockefeller had held were both lost to ACA-opposing Republicans in 2014.

It is impossible to look back on the Senate deliberations without imagining what might have been had Senate Democrats not yoked themselves to the filibuster rule. During the health care reform debate I joined other Democratic state legislators in meeting with Democratic Senator Tom Harkin of Iowa. As Harkin, who announced his intention to retire in 2015 – after 30 years as Iowa's junior senator – noted, "We simply cannot govern a 21st Century superpower when a minority of just 41 senators, representing potentially as little as 11 percent of the population, can dictate action—or inaction—not just to the majority of senators but to a majority of the American people.[88]

Mike Lofgren, a former Republican committee staffer, has a bleak synopsis in his book *The Party's Over*: "Obama and the Democrats essentially stepped into the shoes of the Republicans and followed the same basic policy line, rebranded under the rubric of hope and change."[89] He recounted that as he "watched the health-care debacle unfold in the Senate the nexus between big corporate money and Democratic behavior became manifest. For reasons that may become clear only when we read Obama's White House memoir, the president punted operational control of the legislation to Congress."

5

THE SUPREME COURT

TWENTY-SIX STATES SUED to overturn the ACA, arguing it exceeded the ability of Congress to regulate interstate commerce.

Filed the same day the ACA was signed into law, the multi-state lawsuit (Virginia filed its own) was instigated by Florida's Republican attorney general, Bill McCollum, a former congressman hoping to ride the case into the Florida Governor's Mansion. Yet McCollum became a footnote to his own effort. The anti-ACA tide he helped unleash in Florida propelled a former health care executive, Rick Scott, to the 2010 Republican gubernatorial nomination and, ultimately, into office.

But McCollum's lawsuit lived on.

In a 2011 decision, U.S. District Court Judge Roger Vinson of Florida found arguments against the ACA persuasive, writing, "I conclude that the individual mandate seeks to regulate economic inactivity, which is the very opposite of economic activity. And because activity is required under the Commerce Clause, the individual mandate exceeds Congress' commerce power, as it is understood, defined, and applied in the existing Supreme Court case law."[90] His opinion would have struck down the entire ACA: "I must conclude that the individual mandate and the remaining provisions are all inextricably bound together in purpose and must stand or fall as a single unit."

A split of opinion occurred among circuits of the U.S. Court of Appeals, and U.S. Supreme Court arguments were always inevitable. The Court scheduled three days for them in late March 2012. They were hardly a tour de force for an Obama Administration reeling in the face of hostile questions while explaining the unexplainable. "Solicitor General Donald B. Verrilli Jr. should be grateful to the Supreme Court for refusing to allow cameras in the courtroom, because his defense of Obamacare on Tuesday may go down as one of the most spectacular flameouts in the history of the court" wrote liberal *Mother Jones* magazine.[91]

In the *Washington Post*, Reid Cherlin, a former Obama Administration spokesman, was sympathetic:

> I will say this: having spent a year of my life getting paid to defend the ACA as the White House spokesman on health care, I feel for the guy. Health care reform is very much worth defending, but going about that defense is where things get, well, difficult. . . . It would have been easy for Verrilli—or any of us—to explain single-payer health care. 'Look,' we could have said, 'the government is paying for everyone to have coverage.' End of story. But single-payer is not what our brilliant, world-leading political system gave us.[92]

Nonetheless, on June 28, 2012, the U.S. Supreme Court upheld the ACA, even though Chief Justice John Roberts, in the 5-4 decision, agreed with Vinson that the ACA was unsustainable under the Commerce Clause: "Construing the Commerce Clause to permit Congress to regulate individuals precisely *because* they are doing nothing would open a new and potentially vast domain to congressional authority."

That determination was a vastly more coherent refinement of an incoherent question asked during oral argument by archconservative Justice Scalia: "Could you define the market — everybody has to buy food sooner or later, so you define the market as food, therefore, everybody is in the market; therefore, you can make people buy broccoli?"[93] Yet, it is also a mysterious opinion in many respects. Health care is not broccoli. As law professors Michael Graetz and Jerry Mashaw wrote in the *Harvard Law and Policy Review*, "No one denies that health insurance is interstate commerce. And no one denies that the cross-subsidies of paying customers to non-paying customers are very substantial."[94] The test should be "whether the thing that is being regulated substantially affects interstate commerce."[95]

While rejecting the Obama Administration's argument that the ACA was proper interstate commerce regulation, Roberts nonetheless accepted the Administration's second argument that "even if Congress lacks the power to direct individuals to buy insurance, the only effect of the individual mandate is to raise taxes on those who do not do so, and thus the law may be upheld as a tax." He found that "taxes that seek to influence conduct are nothing new" and the individual mandate was merely "a tax citizens may lawfully choose to pay in lieu of buying health insurance." Thus, the mandate was constitutional.

This reasoning was reminiscent of work under the administration of Franklin Roosevelt to clear the way for what became Social Security. The administration sought the informal advice of a couple Supreme Court justices who might rule on the constitutionality of their efforts. As Kirstin Downey, in her biography of Frances Perkins, Roosevelt's labor secretary, relates:

> Justice Harlan F. Stone had whispered some words of advice as well. At an afternoon party at Stone's home, Frances was drinking tea with the justice when he asked how things were going. She told him they were wrestling with how to establish an economic security program. Stone looked around to see if anyone was listening, then leaned in toward Frances. "The taxing power, my dear, the taxing power," he said in quiet tones.[96]

Fatefully, though, Roberts found the ACA's provisions coercing Medicaid expansion were "a gun to the head" – with states standing to lose all Medicaid funding if they chose not to participate. Under the ACA, Medicaid would be expanded to serve all of those up to 138% of the federal poverty level. Roberts wrote that transformed the Medicaid program, making it "no longer a program to care for the neediest among us, but rather an element of a comprehensive national plan to provide universal health insurance coverage." He ruled: "What Congress is not free to do is to penalize States that choose not to participate in that new program by taking away their existing Medicaid funding." Under his opinion, "States may now choose to reject the expansion; that is the whole point. But that does not mean all or even any will."

Roberts proved too modest. In a manner unappreciated at the time by Democrats celebrating – alongside the insurance and pharmaceutical industries – a victory, or by handwringing Republicans mourning a defeat, Roberts eviscerated a key component of the ACA. In the wake of the ruling, Georgia's Republican Governor Nathan Deal was typical in his reaction: "Today, the highest court in the country let the American people down. While we recognize this is a huge setback for fiscal sanity and personal liberty, we are not giving up."[97]

Revealing an interesting understanding of the separation of powers, enraged Republican Senator Rand Paul of Kentucky put out a press release: "Just because a couple people on the Supreme Court declare something to be 'constitutional' does not make it so. The whole thing remains unconstitutional."[98]

Yet while a battle was lost, the war was not over. After dusting themselves off, Republicans like Deal took Roberts' invitation to not expand Medicaid. In addition, Roberts, with whom the Court's four Democratic appointees were forced to make common cause, effectively diminished the Commerce Clause in a precedent that might prove fruitful for his long-term agenda.

A year following the Roberts' ruling, Margot Sanger-Katz would write in *The Atlantic*:

> When the Supreme Court decided the big health-care case last June, its ruling was seen as a huge win for President Obama. His administration had fended off a challenge that would have dismantled the entire reform effort; it lost on only a small issue to which few people had paid much heed. But a year later, it's increasingly clear that the minor loss is punching a major hole in the law's primary ambition – expanding health insurance coverage to most of the 49 million Americans who lack it.[99]

"The Supreme Court dealt Obamacare a major blow after all," she concluded.

Nor would it necessarily be the last blow. In March 2015 the Court heard arguments as to whether it was legal for the federal government to provide subsidies to those securing insurance through federally-facilitated exchanges as opposed to the state-run exchanges that the ACA had contemplated. That litigation is described later.

6

THE PATIENT PROTECTION AND AFFORDABLE CARE ACT

"LACK OF ACCESS to health care contributes significantly to inequality, and this aspect of inequality in turn is especially important in undermining the performance of our economy" notes the economist Joseph Stiglitz. He writes that health care's "high costs are due in part to rent seeking by insurance companies and the pharmaceutical industry. Other countries have curbed these rents. We have not."[100]

The ACA addresses neither of these "rents."

The act is staggeringly complex. The benefit of the Nixon and Clinton proposals, as compared to the ACA, was the symbolic simplicity of a universal "card" to be used to access health care. No such analogue exists under the ACA. Instead, everything is largely different state-by-state, insurer-by-insurer.

Insurers were prevented from screening pre-existing conditions for children starting in 2011 and adults starting in 2014; setting lifetime spending caps; charging more than $6,350 out-of-pocket per individual ($6,600 in 2015); rating by gender or too greatly by age; or spending less than 80-85% of premiums on medical care. Insurers were required to cover dependents up to age 26.

Tax credits would be available through health benefit exchanges for small businesses and for individuals based upon the relationship of individual or family income to the federal poverty line. Medicaid would be expanded, by states choosing to do so, to cover those below 138% of the federal poverty level.

Plans would be required to reach a certain actuarial value, and provide ten essential health benefits identified by the federal government. States were required to identify a "benchmark" plan.

Preexisting Conditions

Limiting the ability of carriers to deny, or delay, coverage based upon preexisting conditions is a significant market reform. It is what is called "guaranteed issue."

Prior to this change, anyone with a preexisting condition wanted to hold onto health coverage as long as possible so as to avoid a health screening for any new coverage. This was why the protection under the 1986 Consolidated Omnibus Budget Reconciliation Act (COBRA) was so important – a person separating from a job could continue, at their own expense, employer-sponsored health care for themselves and their families for 18 months.

Yet it will be interesting to see how this reform plays out given the federal government's own miserable experiment.

The ACA set up a federally-subsidized Preexisting Conditions Insurance Plan (PCIP) as a bridge to 2014, and allowed states to administer it. Many states already had high-risk pools, although as Robert Laszewski, an insurance expert, had pointed out – in the context of a high-risk pool proposed by Senator McCain during the 2008 campaign – "state-based risk pools for the uninsured have never worked well because they tend to be swamped by people and underfunded."[101] Still, segregating high risk into such pools was originally a Republican idea, and 27 states agreed to administer their own PCIP programs under federal contract. Yet the Obama Administration underestimated how much this population would cost. By February 16, 2013, the federally-run PCIP stopped accepting new enrollment applications, and forced state programs to stop accepting applications two weeks later.

With enrollment frozen, Washington State, one of the nation's most successful PCIP programs in enrollment numbers, provided a good example of the sort of high-risk pool a state-run PCIP program had: Of 1,106 enrollees by April 2013, 474 had HIV/AIDS. Pharmaceutical costs were exorbitant, as one might imagine. Other enrollees suffered conditions such as cancer or diabetes that prevented them from being able to obtain insurance in the pre-2014 market.

A "Helping Sick Americans Now Act" measure to shore up PCIP funding, by taking money from other ACA programs, was introduced by majority House Republicans in April 2013 only to be abandoned after the conservative Club for Growth indicated that to vote for it would count against Republicans on its scorecard. "Fiscal conservatives should be squarely focused on repealing ObamaCare, not strengthening it by supporting the parts that are politically attractive" wrote the group.[102] The Heritage Foundation and Tea Party groups joined in opposition.

This revealed a schism in conservative ranks. The conservative *Wall Street Journal* editorialized in favor of the bill, while the FreedomWorks group led a coalition of signatories, including the so-called Christian Coalition, in a letter of support: "The bill takes $4 billion from an Obamacare slush fund and reallocates part of it to helping sick people the President has turned his back on. The remainder, about $1 billion, goes to deficit reduction. To be clear: this bill defunds Obamacare."[103]

The White House agreed, stating that "[w]hile the Administration would like to extend coverage to as many Americans as possible, rather than finding common ground on a funding source, this legislation effectively would repeal part of the Affordable Care Act."[104]

House Majority Leader Eric Cantor of Virginia was forced to withdraw the bill because of the conservative disunity. In 2014 he would be upset in his Republican primary by a Tea Party challenger.

With money running out, the Obama Administration in April 2013 ordered states administering their own PCIP programs to assume risk themselves above appropriated amounts or transfer vulnerable enrollees to the federal government – where different coinsurance costs and benefits would exist. Enrollees with acute medical conditions risked falling through the cracks if they could not pay higher federal costs.

Indeed, in April 2013 testimony before the Senate Finance Committee, the Administration was no more sympathetic than a heartless insurer, boasting of "aggressively managing costs" of PCIP enrollees by changing provider networks midstream, reducing provider payments, limiting specialty drug access, and jacking up out-of-pocket limits from $4,000 to $6,250.[105] In short, the Administration controlled costs by doing all the things progressives would decry were an insurer to do them.

With a median household income in the United States of $52,762 as of 2011 Census data, one can only imagine the burden of $6,250 in medical costs to the average person. Upon being able to obtain private insurance in 2014, PCIP enrollees faced $6,350 out-of-pocket limits – or greater.

Indeed, in another sign that insurers' health was the ACA's paramount objective, the Obama Administration quietly delayed the $6,350 out-of-pocket limits for certain insurers – allowing them to set their own limits in 2014. In reporting this news in August 2013, the *New York Times* noted "[t]he grace period has been outlined on the Labor Department's Web site since February, but was obscured in a maze of legal and bureaucratic language that went largely unnoticed."[106] An anonymous Administration official defended the delay: "We had to balance the interests of consumers with the concerns of health plan sponsors and carriers[.]" Consumers will always lose in such a "balancing".

Moving forward, the Administration in May 2014 handed insurers another hidden, huge win. It cryptically announced, in its episodic "Frequently Asked Questions" on the ACA (this set was known as "FAQ Part XIX"), that it would allow insurers to not pay for procedures that cost above a set amount – so-called "reference pricing." Even the Administration acknowledged that "such a pricing structure may be a subterfuge for the imposition of otherwise prohibited limitations on coverage, without ensuring access to quality care and an adequate network of providers."

The smiley face the Obama Administration sought to put on the ACA added to confusion about what guaranteed issue really meant for those with preexisting conditions.

On Mother's Day 2013, for example, the White House put out a "Happy Mother's Day from the Affordable Care Act" Facebook meme, stating, "Starting in 2014, it will be illegal to deny coverage to anyone with a pre-existing condition like pregnancy or breast cancer[.]"

While true, it implied something untrue – that insurance access would always be available to anyone pregnant or with cancer. That would only be true if the coincidence occurred where one happened, happily, to be pregnant or, unhappily, afflicted with cancer during open enrollment periods (perhaps three months out of a year). Outside such a period, those pregnant or those with cancer would have no more success buying insurance than they would have had prior to 2014, even if there was nothing overtly discriminatory about their lack of access.

Without finite open enrollment periods, people would buy insurance only when they needed it – "adverse selection" fatal to insurance affordability and the economic reason preexisting condition barriers existed in the first place. Without open enrollment periods, guaranteed issue risked bringing the consequences conjured by the conservative American Legislative Exchange Council: "What it means in practice is that individuals who are in good health can wait to purchase insurance until they are sick. They can use the guaranteed-issue rule to force insurance companies to bail them out at the last minute."[107] However, polling shows that the uninsured are largely unaware of open enrollment periods.

Further, the meme ignored other facts about the ACA: Thanks to the cozy deal struck with the pharmaceutical industry, and the state latitude in regulation, cancer patients could face bankrupting prescription drug costs that were as much a barrier to care as a lack of insurance. To keep premiums down for the healthy, California allowed benefit designs with co-pays of up to 30% for specialty drugs; an advocacy group estimated a patient might pay more than $2,000 a month for one cancer drug.[108] Out-of-pocket limits could be reached through drug costs alone.

Indeed, a December 2013 *Washington Post* article documented the disaffection of "people who expected the new plans to provide pharmaceutical coverage comparable with that of employer-sponsored plans."[109] Compared to the regular private market, for example, exchange offerings had drug benefits that were so pared down that they either did not cover drugs for HIV or required patients to pay as much as 50%, or over $1,000 a month, toward their costs.

In May 2014 two advocacy groups alleged four insurers doing business through the federally-run exchange were discriminating against those with HIV or AIDS through exorbitant out-of-pocket charges; a *New York Times* article reported "patients were shocked when, newly covered, they were asked to pay pharmacy bills of up to $1,000 a month, in addition to the premiums they were already paying."[110] As one advocate related in the *Kaiser Health News*, "A state insurance regulator doesn't have the clinical expertise to know whether the common HIV drugs are covered and how they should be covered on a formulary."[111] Yet no federal anti-discrimination guidelines had been issued.

It may be that those who are sick have no better option than a bad one, and that enough good risk will be added to offset the bad risk. As author Michael Kinsley, who has a preexisting condition, wrote in *Vanity Fair*:

> The theory is that if health insurance is treated like a hot summer day—"Everyone into the pool!"—people with lower-than-average health-care costs will help pay for people with higher-than-average costs, and insurance companies will compete in trying to deliver health care to everyone more efficiently instead of playing hot potato with the bad risks like me.[112]

Yet, as Kinsley observed, "requiring people to carry insurance doesn't solve the adverse-selection problem. As long as the customer has any choice at all, healthier people will gravitate toward less coverage and sicker people will gravitate toward more coverage, and soon we're back in the death spiral."[113] Further, "even if every insurance company obeys the rules and takes anyone who walks, crawls, or wheels in the door, it is unlikely that good customers and bad ones will spread themselves evenly among the various insurance companies, all offering identical benefits."[114] As a result, "the government will have to step in and re-distribute money among the insurance companies."[115] With that much federal government involvement as a consequence of private market complexity and inequity, why not just have a single-payer system?

Metallic Tiers

The ACA classifies health plans based upon actuarial value—that is, how much of your premium pays health care costs. Plans are classified by "metal" tiers. The minimal standard of a Bronze plan would have an actuarial value of 60%, leaving a patient to account for 40% of his or her health care costs out-of-pocket through co-pays or deductibles. In contrast, a Platinum plan has an actuarial value of 90%, a Gold plan has one of 80%, and a Silver plan has a 70% actuarial value.

Beginning January 1, 2014, plans sold in the individual and small group market had to meet at least the Bronze standard. It cannot be overstated what a change this is. Prior to 2014, most people in the individual market had what could be called "tin" plans, of less than 50% actuarial value.[116]

One benefit of creating the metallic tiers – and a threshold for acceptable coverage – is it lets consumers who are not highly-trained actuaries compare plans in ways that were previously impossible. Furthermore, insurers know consumers can do this – which then influences insurers' behavior.

Thus, when health plan rates filed with the Oregon Insurance Division became public in May 2013, two carriers immediately asked for a do-over in recognition of the fact that their rates were uncompetitive. Both carriers were nonprofits. The *Oregonian* reported that the CEO of one carrier stated, "[M]y question when I saw the rates was, 'Can we go in and refile these?' We're going to try to get these to a competitive range" (no good regulator should allow such re-refiling or "shadow pricing" – it enables gaming of rates).[117]

Yet the Oregon example also revealed why the ideal of consumers being able to truly compare "apples to apples" was too simplistic for the insurance marketplace. One health insurer, for example, offered Silver plans less expensive than its Bronze plans. How could an offering from the same carrier that pays 70% of medical costs be cheaper than one paying 60 percent? It was because metallic calculations were based solely upon cost-sharing for the ten federal essential health benefits – a plan might offer *more* than those benefits in any particular metallic tier. Thus, one insurer's Bronze plan might conceivably be better than another's Gold plan.

Health insurance is extraordinarily complex. The same insurer can offer myriad benefit designs, perhaps dozens. The ACA may have established baselines, but it did not erase variations between health insurers or even within a single insurer's offerings. As a 2014 PricewaterhouseCoopers' Health Research Institute report put it: "No two health plans are exactly the same—even if they have the same actuarial value."[118]

Community Rating

With health screening impermissible, a significant market reform was what was referred to as community rating. This includes preventing rating based upon gender, and compressing what are called "age bands."

In the individual insurance market, most states had allowed carriers to charge a 64-year-old five times what a 21-year-old would be charged for insurance. The National Association of Insurance Commissioners (NAIC) had found "overall variation of 5:1 or less is reasonable in the small group market based on the expected claim costs of 22-year-olds and 62-year-olds."[119] The ACA limits this to a factor of three-to-one (H.R. 3200 was originally going to limit age rating to two-to-one).

The consequence is premiums for those older fell while premiums for those younger rose. Those who are younger, however, are more likely to qualify for Medicaid or premium subsidies through purchasing insurance through exchanges. Yet, if a state chose not to expand Medicaid, the young working poor faced rate shock as a result of the new age bands. They were in the worst of all worlds: Commercial insurance had been made unaffordable for them, and yet there was no alternative.

Florida, for example, had allowed that age rating that was actuarially supportable – with a ratio of as much as seven-to-one.[120] And yet Florida had an older population than the national average, with its Medicare-eligible demographic of those 65-and-older, for example, comprising 17.3% of the state's 2011 census. There would be no Medicaid option as a safe harbor for low-income young adults who could not find affordable insurance as a result of the marketplace shift in favor of those older.

The effects of this could be disparate across genders. To give just one example, for 2014 the cost of an Aetna policy in Florida equivalent to a Bronze plan had gone up 119.7% for males ages 21-29.[121] For women in that age bracket, because of new savings based upon the disallowance of gender rating (younger women get pregnant, and childbirth costs money), the increase was only 4.6 percent.

As America's Health Insurance Plans noted in May 2013 congressional testimony, "If higher premiums cause younger and healthier people to delay purchasing coverage until after they are sick or injured, the overall pool of people purchasing health insurance will be weighted more heavily with older and less healthy people — thereby driving up premiums for everyone and destabilizing the market."[122]

Essential Health Benefits

Under the ACA, there are ten essential health benefits (EHB) that are the core package of benefits that health insurance plans, inside and outside of exchanges, must offer in the individual and small group markets:

1. Ambulatory patient services
2. Emergency services
3. Hospitalization
4. Maternity and newborn care
5. Mental health and substance use disorder services, including behavioral health treatment
6. Prescription drugs
7. Rehabilitative and habilitative services and devices
8. Laboratory services
9. Preventive and wellness services and chronic disease management
10. Pediatric services, including oral and vision care

In EHB rulemaking, the Obama Administration gave unexpected discretion to the states. As Robert Pear wrote in the *New York Times*, "The rules lay out 10 broad categories of essential health benefits, but allow each state to specify the benefits within those categories, at least for 2014 and 2015. Thus, the required benefits will vary from state to state, *contrary to what many members of Congress had assumed when the law was adopted.*"[123] (Emphasis added).

This was the absolute floor of what the ACA required — the federal government could have augmented it. The Obama Administration had commissioned the Institute of Medicine (IOM) to study the issue, and related that "[t]he IOM recommended flexibility across States and suggested that States operating their own Exchanges be allowed to substitute a plan that is actuarially equivalent to the national EHB package."[124] And the IOM further recommended that "[c]urrent state insurance mandates—requirements that had previously been established by state law—should not automatically be included in the EHB package but reviewed in the same way as other potential benefits."[125]

In other words, autistic kids – and others protected by state insurance mandates – might be out of luck if their benefits did not fit under what the federal
government was willing to subsidize through exchanges. That would certainly be
fine with insurers, who oppose such mandates. A report from the Pew Charitable
Trusts noted that "[a]utism advocates celebrated what they thought was a major victory when President Barack Obama signed the Affordable Care Act in 2010: They
expected the law to require all insurance companies to cover pricey, potentially
lifelong treatments for those with the incurable condition." Instead, "critics say the
ACA will add a new layer of complexity" to procuring care for autism.[126]

Even the IOM had believed the federal government would flesh out the essential health benefits rather than simply reissue, through its "guidance," the skeletal,
undefined list of ten criteria from the ACA. The IOM had recommended that "[i]
nitial guidance by the Secretary on the contents of the EHB package should list
standard benefit inclusions and exclusions at a *level of specificity at least comparable to
current best practice* in the private and public insurance market."[127] Apparently that
was too exhausting for the Obama Administration. As one account noted:

> Consumer advocates and some provider groups also had sought
> a national standard to reduce variation from state to state and to
> ensure a sufficient minimum benefit package. They complained
> that HHS's approach does not address the fact that many health
> plans have inadequate benefits. More than 2,400 doctors, nurses,
> and health advocates signed a letter to HHS dated December 1,
> 2011, saying that the department's approach would "enshrine these
> skimpy plans as the new standard."[128]

On February 6, 2012, alarmed House Democrats – including Henry Waxman
and John Dingell – sent a letter to the Obama Administration. They asserted that
"[w]hen creating the EHB package, we intended this to be a federal decision. We had
not anticipated your decision to delegate the definition of the EHB package to states.
. . . Without very careful protections, we have serious concerns about delegating the
decision for the EHB to the States and providing even further discretion to insurers."
They noted that "plans are not required to meet state benefit mandates in many states
and have not had to meet mental health parity or other insurance requirements."
They also asked, "If states are free to define the EHB benchmark, what happens if they

either fail to select a package that meets the ACA requirements or fail to enforce the adherence to that package by health insurers?"[129]

Yet even the Obama Administration's laissez-faire approach was too much for the NAIC, which wrote: "State insurance regulators strongly support a process that continues to rely on states and policies sold in the marketplace to determine the EHB." The primary concern of the NAIC was not consumers, but "the amount of data requested of issuers and the administrative burden and cost that is being placed on them."[130]

The essential health benefits did not address hearing, or vision for adults, whatsoever. The failure to cover hearing, particularly, is a notable omission. According to the National Institute of Deafness and Other Communication Disorders, "One in eight people in the United States (13 percent, or 30 million) aged 12 years or older has hearing loss in both ears, based on standard hearing examinations."[131] That loss becomes more disabling as you age. While 14 percent of those aged 45-54 have hearing loss, for example, the loss is considered disabling for just 2 percent of that age demographic. The percentage of those for whom hearing loss is disabling grows to 8.5 percent for those aged 55-64. After that the progression is quick into your Medicare years. A quarter of those aged 65-74 have disabling hearing loss, and over half of those over 75.

Hearing aids are prohibitively expensive for most people, given that they are generally not covered by insurance and are not covered at all by Medicare. Instead of receiving medical care through audiologists, far too many with hearing loss are forced to buy faux hearing aids (really just sound amplifiers) from magazine ads, online sites, or big box stores. These devices are not fitted to their medical needs, and are outside of the care and diagnosis of a clinically-trained audiologist. Hearing loss is far more subtle than just turning up the volume, and why is the ability to hear not considered essential to whole health?

Only three states require insurance coverage for adult hearing aids. When, having replaced her husband John, Democratic Congresswoman Debbie Dingell of Michigan introduced the Medicare Hearing Aid Coverage Act of 2015,[132] to repeal the exclusion of, and allow coverage for, hearing aids and examinations for them, only three other Democrats signed on in the first few months following introduction. Coverage of hearing aids would, especially, reduce the profits for Medicare Advantage insurers. Yet, if such a benefit is not covered through Medicare, the chances are nil of state politicians compelling it through the private market.

Dental coverage is one of the ACA's greatest shortcomings. While one of the essential health benefits was pediatric dental care, the Obama Administration somehow determined that this coverage as offered by stand-alone dental insurers fell outside the ACA's out-of-pocket limits.

In the April 2013 Senate Finance Committee confirmation hearing for Marilyn Tavenner, President Obama's nominee as Medicare and Medicaid administrator, an incredulous Democratic Senator Benjamin Carder of Maryland unloaded: "Congress did not intend to create a market advantage for stand-alone dental plans over an affordable pediatric dental benefit embedded in a comprehensive plan." He criticized her for allowing "each state to determine its own separate pediatric dental out-of-pocket limit, creating a patchwork of unequal benefits across the nation. Congress did not permit states to set their own out-of-pocket limits for comprehensive health plans – *why are you discriminating against oral health?*"[133]

Tavenner responded that "stand-alone dental plans are not subject to the insurance market reforms" and declared that for 2014 "a reasonable limit" on cost-sharing was $700 per child enrollee or $1,400 for two or more children.

Tavenner was a former executive at the world's largest operator of health care facilities – Tennessee-based Hospital Corporation of America – a company that pled guilty to 14 felonies, and paid $1.7 billion in penalties, for overcharging government after future Florida Governor Rick Scott left as its CEO amidst federal raids over evidence of double bookkeeping.[134]

The effect of Tavenner's position, Cardin opined, was "to eviscerate consumer protections for children enrolled in stand-alone dental plans" given that surely oral health was essential to a child's whole health. Nonetheless, every Senate Democrat voted to confirm her.

As there is no ACA requirement of adult dental coverage, far too many adults will continue to go to emergency rooms for full-blown oral health complications.

Medical Loss Ratio
Ostensibly the ACA protects against insurance price-gouging with a mechanism called a medical-loss ratio (MLR) – where the amount of a premium that must be spent on medical care is specified as 80% in the individual and small group markets and 85% in large group markets. If insurers do not operate at this modest level of efficiency, policyholders receive rebates by fall of the next year. In practice, insurers can make vast sums of money within this construct.

Premiums exceeding the MLR for 2012 returned $504 million to policyholders nationwide in 2013 – of which $192 million was attributable to the individual market.[135] Contrast that meager return to the roughly $1.2 trillion in health insurance subsidies that the Congressional Budget Office projected the federal government will provide under the ACA from 2014-2022 – a projected taxpayer subsidy of $35 billion, or $5,510 per exchange enrollee, in 2014 alone.[136]

To offer another comparison to a nationwide refund of $504 million for policyholders, net revenues for UnitedHealth Group alone in 2013 were $122.5 billion, with income at $9.6 billion.[137]

Yet even the generous MLR was too great a curb on insurer profitability for insurance regulators.

Beginning with a June 2010 letter to Secretary Sebelius, the NAIC began complaining about the medical loss ratio: "The medical loss ratio and rebate program in PPACA have the potential to destabilize the marketplace and significantly limit consumer choices if the definitions and calculations are too restrictive."[138]

The American Legislative Exchange Council (ALEC), in a 2011 publication, *The State Legislators Guide to Repealing Obamacare*, encouraged states to seek MLR waivers as a stalling tactic.[139] The Obama Administration did grant time-limited waivers from MLR requirements to states with limited insurer competition. For example, Maine, with just two carriers, was granted a MLR of 65 percent for 2011 and 2012, but had its waiver rejected to continue that MLR for 2013.[140]

Texas was among states to have its waiver request rejected; Republican Governor Rick Perry's administration sought to lower the MLR to 71% for 2011, 74% for 2012, and 77% for 2013.[141] The insurance regulator for Republican Wisconsin Governor Scott Walker made the same case.[142] The Obama Administration rejected these appeals for even greater insurer profitability.

In Florida, where former health care executive Rick Scott was governor, the Obama Administration rejected the argument that the withdrawal of six health insurers from Florida's market, with a combined market share of less than 1%, would destabilize the individual market or, for that matter, even was precipitated by the MLR.[143]

Governor Scott's regulator making that unlikely case was the NAIC president, Kevin McCarty. McCarty sought to lower the MLR to 68% in 2011, 72% in 2012, and 76% for 2013. Although McCarty claimed a public hearing demonstrated "remarkable unanimity" of support for lowering the MLR, the Obama Administration noted consumers were not allowed to speak at the hearing – only insurance industry representatives. At McCarty's urging the NAIC also passed a resolution urging the federal government to treat insurance brokers' commissions "as a health care quality expense" for purposes of calculating the medical loss ratio.[144] Such a change would have effectively erased the ACA's one modest curb upon insurers' profiteering.

In most states the MLR was no imposition. There was no reason to believe ALEC's claim that the MLR would "lead to less consumer choice and higher prices" because "many small insurers may be ill-equipped to comply with the new rules." If carriers, of whatever size, were so inefficient, why should they be licensed to sell insurance? And why would efficiency, through spending a baseline proportion of premium dollars on care and not administration, raise consumer prices?

Cooperatives

The only surviving language of the ACA providing anything close to a public option allowed for $6 billion in loans to start non-profit health insurers in each state, run by consumers themselves, called Consumer Operated and Oriented Plans (CO-OPs). Coverage could be offered inside and outside of exchanges. For any CO-OP, the customers would elect a board of directors, with boards to have majority-customer composition. The CO-OPs could only use profits to lower premiums, improve benefits, or improve care quality.

Washington State has the nation's best example of a longstanding cooperative, Group Health, founded in 1947 with over a half-million members. Group Health, a health maintenance organization highlighted in President Clinton's proposed 1993 health care reform, directly employs care providers and operates its own facilities.

The original $6 billion to establish CO-OPs was reduced to $3.4 billion in Obama Administration deal-making with Congress, and then, after only $1.9 billion had been expended, the Administration, without explanation, unilaterally surrendered remaining funding for the program in a January 2013 "fiscal cliff" deal with Congress celebrated as a triumph of bipartisanship.

The capitulation left only 24 CO-OPs that had already received funding, with at least as many others with pending applications out in the cold despite incurring expenses in good faith. Loans would have had to be repaid in five years, making the CO-OPs an uncertain business model in the best of circumstances, but the ACA's quasi-public option had been killed without ceremony.

Those CO-OPs able to start hinted at the promise of a public option – one in Oregon was offering 2014 rates competitive with big insurers, even though it lacked their buying power relative to health providers.[145] Like other CO-OPs that were able to get going before the plug was pulled, it promised a more customer-friendly experience. A CO-OP in New Mexico was going to pay community health workers to visit enrollees in their homes, instruct them in nutrition, and help them manage chronic conditions like diabetes so as to keep them out of hospitals. By February

2014, a CO-OP in Kentucky had enlisted more than 60% of that state's exchange enrollment, while one in Maine had captured more than 80 percent.[146]

Even before funding was rescinded, the fate of CO-OPs was not bright. The *Washington Post* noted, in an October 2013 article, that due to insurance industry opposition "Congress saddled its new creations with onerous restrictions that, experts say, doomed the co-ops to failure."[147] Loans were issued on such a tight timeline that they might be impossible to pay off. At the time of the Senate's 2009 consideration of the ACA, Nebraska's Ben Nelson was critical to assisting the insurance industry in watering the co-op provisions down. The *Post* quoted former Democratic senator Kent Conrad of North Dakota, the Senate's leading advocate for co-ops in 2009: "The long knives were out for this. No money could be used for marketing? Really? That was clearly intended to be a poison pill."

In at least one case, online exchange problems may have doomed a CO-OP. A March 7, 2014 *Washington Post* article described how one doctor's dream was imperiled by the disastrous rollout of Maryland's exchange.[148] Hardly anyone was able to get through to enroll in his vision of a CO-OP combining insurance and health centers where doctors would be paid flat salaries (reducing the incentive to over-treat) and "[t]iny waiting rooms would reinforce the message that all patients would be seen quickly." A wellness emphasis was to include lifestyle coaches and free yoga.

Individual Mandate

The unpopularity of an individual mandate approach was never a mystery. In June 1994 a memorandum from Ira Magaziner to Hillary and President Clinton stated "[i]t is a radical departure from today's system, and workers are not likely to believe that their employers will continue providing coverage, particularly during a time when employers are dropping coverage and reducing benefits."[149]

Yet, if the paradigm of guaranteeing health care access through the commercial insurance market was to work, an individual mandate was necessary.

Under Section 1501 of the ACA, Congress found that without an individual mandate

> many individuals would wait to purchase health insurance until
> they needed care. By significantly increasing health insurance cov-
> erage, the requirement, together with the other provisions of this
> Act, will minimize this adverse selection and broaden the health

insurance risk pool to include healthy individuals, which will lower health insurance premiums.

"This was the first time in American history that the federal government ordered the general population to purchase a commercial product" wrote the National Federation of Independent Business (NFIB).[150]

For 2014, the penalty for not buying insurance would be $95 per uninsured adult ($47.50 per child), or 1% of family income, whichever was greater. That amount would increase to the greater of $325 ($162.50 per child), or 2% of family income, in 2015, and $695 ($347.50 per child), or 2.5% of family income, in 2016.

The group most at risk of being willing to pay the penalty is the group that the ACA needs most to succeed: So-called "young invincibles." If healthy young people opt out of health care reform, exchanges would be full of the older and sicker – starting an inexorable rate spiral. The higher rates go, the less likely young people will participate – what Ezekiel Emmanuel calls "a negative reinforcing cycle that undermines the entire exchange system."[151] And by July 2014 a poll showed that voters of ages 18-29 – young voters so critical to putting President Obama into office – were the age demographic most disenchanted about Obama's handling of health care. Sixty-one percent disapproved.[152] A poll of young voters released in October 2014 by the Harvard Institute of Public Policy showed them barely trusting Democrats more than Republicans on health care: 33% trusted Democrats and 25% trusted Republicans.[153]

With a key demographic so alienated, it remained to be seen whether the relatively-meager individual mandate penalty would serve the objective of avoiding adverse selection. As the NAIC has observed, "In a guaranteed issue, no pre-existing condition environment, the reward for waiting to obtain coverage until it is needed, or switching coverage to minimize cost and maximize benefits will always exist, even with the tax penalties in federal law."[154]

As the Obama Administration retreated from ACA enforcement, by June 2014 the Congressional Budget Office was estimating only 13% of those who were uninsured would even pay the penalty.[155]

Employer Penalty

Under the ACA, employers of at least 50 full-time employees are required to provide health insurance or pay a penalty that would, initially, be $2,000 a year. That coverage would have to be at least at the Bronze level; in other words, paying at least 60% of covered health care expenses. That is richer than much employer coverage in existence prior to 2014. Upon crossing the 50 employee threshold, employers would be subject to a complex calculation where they could subtract 30 employees from their total in paying the penalty.

The NFIB correctly notes a result of this arbitrary Rubicon: "The mandate makes it extremely expensive to cross the 50-employee threshold. For example, a midsized restaurant that goes from 49 to 50 employees will face a $40,000 per year penalty. A business can avoid the penalties by firing employees, by not hiring new ones, by replacing full-timers with part-timers, or by outsourcing." A 2014 Congressional Research Service report referred to this as a "cliff": "In other words, a firm that employed 49 full-time workers and then hired a 50th full-time worker would be subject to a penalty based (in part) on 30 full-time workers."[156]

The employer penalty itself was not enormous relative to the costs of health care. As 2014 approached, there was considerable publicity over the question of whether employers would drop health insurance coverage for employees and simply pay the penalty – or game their way past the coverage requirement for full-time employees by reducing the hours of their employees to part-time status. The Obama Administration then decided to not enforce the penalty in 2014, and later announced it would largely exempt from it in 2015 all employers of fewer than 100 full-time employees. This is the subject of later discussion.

Multi-State Plans

The most objectively absurd aspect of the ACA is a provision where the federal government offers what are called "multi-state plans," ostensibly to boost competition in states without enough health insurance options. Yet, as an April 2013 report for the Robert Wood Johnson Foundation noted:

> [A]lthough one of the goals of the Multi-State Plan Program was to increase competition, it is possible that the program could have the opposite effect and increase dominant players' share of an already concentrated market. The reason is that only a handful of insurance companies are currently in position to participate. The issuers participating in the Multi-State Program must be licensed in each state and have sufficient provider networks and financial reserves

and an adequate information technology structure in place to meet enrollees' needs nationwide.

To put it more plainly, as law professor Timothy Jost, a leading expert on health care reform, did in the *New York Times*, "If you've got Blue Cross competing with Blue Cross, it doesn't give you much competition."[157]

Indeed, in Washington State, the multi-state plan that sought admission to the exchange was offered by Premera Blue Cross – the carrier already dominating Washington's market. The *only* difference under the ACA from Premera's normal offering was a plan that did not cover abortion. It is hard to regard this distinction as a win for consumers.

By the close of 2014 open enrollment, Premera, and a wholly-owned Premera subsidiary, accounted for three-fifths of exchange enrollees in Washington (the next-closest insurer had 17%).[158]

Exchanges
The idea of health insurance exchanges had its genesis in conservative free market thought.

In a May 5, 2009 statement to the Senate Finance Committee, Stuart Butler, a Heritage Foundation vice president, argued that "[t]here is broad support for a health insurance exchange to improve the functioning of a competitive market for plans."[159] Instead of an individual mandate, he suggested tricking families into enrolment by making "automatic enrolment in private plans the default for working families. In this arrangement, working families would automatically be signed up to the employer's plan or to one of a group of plans chosen by the state and would have to actively decline coverage if they didn't want it.... Inertia is very powerful."

The multi-state litigation challenging the ACA centered upon the individual mandate to purchase health insurance, while the U.S. Supreme Court decision upholding the ACA was notable for affording states the choice of whether to opt in, or out, of Medicaid expansion. Health benefit exchanges were ignored, yet are the very portals through which health care reform succeeds or fails.

Contrary to rhetoric about "Obamacare" and the specter of a federal health care takeover, almost all lines of insurance—including much of health insurance—are still regulated by individual states. An exception is employee benefit pension plans governed by the Employee Retirement Income Security Act. Health care reform is more carrot than stick. The penalties are much lighter than the inducements.

Exchanges are the conduit through which federal tax subsidies for insurance are available for those ineligible for Medicaid expansion. The familiar example used was of a shopping website like Expedia, where the user submits parameters to find the best deal. Exchanges fill a similar role relative to health insurance options for the individual and small group markets. By 2017, large group plans may also be procured through exchanges.

The "carrots" of exchanges are tax subsidies available to those with incomes up to 400% of the Federal Poverty Level who purchase insurance through them. Premium tax credits are both refundable, for those who have no tax liability, and advanceable at the time of insurance purchase for those who do.

No one is required to purchase insurance through such exchanges, and the pre-existing insurance market continued outside of them.

Exchanges can be established as either public or nonprofit private entities. Some states set them up as hybrids. States may also partner with the federal government by having it administer some aspects of an exchange through a "state partnership exchange." In the event a state is not ready, or is unwilling, to operate an exchange, the federal government runs a "federally-facilitated exchange" for the state.

Because insurance is otherwise state-regulated, it is ironic that so many critics of "Obamacare" made federal intervention in their state's private health care market inevitable by not affirmatively setting up a state-run exchange. A Heritage Foundation piece acknowledged as much in 2011: "[R]efusing to create an Obamacare state exchange, while politically appealing, would leave state health insurance markets vulnerable to even more federal interference and disruption over the next two years."[160]

"States had served as the primary regulators of insurance markets for decades, so there was widespread expectation they would want to operate the new insurance exchanges, too" noted one *Washington Post* analysis.[161] Yet that turned out not to be the case, as a later chapter describes, and was born out of a naïve analysis.

The individual insurance markets in most states are dominated by one or two different insurers — 29 states have a single carrier writing over half of the health insurance coverage in the individual market.[162]

The ACA will not substantially change this, at least in the near term.

Indeed, UnitedHealth chose only to file to participate in a dozen state exchanges in 2014, as compared to the 25 it had said it might sell in, and Aetna filed to participate in fourteen. Cigna would participate in five states. Most exchange shoppers would only find products that were in their states all along.[163] A June 2013 *New York Times* article noted that options in many states might "be limited to an already dominant local Blue Cross plan" and many citizens "may not have the robust choice of insurers that the law sought as a way to keep premiums lower and customer responsiveness higher."[164]

This may have been a clever way to avoid taking on the risk that guaranteed issue would initially bring. By coming later into a market, insurers might avoid those with preexisting conditions who rushed to sign up for insurance in 2014. Put more plainly, they avoided sick customers. By coming in the market later they could effectively cherry-pick, even though they were technically prevented from health screening anymore.

Insurers are by nature risk-adverse, and nothing within the ACA compels them to change that behavior. Indeed, they have a duty under state solvency regulations to avoid excessive risk.

What if you live in a rural county, have a mandate to purchase health insurance, and yet have no insurers in your county contracting with providers? This is a concern that would not have arisen with a single–payer system, just as it does not arise with Medicare. Yet it is a problem inherent in taking a commercial insurance market approach to procuring health care access. And it is an issue as consumers look to use their tax subsidies in exchanges.

In Mississippi, it initially appeared so few insurers would participate in a federally-facilitated exchange that 36 of the state's 82 counties would be left with no insurance coverage whatsoever in 2014 through the exchange.[165] Finally, one carrier – Humana – decided it would offer coverage in all counties.[166] Thus the ACA had simply obligated Mississippians without health coverage to buy Humana insurance. As *POLITICO* reported, "when the federal website, HealthCare.gov, made its disastrous debut on October 1 [2013], just four counties had two insurers competing for business; the rest had only a single choice."[167]

The *New York Times* studied data for 2014 and found rural areas were especially beset by a lack of insurance competition through the federally-facilitated exchanges.[168] In Michigan, the *Detroit Free Press* documented the difference between a county with one insurer and those counties where that insurer had competition: "The least expensive basic plan for a 40-year-old couple with two children costs $761 in Delta County, compared with $462 a month for a comparable plan in Kent County[.]"[169]

Accordingly, Americans losing non-ACA compliant health insurance plans in 2014 faced sticker shock because they lacked options. Beyond Mississippi, consider what the individual mandate meant for many of those hoping to use tax subsidies purchasing through exchanges. In all but three Alabama counties you had to buy Blue Cross and Blue Shield of Alabama. In three-fifths of North Carolina you had to buy Blue Cross and Blue Shield of North Carolina. In New Hampshire you had to buy Anthem. In West Virginia you had to buy Highmark. Rural county residents in many other states, including my Washington, have a single choice. In 22 Northern California counties 91% of all exchange coverage for 2014 was purchased through Anthem Blue Cross.[170]

How did ensuring such monopolism work out for Democrats? Not so well for Senator Kay Hagan of North Carolina, who lost her seat in 2014 after dominant carrier Blue Cross and Blue Shield, in a classic "October Surprise," announced it was raising rates 13.5% for 2015.[171] Hagan's seat was but one of several Democratic seats lost in monopoly or near-monopoly states.

Monopolism will only be reinforced by federal subsidies, as entering a market, and building a network of doctors and hospital, is a difficult proposition for any insurer. In Washington, for instance, the ACA cemented the monopoly of Premera Blue Cross – a fact unmentioned by politicians heralding enrollment while cashing Premera campaign contributions. As a story in the *Puget Sound Business Journal* related, "On the chessboard of Olympia politics, Premera is a queen: nimbly moving in every direction, knowing when to strike and outmaneuvering opponents of all kinds."[172]

At least for 2014, rates in exchanges were based upon conjecture, as Ezra Klein wrote in the *Washington Post*:

> The problem is that insurers don't know what their costs will be next year. So they're guessing. They're guessing who will enter the exchanges. They're guessing who will choose to buy their coverage. They're guessing whether healthy, young people will obey the individual mandate or pay the penalty. They're guessing what price they'll need to be competitive against other insurers, given differences in the networks, benefits, etc.[173]

After the consulting firm Avalere Health studied the 2014 rates, Caroline Pearson, Avalere's health reform vice president, related in the *Post* that, even where rates were lower than expected, "enrollees on exchanges are likely to face very high out-of-pocket costs before they hit their cap, and they are at risk of being in very narrow network plans that may or may not include all the providers they need access to."[174]

Obviously this would be dreadful for those with health conditions, and it was yet another sign of how the complexity of insurance products – much more complicated than premiums alone – is not easily reducible to media declaration of winners and losers. For 2014, the Avalere study found that "[f]or a single individual enrolled in a Silver plan, the average annual deductible before any plan coverage begins will be $2,550, which is more than twice the average deductible in employer-sponsored coverage."[175] It wasn't impossible that the deductible before care could be accessed might be the entire out-of-pocket limit of $6,350 – a "limit" that increased to $6,600 in 2015 (or $13,200 for a family).

It is also worth noting that out-of-pocket limits only apply to care in an insurer's network – in Washington State, for example, carriers in the exchange doing business in Seattle were allowed to omit from their networks the state's major trauma center, the pediatric hospital, the Seattle Cancer Care Alliance, and the only Seattle hospitals where childbirth occurs.[176]

Indeed, omitting cancer treatment facilities became a common practice among exchange offerings throughout the country. As the Associated Press reported on a survey it conducted, "Cancer patients relieved that they can get insurance coverage because of the new health care law may be disappointed to learn that some the nation's best cancer hospitals are off-limits."[177] As the article noted, "By not including a top cancer center an insurer can cut costs. It may also shield itself from risk, delivering an implicit message to cancer survivors or people with a strong family history of the disease that they should look elsewhere."

The effective death sentence this could deliver did not trouble the Obama Administration, which made clear that "[a] plan *may*, but is not required to, count out-of-pocket spending for out-of-network items and services towards the plan's annual maximum out-of-pocket limit."[178] (Emphasis added).

There is no tax assistance under the ACA toward exorbitant out-of-pocket costs, only toward premiums. While plans with premiums that exceed 8% of household income are deemed unaffordable for purposes of enforcing the individual mandate, no consideration whatsoever is given toward deductibles or other out-of-pocket costs that are the way insurers can game premium costs down.

This made President Obama's sunny assurances in an October 21, 2013 Rose Garden media event terribly misleading: "Through the marketplaces, you can get health insurance for what may be the equivalent of your cell phone bill. Or your cable bill."[179] That representation only factored in premiums; presumably most families did not have a monthly cell phone bill of as much as $12,700 (the 2014 deductible limit). And even low premiums would only be guaranteed for those qualifying for the highest levels of premium assistance.

While the federal government considers it "affordable" for an individual to pay insurers up to $6,600 in out-of-pocket expenses, it is not that understanding if the individual owes the federal government itself money. The same Internal Revenue Service (IRS) that would penalize an individual for not buying insurance with a $6,600 out-of-pocket deductible would – under the "Total National Standards for Out-of-Pocket Health Care Costs" – only allow them to incur $60 a month in such costs if they owe the IRS itself.[180]

Defenders of the ACA, like Sebelius, had derisively referred to the health insurance that predated it as "mortgage protection." Yet what sort of protection was a policy that, even after a tax subsidy toward premiums, required a $6,600 deductible before care could even be accessed? The Federal Reserve found only 48% of Americans could cover a medical emergency costing $400 without selling something or incurring a loan.[181]

In January 2015 *USA Today* ran a well-reported front-page article entitled "Dilemma over Deductibles: Costs Cripple the Middle Class." With Americans skipping needed health care because of deductibles, or falling into financial hardship, the indifferent response of an insurer spokesperson was that high deductibles meant consumers had "'skin in the game.'"[182]

Even a Nobel Prize-winning economist like Paul Krugman, normally thought of as an economic justice champion, could fall prey to cheerleading about premiums while ignoring all other costs. In an October 2014 *Rolling Stone* piece Krugman asked, rhetorically, "What about the costs? Here, too, the news is better than anyone expected. In 2014, premiums on the insurance policies offered through the Obamacare exchanges were well below those originally projected by the Congressional Budget Office[.]"[183] He made no mention of deductibles or what value consumers were actually receiving. Again, the obsession with premiums suggested they were all that mattered relative to health insurance.

Indeed, it was not easy to discern what even seemingly-good ACA news – such as the fact that premium rates would not go up as much as feared in some places for 2015—*really* meant for consumers. To what degree were rate increases mitigated by narrowing networks and/or raising deductibles? In Florida, for example, rates had gone up so high in 2014 – 48.3% in the case of Blue Cross Blue Shield of Florida – that some 2015 relief would have seemed inevitable.[184] Yet, for 2015, the average increase in the individual market in Florida was to be 13.2 percent – still a staggering increase.[185]

For 2015, PreferredOne, the largest insurer in Minnesota's MNSure exchange, announced it was both pulling out of the exchange and raising its rates 63 percent.[186] The company had sold 60% of the policies in the exchange – with its exit MNSure conveniently left the PreferredOne rate increase out of the average 2015 rate increase it announced. Even without PreferredOne included, insurance agents argued that improper weighting by the state meant that the announced 4.5% rate increase on exchange offerings was really 11.8 percent.[187] Was this the "Change We Can Believe In" first promised by President Obama's 2008 campaign?

Contrary to President Obama's untenable guarantee that those who liked their health insurance plans could keep them, insurers around the country cancelled plans in 2013 – forcing consumers into more expensive options. What Obama's promise had not conveyed was that only "grandfathered" plans – plans in existence at the time of the ACA's passage – did not have to meet the ACA's standards. Insurers reinvent their plans all the time. Were they to not do so they would have no new customers and plans would, inevitably, go into death spirals.

Grandfathered plans, in other words, could not continue indefinitely. Statements to the contrary were false. Obama had declared, for example, that "if you like your insurance plan, you will keep it. No one will be able to take that away from you. It hasn't happened yet. It won't happen in the future."[188] Yet that was not true for millions of Americans.

While I support the requirement that health insurance meet certain basic standards, the effect of this should have been made clear. Making an impossible promise in the first place, and then initially failing to acknowledge it had been broken, only deepened distrust of government. And the absence of a public option could mean a single choice for many consumers who felt jammed by higher prices and had incomes above the eligibility threshold for subsidies.

In an appearance on liberal comedian Bill Maher's *Real Time* talk show, Congresswoman Debbie Wasserman Schultz of Florida, the Democratic National Committee chair, dismissed as "arguing over minutiae" the question of whether the president's words misled the estimated 14 million Americans at risk of losing plans they were assured they could keep.[189] "To a lot of Americans, it's not minutiae and I think they're insulted" to hear such an assertion, retorted Maher.

Finally, the firestorm of criticism became so overwhelming that the president was forced to stage a mea culpa White House press conference on November 14, 2013, in which he announced that insurers – provided state regulators approved – would be allowed to keep their pre-ACA policies in force through 2014. The president admitted "we fumbled the rollout on this health care law" and that "those who got cancelation notices do deserve and have received an apology from me, but they don't want just words."[190] By this point, however, it was impossible for many states to keep the president's promise without disrupting already-volatile insurance marketplaces.

Predictably, however, the Obama Administration used this embarrassment as an occasion to further enrich insurers. As Robert Pear reported in the *New York Times*, "The White House is offering more money to insurance companies as an incentive for them to let people keep insurance policies that were to have been canceled next year."[191] This, of course, would be on top of subsidy payments in excess of $1 trillion that insurers were already scheduled to receive over the first decade.

In March 2014, the Administration announced it would allow consumers to keep grandfathered plans – where regulators allowed – through 2016 (and the next presidential election). This reinforced concerns about how much of the ACA could simply be ignored based upon the whims of whoever was president. Jonathan Turley, a George Washington University law professor, told the *New York Times* that "what the president is doing is effectively amending or negating the federal law to fit his preferred approach" – a disturbing precedent on many fronts.[192]

As to premiums, I was actually concerned that carriers might underprice their products for 2014 to lure new customers. After hooking them they could then increase rates with relative impunity in almost any state. For 2014 they could either eat losses through reserves, or have them subsidized through a "risk corridor" program requiring the federal government to give direct appropriations to insurers that set their exchange premium rates too low.

The likelihood of any insurance regulator telling an insurer to raise rates, even if that regulator had the power to approve them in the first place, was slim. And insurers very significantly increased rates in the run-up to 2014 – giving them a cushion to lessen sticker shock for new customers.

Moreover, against what benchmark would lower-than-expected rates even be measured? Improvidently, during his 2008 presidential campaign, Obama had pledged his plan would "bring down the cost of health care and reduce a typical family's premiums by as much as $2,500 per year." There was no instance I am aware of where 2014 premiums fell relative to 2008 (or even 2013) levels.

Exchanges can either be active purchasers or passive clearinghouses of insurance choices. Without active purchasing, exchanges, in effect, indiscriminately shovel consumers and tax dollars alike into the insurance industry's gaping maw.

The American Medical Association (AMA) opposes the active purchaser model. In a 2011 position paper, the AMA wrote that "[i]f state officials are negotiating price and other issues with plans . . . then they are likely to eliminate certain options for patients and may restrict the benefit structures or cost-sharing levels available to patients, and these actions could limit patient choices regarding health insurance coverage options." The concern is that with fewer plans providers get squeezed more. In the alternative, the AMA argued, an "open marketplace" model "would allow smaller health insurance issuers to challenge the monopolies that large health insurance issuers have in many markets now."

This sanguine analysis does not grasp the limitations of insurance. Smaller plans are unlikely to have provider networks in place to offer meaningful competition.

As one 2011 report on active purchasing by Sabrina Corlette related: "Large employers that engage in active purchasing, such as the California Public Employees' Retirement System (CalPERS), use the contracting process extensively to extract the best possible value from participating plans."[193]

That might not work in a state with few options, as an analysis prepared for Arkansas noted: "A review of the current Arkansas health insurance marketplace raises some flags about the potential efficacy of selective contracting and price negotiation in the state. Given the lack of competition in the market, negotiations may prove difficult. The marketplace is concentrated and there may not be enough plans to negotiate with."[194] Yet there could still be some benefit for consumers: "Arkansas may want to utilize the active purchaser option to make sure that consumers are not overwhelmed by apparent choices in the Exchange that, in reality, are not very different." Otherwise, a single company "could take steps to offer a multitude of products in an effort to prevent other companies from entering the state and offering plans on the Exchange."

States choosing the active purchaser model for exchanges included California, Connecticut, Massachusetts, Oregon, Rhode Island, and Vermont – as well as the District of Columbia. In Oregon, the list of 22 health plans that had applied to sell on the exchange was pared down to 12.[195]

California has the most obvious chances of success as an active purchaser. "The larger the exchange becomes, the more likely it can exercise leverage in the marketplace," writes Corlette.[196] Indeed, the rate filings for the Cover California exchange for 2014 showed only modest increases in rates for participating insurers.[197] While President Obama flew out to California to celebrate, Sarah Kliff, the Washington Post's then-prolific health policy reporter, put the news in context: "We know that that lower-than-expected premiums in California will matter to Californians. As to what the numbers mean for residents of other states, it's worth striking a note of caution in generalizing. California's health-care marketplace isn't like those being set up elsewhere in the country."[198] As Kliff pointed out, "In an active purchaser exchange, health plans know that they're competing against others for the chance to access millions of customers with tax subsidies." In most states "this downward pressure doesn't exist."

Yet even a proponent of active purchasing on the Cover California board acknowledged "[n]o single purchaser alone is going to transform the marketplace."[199] And, in a press release, California Insurance Commissioner Dave Jones expressed disappointment in the number of exchange offerings for 2014: "There are only three statewide health insurers selling in Covered California, which means less statewide competition than we'd hoped to see in the new marketplace. Major national health insurers like Aetna, United Healthcare and CIGNA are not participating in the Exchange."[200]

Indeed, Aetna, which had been the fourth-largest insurer in California's individual market with a 5.2% market share in 2011, pulled out of the individual market altogether for 2014 – further putting that market under the control of three carriers that held 87% of the market share.[201] Thus 2014 would dawn with even fewer choices for California consumers.

April 2013 testimony before the Senate Finance Committee made it clear the federal government had no inclination to be an active purchaser on behalf of federally-facilitated exchange states. Instead, it would just rubber-stamp all qualified health plans (QHPs): "To ensure a robust QHP market, and to promote consumer choice among QHPs, in the first year, HHS intends to certify as a QHP *any* health plan that meets all certification standards."[202] (Emphasis added). Further, the federal government would simply "rely on states' reviews of market reforms as part of its QHP certification process."

In other words, those states most hostile to the ACA, and least inclined to protect consumers from insurers, would be able to dictate which carriers met ACA standards to participate in insurance marketplaces run by the federal government itself.

Even in a state like Washington, with its own exchange and a record of consumer protection, "competition" wasn't always what it appeared to be. For example, Regence BlueShield is held by a corporation called Cambia that holds two other insurers, Asuris Northwest Health and BridgeSpan, both of which offer insurance in "competition" with Regence. Premera Blue Cross offers insurance under its own name and that of LifeWise Health Plan, with LifeWise a "separate" corporation in the eyes of regulatory law. These permutations allow insurers to segregate risk.

In Washington, the Healthplanfinder exchange delayed, in August 2013, accepting filings from four companies until its board could understand why another five were rejected by the insurance commissioner. As the *Seattle Times* reported:

> Member Don Conant noted that Lifewise, one of the four approved carriers, is a subsidiary of Premera, another approved carrier.
>
> "I'm choosing to see these as one carrier," said Conant, general manager at Valley Nut and Bolt in Olympia and an assistant professor in the School of Business at St. Martin's University. "It's sort of a choice without a distinction."[203]

In the face of bad publicity, and after the rejected carriers filed legal challenges, four more carriers were approved by the insurance commissioner in settlements. Yet some of the carriers had very limited provider networks, and Seattle Children's Hospital sued over having been left out of the networks for plans permitted to enroll exchange participants in the state's most populous county that includes Seattle.[204] After an independent hearing officer alleged she was subjected to undue influence by the insurance commissioner, who wanted her to uphold his omission of the hospital's care from plans, she was put on leave – she ended up receiving a $450,000 settlement from the insurance commissioner's office. [205]

The two largest plans in Eastern Washington were allowed to omit Eastern Washington's largest hospital, in Spokane, and around 500 of its affiliated doctors from their networks.[206] Similar developments occurred in other states, defying another improvident promise which President Obama had used to sell the ACA: "We will keep this promise: If you like your doctor, you will be able to keep your doctor. Period."[207]

While Republicans liked to jab President Obama with that promise, a 2014 ballot initiative in South Dakota to require health insurers to cover out-of-network providers split the Republican ranks – with most favoring insurers and big hospitals over smaller specialty hospitals and providers.[208] Opponents included the South Dakota Chamber of Commerce and Industry.[209] However, voters overwhelmingly supported the "choose your doctor" Measure 17.[210]

7

THE ACHILLES HEEL OF
STATE REGULATION

A SERIOUS CHALLENGE for the ACA is that it delegates so much authority to state insurance regulators who are predominantly appointed by governors hostile to the ACA. The organization of which they are a part, the NAIC, began pushing back as early as 2010 against many of the consumer protections of the ACA – a posture unchanged upon Ben Nelson taking the NAIC's helm following his U.S. Senate exit.

As shown by the previous examples of medical loss ratio waiver requests, many insurance commissioners do not even want to limit insurers to a generous 20% margin for administration. Further, even those commissioners willing to comply may not be up to the task.

"Charged with making sure the prices are justified, state insurance departments often have far less actuarial expertise at their disposal than the insurers" noted one analysis in *Kaiser Health News*.[211] And state regulators are the only hope. Consumer groups do not have capacity or expertise to review health insurance rates, and those buying insurance individually have no moneyed entities lobbying for them. Political power and mathematical acumen resides with insurers and their actuaries.

As Senator Schumer had asked during the single day of Senate debate allotted consideration of a public option: "If the State Insurance Commissioners are doing such a good job, then why are the costs going through the roof?" The imperative for insurers is simple. "The job of a private insurance company . . . is to add a profit margin to everything it can, and to avoid paying bills to the degree possible" writes the economist Gar Alperovitz.[212]

Robert Reich, the former United States labor secretary, argues that "America's giant insurers outgrew state regulation" despite their decades-long exemption from federal antitrust laws that was based "on the assumption they'd be regulated by state insurance commissioners."[213] Indeed, the ACA was adding to the imbalance. In July 2015 it was announced that Aetna was buying Humana for $37 billion, which, among other things, would help it corner the lucrative Medicare Advantage market. Aetna had already devoured rival Coventry Health Care in 2013 for $5.7 billion. At that time of the announced Humana purchase, Cigna had rebuffed Anthem's $47 billion takeover offer, although it was still in discussions with its suitor, while Centene had just purchased rival insurer Health Net for $6.3 billion.[214]

By May 2013, 44 states were deemed "effective rate review" states by the federal government. Allegedly they could determine the reasonableness of a rate increase in their individual or small group markets under a state regulatory or statutory standard. The federal government initially conducted such reviews in six states: Alabama, Louisiana, Missouri, Oklahoma, Texas and Wyoming.[215] Louisiana now conducts its own rate review.

Yet being deemed "effective" at rate review implies more than is true. Under the ACA, insurers must "justify" rate increases in excess of 10 percent. In practice, this is easy enough to do with actuarial math. And any increase below that level, up to 9.9%, can go without any scrutiny whatsoever, given both the ideology of many insurance regulators coupled with the fact that many have no authority to challenge rates.

Nor can even the federal government deny rate increases of 10% or more. The Obama Administration acknowledged the ACA "only provides CMS with the authority to require justification and disclosure of proposed rate increases."[216] In its rule-making, the Administration noted that "[t]he rate review program established by this rule defers to State law and provides that, for States with Effective Rate Review Programs, CMS will adopt their determinations as to whether rate increases are unreasonable."

The Obama Administration also acceded to insurance industry lobbying against a "requirement to report executive and employee compensation data" – reasoning "these amounts would represent only a very small proportion of an overall rate increase when allocated by product and member month, and, consequently, would not be helpful to consumers in showing the primary rate increase drivers." In other words, too much disclosure is dangerous for the consumer.

The Obama Administration related consumer concern "that States with limited review capabilities could be designated as having effective programs." Yet, because the ACA did not provide the federal government with meaningful rate review, it would not mandate it for states:

> Section 2794 of the PHS Act requires CMS to establish a process for reviewing unreasonable rates; it does not provide CMS with prior approval authority. We therefore did not think it would be appropriate for CMS to mandate that States have prior approval authority in order to qualify as having Effective Rate Review Programs.

In fact, rate review was left out of the ACA by design. In 2011, Democratic U.S. Senator Diane Feinstein of California introduced a Health Insurance Rate Review Act to grant the federal government authority to block unfair rate increases in the states where regulators lacked authority to do so. Although eight other Senate Democrats signed Feinstein's bill it died without a hearing. In 2013 she re-introduced the bill, noting regulators in California and 14 other states had no "authority to block or modify" rate increases.[217] Again, no hearing was given the bill by the Democratic Senate.

An emboldened Florida Governor Scott signed legislation in 2013 suspending the state's ability to disapprove rates for 2014 and 2015.[218] Companies could charge whatever they wanted to. Under the Florida law, insurers would be required to "include a notice describing or illustrating the estimated impact of PPACA on monthly premiums with the delivery of the policy or contract or, upon renewal, the premium renewal notice."[219] Thus consumers would not be protected from insurers, and insurers could blame everything on the ACA.

"To eliminate the Florida insurance commissioner's authority to turn down rate increases is unbelievable and unconscionable," fumed Democratic Senator Bill Nelson of Florida – a former insurance commissioner.[220] Yet the ACA that Nelson voted for allowed that possibility.

In a December 2012 consumer publication, the Texas Department of Insurance noted that "[c]ompanies set their own premiums. TDI doesn't regulate or approve health plan rates."[221]

The federal government was defensive of Texas regulators' resistance to even fulfill their ACA duty to help determine whether rate increases in excess of 10% were reasonable or unreasonable (an empty enough exercise with no way under Texas law to stop unreasonable increases). Of the Department of Insurance, one advocate in 2012 told *KUHF* public radio: "They've been very unresponsive. They have not returned calls. They have not returned repeated requests. And it really took having over 1,600 Texans signing on to a petition to say, 'Hey, this is something we care about and we need to know what's going on with this.'"[222]

When President Obama capitulated on allowing states to approve non-compliant plans in order to maintain his ill-fated promise to allow citizens to "keep their insurance," the *Washington Post* reported that "[s]ince Texas has refused to implement the health law's new regulations, it has also said it would not stop non-compliant plans from selling in its market. That was true before the president's announcement, the Texas Department of Insurance says, and afterward."[223]

California was deemed an effective rate review state, though Commissioner Jones, an elected Democrat, put out a May 2013 press release conceding he was powerless when it came to rate increases:

> I remain very concerned that there is no legal authority in California to reject unreasonable and excessive rate hikes. Health insurance rates have increased dramatically over the last several years, and are likely to continue to climb unless California law is changed to provide consumer protection through effective health insurance rate regulation, which means the authority to reject excessive rate hikes.[224]

California's Democratic Legislature defeated efforts to give Jones that authority. Thus, for 2014, the three largest states – California, Florida and Texas – representing over one-quarter of the U.S. population, were incapable of reviewing health insurance rates.

New York law represents a prior approval standard: "The superintendent may modify or disapprove the rate filing or application if the superintendent finds that the premiums are unreasonable, excessive, inadequate, or unfairly discriminatory, and may consider the financial condition of the corporation in approving, modifying or disapproving any premium adjustment."[225]

Note the filing is not required to be disapproved or modified under those circumstances. Thus, depending upon a regulator's predilections, even an "unreasonable" or "unfairly discriminatory" rate filing *could* be approved in a progressive state like New York, where, instead, the superintendent of the Department of Financial Services was able to announce that a 19.96% increase requested by Aetna for 2015 was lowered to 5.32 percent.[226]

Further, New York was a "file-and-use" state prior to the ACA – which meant carriers simply filed their rate increases and implemented them. It only switched to prior approval regulation after the ACA's enactment. That was true in other states, too, like Michigan. Accordingly, the mere possibility of exacting rate review was new. And many states remain file-and-use states, at least in part. Most states are far more accustomed to responsibly regulating property and casualty insurance filings – such as auto or home insurance – than they are the complexities of health insurance.

The federal government contemplated making a component of "effective rate review" public ability to comment on proposed rate increases during state review. The NAIC's response was too much information could be harmful: "This is a decision that should be left to the states. Each state has different laws relating to trade secrets and public information, and a public comment process during the review period is not possible if the rates or the insurer's supporting information are still confidential at that time."[227] The Obama Administration yielded to this advice.

Some states, including Colorado, New York, Oregon, and Washington, took federal rate transparency grants and used them to make all rate filings public and allow comments. One report noted that "[p]erhaps no state has done more to engage consumers in the rate review process than Oregon. The Insurance Division instituted a public comment period for rate filings, contracted with a consumer advocacy group to weigh in on rate filings on behalf of consumers, and initiated public hearings."[228]

Yet other states are secretive. In Pennsylvania, for example, only filings where a carrier requests a rate increase of 10 percent or greater are available for public review and comment.[229] In Florida, *Health News Florida* noted, rate "requests do not include the rationale behind them, as that is considered a trade secret and not open to the public."[230] Some states redact heavily even where they do share rate filing information. In Washington State, I actually heard an insurance lobbyist refer to rate components as "secret sauce."

Most insurance regulators are appointed, not elected – with considerable churn. With 11 new governors elected in 2014, for example, there might be 11 new insurance commissioners in 2015 (in addition to a new commissioner elected in Kansas).

Consider the appointments made following the 2010 election. Many insurance regulators came straight from the insurance industry – as was the case when Wisconsin Governor Walker, upon taking office in 2011, named as his insurance commissioner Ted Nickel, the government affairs director for an insurance company, past chair of the Wisconsin Insurance Alliance, and past Republican candidate for the Wisconsin Assembly. As deputy commissioner Walker appointed Dan Schwartzer, another insurance industry lobbyist.[231]

In Michigan, Republican Governor Rick Snyder's top insurance regulator, Kevin Clinton, had come to regulation from serving six years as president and CEO of American Physicians Capital – a publicly-traded medical liability insurance company.

In Pennsylvania, Republican Governor Tom Corbett's insurance commissioner, Michael Consedine, came to his post straight from being a partner, and insurance practice group vice chair, in a law firm that represented insurers.

In South Carolina, Republican Governor Nikki Haley appointed as her Department of Insurance director Ray Farmer, the vice president of the American Insurance Association, which bills itself as "the voice of the property and casualty insurance industry."[232]

A predecessor to Farmer as South Carolina's insurance regulator, Eleanor Kitzman, lost a 2010 race to be Haley's lieutenant governor.[233] Kitzman then was appointed as Texas's insurance commissioner in June 2011 by Republican Governor Rick Perry, yet was so conservative that even the Republican Texas Senate would not confirm her. Among other things, Kitzman removed consumer protections for health insurance, including disclosing which providers were in a carrier's network. As the *Dallas Morning News* asked, "What part of consumer protection doesn't she get?"[234]

In Utah, Republican Governor Bob Herbert's insurance commissioner Todd Kiser was a former Republican legislator who came to his post from running his own Kiser Insurance Agency for 35 years.

It might be assumed that political appointees hailing from backgrounds where they worked for, or ran, insurance companies, would be returning to that sector after their political patrons' terms were up. Thus, regulatory crusades may foreclose post-government career options. For example, the Tennessee insurance commissioner, Julie Mix McPeak, appointed by Republican Governor Bill Haslam in 2011, had previously served a Republican Kentucky governor ousted by voters. During the interval between government regulatory positions she defended insurance companies against consumers as an attorney.

Insurance departments can be a parking ground for failed larger aspirations. While I have known many regulators with insurer backgrounds who seemed like decent, honest people, the hostility of some toward government (even though government was their employer) can be palpable at NAIC meetings. I recall having sat with some of them at a dinner breakout at my first NAIC conference at a luxury golf resort in Indian Wells, California. Not knowing who I was, they were deriding government generally and Democrats in particular.

The NAIC conferences allow state regulators to showcase themselves before insurance lobbyists who attend the breakout sessions, buttonhole regulators in halls, take regulators to dinner, and attend the receptions that the association puts on in luxury resort hotels. The NAIC held its February 2013 retreat for commissioners in the Virgin Islands, a destination more accessible to insurance lobbyists than consumer advocates. The 2014 NAIC conference in Louisville, Kentucky featured a private event at Churchill Downs.

In circumstances where a governor who appoints an insurance commissioner is not seeking re-election, or has been defeated, NAIC conferences become jobs fairs for commissioners, and many at-will regulatory staff, still in positions to endear themselves to prospective employers. This is especially overt following a governor's defeat, where you might face only two or three months of remaining job tenure in the insurance department. In such circumstances I have seen "lame duck" regulators sleep during meetings so as to be perky for dinner functions that might land them the next opportunity.

Often there is not even rhetorical focus on consumer protection. For example, Ohio's Republican Governor John Kasich assigned his lieutenant governor, Mary Taylor, dual roles as head of an anti-regulatory Common Sense Initiative Ohio and as the director of the Ohio Department of Insurance, where, her NAIC bio noted, "CSI Ohio will review Ohio's regulatory system to eliminate excessive and duplicative rules that stand in the way of job creation, and the regulatory mission of the Department of Insurance is a good place to start."

When rate filings came in, Taylor put out a press release heralding the fact that rates were up 88% – vindicating her anti-ACA position.[235] In an accompanying polemic, she argued her case: "Under the ACA, all Ohioans will be lumped together for the purposes of pricing thereby eliminating the benefits of healthier choices. This method of rating is commonly known as 'community rating' – an approach some states incorporated before the ACA. Because Ohio is being forced into this type of pricing, health insurance costs are increasing in 2014."[236]

Taylor's arguments, and blame of the ACA for the increases, foreshadowed she would not exercise her limited rate review discretion. So long as "the benefits provided are not unreasonable in relation to the premium charged" Ohio law did not allow disapproval anyway.[237]

For 2015, insurers received rate increases averaging 12% for Ohio's individual market and small businesses.[238] "Obamacare is hitting us harder and driving our costs up significantly" declared Taylor in a press release.[239]

Direct election of insurance regulators does not necessarily bring consumer advocacy on health insurance rates.

The biography for Georgia's elected Republican insurance commissioner, Ralph Hudgens, notes Hudgens' foremost priority is being "100 percent pro-life and a champion of various pro-family causes."[240] Hudgens' second-highest priority appeared to be working to impede ACA implementation. Oklahoma's elected Republican insurance commissioner, John Doak, was a former insurance executive who touted, as an accomplishment, "[r]eturning the nearly $1 million federal grant for conducting health insurance premium rate reviews[.]"[241]

It could be worse. Louisiana's elected Republican insurance commissioner, James Donelon, had at least served with integrity since his first 2007 election without being sent to prison – as predecessors were.[242]

Commissioners declining to seek, or exercise, rate review authority would likely argue, in their defense, that rate review would conflict with their duty to preserve insurer solvency – which also protects consumers. They would also note, correctly, that there is nothing in the ACA, or their own state statutes, requiring them to set aside free market orthodoxy in favor of aggressive regulation.

The best state for rate review is Vermont.

In Vermont, the commissioner of the Department of Financial Regulation has a broad grant of authority "to determine whether a policy or rate is affordable, promotes quality care, promotes access to health care, and is not unjust, unfair, inequitable, misleading, or contrary to the laws of this state."[243] The commissioner then makes a recommendation on rate increases to the Green Mountain Care Board, which is free to accept, modify or reject the recommendation – applying criteria that include "changes in health care delivery" as well as "other issues at the discretion of the Board."[244]

The public has the right to comment on rate increase requests of 5% or more for three weeks from the date the state posts the rate request to its website. At least twice a year, the Board also holds public forums exclusively on insurance rates.

THE ACHILLES HEEL OF STATE REGULATION

Even where rate review authority exists, and is exercised, it allows enormous profits.

Washington State, for example, is dominated by three nonprofit health carriers. For 2012, only $785,946 in rebates was paid under the MLR in 2013 by for-profits with very small shares of the state's health insurance market.[245] Each of three major nonprofits was already under the MLR, and yet realizing large profits even in a state where the insurance commissioner has authority to review rate increases. That was because, in reviewing rates, the Washington commissioner legally cannot factor in the surplus cash carriers have stockpiled. Those surpluses, by 2013, exceeded $1 billion apiece for the Blue Cross and Blue Shield nonprofits.

Washington's Democratic elected insurance commissioner sought authority to review nonprofit carriers' surpluses. In 2011 and 2012 bills to allow that review died in a Democratic Senate; in 2013 the bill died in a Democratic House. As it turned out, for the formidable Premera Blue Cross the cost of keeping scrutiny away from a billion dollars was not great. As the Puget Sound Business Journal reported, "Between 2010 and 2013, Premera directly donated $726,850 to politicians and party committees."[246] Its bounty was spread fairly evenly between both parties.

Meanwhile, between October 1, 2011, when Regence BlueShield obtained an 11.4% rate increase (it had asked for 12.7%) for Washington State's individual market, and October 1, 2012, when it was granted another 13.5% rate increase (it had asked for 14.7%), the nonprofit's surplus had grown from $957 million to $994 million.[247] And that was under the ACA.

For 2014, as the state's exchange came online, the average rate increase for health insurers in Washington's individual market was 11.2%,[248] far-outpacing personal income growth of only 2.57% by the last annual measure.[249]

With the market share of Premera Blue Cross assured by taxpayers, and over three-fifths of exchange enrollment through Premera or its wholly-owned subsidiary LifeWise, the company was allowed by the insurance commissioner to ignore a mental health parity law requiring them to serve kids with autism; only private class-action litigation forced a settlement.[250]

Washington was not alone in the unhealthy profiteering of nonprofit insurers. In tiny Idaho, a March 2013 article in the *Idaho Statesman* reported "Idaho's two major health insurance companies are using money from double-digit rate increases to build savings and investment accounts that now top $600 million."[251]

Consumers Union studied the issue in 2010 and found nonprofit Health Care Service Corporation – doing business as Blue Cross Blue Shield in Illinois, New

Mexico, Oklahoma and Texas – increased its surplus to $6.7 billion in 2009, five times what solvency required, from $4.3 billion in 2005. Meanwhile, like other surplus-accumulating nonprofits Consumers Union studied, the insurer had pounded customers with huge rate increases.[252]

Regulators in most states lack authority to account for such surpluses. If insurers can limitlessly accumulate surplus profits free from regulatory oversight, "rate review" is a hollow exercise.

In 2014, a Seattle Times editorial noted that "Premera Blue Cross cooed its approval" after the Washington State Senate, at Premera's behest, gutted a bill – supported by consumers, medical practitioners, Boeing, and even the ACA-opposing National Federation of Independent Business – to simply require insurers to create access to a "basic health price and quality information" database.[253]

In Alaska, a gigantic Premera Blue Cross rate increase helped torpedo incumbent Democratic Senator Mark Begich in the 2014 election. As the company stated in a press release, "We need a 71.5% average rate increase to break even in 2015. We have instead filed for and received approval for a 37.3% average rate increase."[254] There was no regulatory requirement they use their surplus cash to mitigate or avoid this, and the ACA-supporting Begich was narrowly defeated.

8

THE BATTLE AGAINST
STATE EXCHANGES

WHILE THE INDIVIDUAL mandate under the health care reform law has been the subject of litigation,[255] one might think the requirement of exchanges would be uncontroversial. After all, what could be more consumer-friendly than a one-stop-shopping site where one can compare and price health insurance coverage? Exchanges are even required to have toll-free numbers, quality ratings, and electronic calculators for consumer assistance. As conservatives were the original proponents of exchanges, you might assume this aspect of health care reform was free from opposition.

Wrong.

When a Republican anesthesiologist, Representative John Zerwas, introduced a bill establishing an Exchange in Texas,[256] Governor Perry promised a veto. Zerwas's intentions were benign and imminently conservative—he wanted to avoid a federal takeover of health care. While Zerwas opposed federal health care reform, he stated his goal was "to keep the cost of coverage down by promoting competition and ensuring Texas families and Texas employers have the right to choose their own coverage."

Yet, following Perry's threat, Zerwas's bill was scuttled. Opined the *Dallas Morning News*: "It isn't like health care exchanges are a socialistic plot to take over health care. They instead create marketplaces where consumers and small businesses can compare health insurance plans. Republicans as well as Democrats have favored this competitive approach."[257] With a legislature that only meets in odd-numbered years, Texas was among states where, as early as 2011, resistance to federal health care reform had, ironically, made federal intervention in state health care markets inevitable (in 2013, Zerwas would unsuccessfully try to expand Medicaid).

Nor did the 2012 presidential election results alter intransigence. Following the election, Perry, himself a failed 2012 Republican presidential candidate, informed Secretary Sebelius that "Texas will not implement a so-called state exchange."[258]

Texas has the nation's highest rate of uninsured residents.[259] Not only would it not establish an exchange, but it refused to provide any state assistance to promoting the federally-facilitated exchange.

In her 2013 State of the State Address, South Carolina Governor Haley declared that "[d]espite the rose-colored rhetoric coming out of D.C., these exchanges are nothing more than a way to make the state do the federal government's bidding in spending massive amounts of taxpayer dollars on insurance subsidies that we can't afford."[260]

To even express willingness to establish an exchange could be toxic. In Georgia, Governor Deal rescinded a push for exchange legislation after Tea Party protest.[261] In a contrite statement, his office explained "[t]he governor understands Georgians' suspicions about any legislation associated with Obamacare."[262]

After the Republican-controlled Montana Legislature killed legislation to begin creating an exchange, the disappointed Democratic insurance commissioner, Monica Lindeen, stated "[t]hey've basically handed off the health exchange to the federal government."[263] Lindeen wasn't alone in her disappointment. As the government relations director for the Montana Chamber of Commerce wrote: "Having a Montana-based exchange is certainly preferable to a one-size-fits-all approach that Washington, D.C. would hand down to us."[264] Yet many states chose that default due to their legislatures' political gestures.

Beginning in 2010, voters began expressing their view of the ACA via legislatively-referred measures. Each purported to exempt states and their citizens from the ACA's individual mandate and penalties. In Arizona, voters approved Proposition 106, the Arizona Health Insurance Reform Amendment, a legislatively-referred constitutional amendment.[265] Oklahoma voters approved the Oklahoma Health Care Freedom Amendment, Question 756, a legislatively-referred constitutional amendment.[266] Additionally, Missouri voters approved Proposition C, a legislatively-referred state statute,[267] by a 3-1 margin despite the fact that the Missouri Hospital Association spent over $300,000 trying to defeat it.[268] In 2011, Ohio voters overwhelmingly approved a state constitutional amendment, Issue 3,[269] which declared "[n]o ... law or rule shall compel, directly or indirectly, any person, employer, or health care provider to participate in a health care system."[270]

In 2012, Alabama voters narrowly-approved the Alabama Health Care Amendment, Amendment 6, a legislatively-referred constitutional amendment (while also refusing, with another measure, to remove school segregation language from the constitution).[271] Wyoming voters approved their own legislatively-referred constitutional amendment, Amendment A.[272] Further, Missouri voters revisited the issue and took a different approach in amending their constitution through Missouri Health Care Exchange Question, Proposition E, which "prohibits the establishment, creation, or operation of a state-based health insurance exchange unless the exchange is created by a legislative act, an initiative petition, or referendum."[273] Specifically the measure forbids the governor from unilaterally establishing an exchange.[274]

In 2011, Montana adopted a statute that ostensibly prohibits "[t]he state or federal government" from requiring the purchase of health insurance or imposing penalties for not purchasing insurance.[275] In language obviously aimed at the elected ACA-supporting insurance commissioner, the law also prohibits even "participation by a state official" in efforts to implement the ACA.[276] This made a legislative-referred 2012 statutory ballot measure against the individual mandate and penalties redundant, although it also passed.[277]

These measures are only meaningful as expressions of discontent. Any state statute or constitutional provision purporting to exempt a state's citizens from federal law is federally preempted. However, the fact that voters have "spoken" on the issue could rob federal progress of legitimacy in such states.

In a sign that perhaps the threshold question of the ACA's very existence was no longer as contentious in some places, Florida voters in the 2012 election rejected the symbolic Florida Health Care Amendment, Amendment 1, a legislatively-referred constitutional amendment pushed by Governor Scott to ostensibly exempt Floridians from the ACA's individual mandate.

Yet, even following an election where President Obama won 58% of his Democratic state's vote, Republican New Jersey Governor Chris Christie vetoed, for the second time, legislation to set up a state-run exchange.[278] His justification in vetoing a bill in May 2012 was uncertainty over the Supreme Court case and presidential election outcome,[279] and his continued inflexibility showed Republicans would continue to fight the ACA even where Obama was popular.

Two elected Republican insurance commissioners desiring to set up exchanges battled their Republican governors.

In Kansas, Governor Sam Brownback, who as a U.S. senator voted against the ACA, returned to the federal government $31.5 million for a state-based exchange. Insurance Commissioner Sandy Praeger then submitted a grant application to create a state-federal partnership exchange. Brownback refused to support her, asserting "we will not benefit from it" – a position that drew a retort from Nile Dillmore, a Democratic state representative: "Why would he give up a Kansas-based exchange for a federal government exchange? I thought he was the governor who said the federal government can't do anything right?"[280]

Not seeking re-election in 2014, Praeger endorsed the Democratic challenger to Brownback, her fellow Republican, and also endorsed the Democratic nominee for her position. However, both Brownback and the Republican running for Praeger's spot, Ken Selzer, won. Selzer, an accountant who had largely worked for the insurance industry, made it clear his priority as insurance commissioner would be working to undermine the ACA.[281]

In Mississippi, Insurance Commissioner Mike Chaney engaged in a public feud with Governor Phil Bryant. Chaney asserted he had authority to set up an exchange, and submitted an application to do so.

Defending his actions in a Republican state, Chaney, who already had an insurer offering coverage through his One, Mississippi exchange, warned that "[i]f you default to the federal government, you forever give the keys to the state's insurance market to the federal government."[282] Yet he admitted, after one televised confrontation with an anti-ACA Cato Institute staffer following a luncheon, "I was invited to the picnic, and I was the main course."[283]

The state's attorney general backed Chaney's authority to establish an exchange, but Bryant wrote separately to Secretary Sebelius to share his unwillingness to cooperate. It became the only such application rejected by the federal government, which wrote Chaney it was due to "the Mississippi Governor's stated intent to oppose implementation of a State-based Exchange." Triumphant, Bryant issued a statement: "I have said repeatedly that the health insurance exchanges mandated by ObamaCare are not free-market exchanges. Instead, they are a portal to a massive and unaffordable new federal entitlement program."[284]

Bryant's triumphalism was consistent with an edict laid down by the Mississippi Tea Party's co-founder: "To resist by all means that are right in the eyes of God is not rebellion or insurrection, it is patriotic resistance to invasion."[285] Unlike his Republican predecessor as governor, deal-making lobbyist Haley Barbour, Bryant was a Tea Party absolutist. The federal government did not help matters, giving scarce grant money to help navigate the federally-facilitated exchange to a mysterious church First Lady Michelle Obama reportedly liked because its pastor "banned fried chicken in an effort to help parishioners lose weight."[286]

Louisiana's elected Republican insurance commissioner, James Donelon, did not go as far as Praeger and Chaney, but he had also favored the establishment of an exchange, noting that "[i]t's almost a lose-lose situation for us. If we don't do anything and the (presidential) election doesn't come out such that the law can be changed, then the federal government will do it and we will be at their mercy under the federal law to comply with whatever they require."[287] Yet Republican Governor Bobby Jindal refused to pursue an exchange.

In addition to refusing to set up exchanges, many states, including large ones like Florida and Ohio, actively worked to subvert federally-facilitated exchanges. Georgia's elected insurance commissioner, Ralph Hudgens, vowed to be "an obstructionist."[288] Given the regulatory powers states exert over insurance, including the marketing of it, there are many creative ways in which they could thwart exchange enrollment. In Hudgens' case, it was by requiring state insurance agent tests for the "navigators" that the ACA funds to assist consumers in exchange enrollment. Florida also required criminal background checks and fingerprinting for those navigators.[289]

Litigation was brought against the federal government based upon the argument that tax credits could only be available where a state exchange existed, as the ACA specifically stated such subsidies were available for those "enrolled in through an Exchange established by the State[.]"

In a 2-1 decision, a panel of the U.S. Court of Appeals for the District of Columbia Circuit ruled, in July 2014, that an IRS regulation allowing subsidies through federally-facilitated exchanges was contrary to the ACA's plain language. Arguably this was an elevation of form over substance, as the ACA also provided for the role of the federal government in facilitating exchanges and it would seem improbable that there was an intent that these would operate without any incentives for taxpayer participation.

Yet the fact that there was even an argument was further evidence that the ACA was more akin to a rough draft than a finished product. The D.C. Circuit opinion was not inconsistent with a 2012 presentation from economist Jonathan Gruber, the immodest ACA architect, who had stated "if you're a state and you don't set up an Exchange, that means your citizens don't get their tax credits. But your citizens still pay the taxes that support this bill."[290]

The D.C. Circuit opinion also shared, in an expansive footnote, a fascinating new argument by the Obama Administration in defense of the ACA. According to this argument, the disputed ACA provision was "the product of legislative compromise to secure the support of Nebraska Senator Ben Nelson, the crucial sixtieth vote needed to avoid a filibuster. Nelson opposed House plans for a national, federally-run exchange, fearing that it would set the United States down a path to a single-payer system."[291] The court panel rejected the Nelson-Made-Us-Do-It defense, stating, "Senator Nelson may have opposed a single, national exchange, but it does not necessarily follow that he opposed making subsidies available on federal fallback Exchanges in uncooperative states." Because the plain language of the ACA only referenced state exchanges, any arguments about what Ben Nelson may, or may not, have intended were irrelevant to the court.

The decision of the three-judge D.C. Circuit panel was vacated by the full D.C. Circuit court sitting en banc, and the U.S. Court of Appeals for the Fourth Circuit also rejected a similar case against the subsidies – even though the Fourth Circuit decision admitted the "the applicable statutory language is ambiguous and subject to multiple interpretations."[292] Despite there not being a conflict between circuits, the U.S. Supreme Court heard arguments in March 2015 on the subject – eliciting another avalanche of amicus briefs both for and against the ACA.[293]

In the end the risk to the ACA was exaggerated, as justices were clearly not unmindful of the chaos that might be unleashed were millions of Americans using tax credits to be cast into the wind. The Obama Administration's position was upheld in a 6-3 decision in June 2015.[294]

Writing for the majority, Chief Justice Roberts, again the ACA's savior, conceded the statutory tax credit language was "ambiguous" and attributed that to the fact that "the Act does not reflect the type of care and deliberation that one might expect of such significant legislation." Acknowledging the "strong" arguments about the "plain meaning" of the statutory language, Roberts found that the tax credits must apply to the "Federal Exchanges" as well as state-run ones lest insurance markets be destroyed – "the type of calamitous result that Congress plainly meant to avoid."

In a bitter dissent, Justice Scalia accused the majority of "interpretive jittery-pokery" and "rewriting the law under the pretense of interpreting it[.]"

9

WASHINGTON STATE: WHAT A STATE EXCHANGE LOOKS LIKE

DETERMINED TO GO its own way, Washington State, as early as 2011, was recognized as one of a dozen "pace car" states in implementing the ACA and establishing its own exchange.[295] Progress brings with it challenges, as illustrated by the Washington example, including the fact that, although established through federal grants, exchanges are required to be self-sufficient by January 1, 2015, with no further federal grants available.[296]

On the surface, Washington State appears to be the bluest of blue states. It has not had a Republican governor since 1984, nor delivered Electoral College votes to a Republican presidential candidate since that year. Since the 2000 election the state has been represented by two Democratic women in the U.S. Senate.

Yet the state's absence of term limits has created a play-it-safe conservatism on the part of the Democratic hegemony. The state easily has the nation's heaviest tax burden upon the poor.[297] It is Washington voters who, through their power of initiative, have accomplished most of the progressive things the state is known for, such as a toxics cleanup act; the nation's highest minimum wage, indexed to inflation; a strict indoor smoking ban; a clean energy law; a firearms background check law; and legal assisted suicide and marijuana. Progressive voter-passed initiatives that actually cost the state money – expanding a Basic Health Plan through a dedicated cigarette tax increase; reducing class sizes; giving annual salary increases to teachers and K-12 staff; or training long-term care workers to avoid negligence – have been repealed, or suspended, by legislators.

In 2013 the Democratic governor, Jay Inslee, and legislators passed a multi-billion-dollar tax break for Boeing – the nation's largest tax break ever – while also browbeating Boeing machinists into giving up pensions. Poignantly, the governor was already drawing a congressional pension while adding to the same defined-benefit state pension his legislative allies enjoyed. Following the granting of the largely-unconditional tax break, and the pension surrender, Boeing announced it was still moving thousands of jobs elsewhere. The tax break boondoggle was financed in no small part by a failure to fund K-12 education so egregious that it earned the legislature a 2014 contempt of court citation from the Washington Supreme Court. Washington voters in 2014 passed progressive measures even as they kept their Senate in Republican hands and reduced the Democratic House majority; neighboring Oregon actually saw its Democratic legislative majorities expand as Democrats were willing to push big ideas.

However, in the halcyon health care reform days of 1993 the state got ahead of the nation in enacting its own reform, even as President Clinton's efforts faltered. The story is now a cautionary tale. The law guaranteed access to insurance immediately, regardless of preexisting conditions. Its individual mandate, however, was not to take effect until 1998, and was repealed in 1995 when Republicans took rare control of the Legislature. Rates soared as residents purchased insurance only when they needed it. It was a classic marketplace death spiral. Eventually the individual and small group insurance markets collapsed.[298] The Washington experience was heavily relied upon in the insurance industry's amicus brief before the Supreme Court on the ACA.

Washington State's 2011 law creating a public-private Washington Health Benefit Exchange (now known as the Washington Healthplanfinder) took a uniquely bipartisan approach.[299] It limited the Governor to choosing eight voting board members from names nominated by the House and Senate Democratic and Republican caucuses.[300] Each of the four caucuses forwarded five names to then-Governor Christine Gregoire, a Democrat, from which she had to choose two.[301] A governor-chosen chair was to vote only in the case of a tie on a board split evenly between the two major political parties.[302]

Compared to other states, Washington was the one state where the party controlling the executive and legislative branches of government yielded any control of an Exchange board to the minority party. Even the Democrats controlling Nevada's legislature had only been able to obtain two appointments relative to the Republican governor's five.[303] Tactically, this was risky, particularly given that a governor-appointed chair could break tie votes.[304] As early as 2011, the foreseeable Republican nominee in the 2012 governor's race was Attorney General Rob McKenna—who joined the multi-state lawsuit to overturn the ACA.

With Republicans nationally working to undermine the ACA, Democrats in Washington gave Republicans tools to help dictate the ACA's success or failure in their state. Seeing the advantage, Republicans broke free of their reflexive opposition to everything ACA-related – 20 House Republicans joined six Republican senators in voting for the Exchange's enabling law.

The party caucuses must each nominate at least one person with a certain aptitude— with Republicans responsible for nominating at least one health economist or actuary and one small business representative, and Democrats responsible for nominating at least one employee benefit specialist and one representative of health consumer advocates.[305] It is not clear why this concession of expertise on the part of one or the other party was made. For example, are we to believe small business owners are only Republicans?

Service on the board is prohibited for those with a personal or professional financial stake in decision outcomes.[306] Three of the initial Republican appointees, however, included two with active insurance brokerages and one who was the immediate past president of a statewide trade association (the Washington Farm Bureau) with a health plan problematic under the ACA's consumer protections. The Republican appointees were fond of referring to the taxpayer-financed Exchange as a "private business" and begrudging any legislative oversight of its functions. Even the governor's chair appointee was a past executive of one of the Washington's largest health insurers.

The real work of tasking the Exchange occurred during the 2012 legislative session, when an ACA-implementation bill, requested jointly by Governor Gregoire and Insurance Commissioner Mike Kreidler, both Democrats, passed into law.[307] The new law made it clear that the Exchange must be self-sustaining, required at least annual reporting to the Legislature, and allowed Exchange employees to participate in state retirement and health care plans while otherwise exempting them from state civil service laws.[308]

The Exchange law provided a clear victory for consumers by prohibiting carriers from "gaming" the system when choosing what plans to offer—that is, carriers cannot manipulate their exposure by exclusively offering low-cost plans outside the Exchange.[309] The insurance business plays on the law of averages; the theory being the bigger the pool, the wider the risk-sharing, and, therefore, the lower the cost. As the U.S. Department of Health and Human Services notes: "Successful Exchanges will avoid adverse selection by ensuring that those who buy through the Exchange are a broad mix of the healthy and the less healthy."[310]

Avoiding adverse selection is really where the promise of health care reform breaks down, particularly if a state elects not to expand Medicaid. If a state chooses not to expand Medicaid, the exchange should be the main conduit to provide health coverage for the uninsured. However, a penalty of as little as $95 a year is not enough to incentivize personal responsibility. Because states retain their prerogative to regulate insurance—with the ACA providing, at most, light interference—states hostile to the ACA, and friendly to insurers, could choose to set up an exchange where insurance companies dictate coverage offered through the exchange. Thus, an exchange could simply become a federally-subsidized purgatory of high risk and high premiums.

Washington's 2012 law requires that for any plan or policy year beginning after January 1, 2014, those carriers offering a Bronze plan outside the Exchange must also offer Gold and Silver plans outside the Exchange.[311] Bronze plans are less expensive because of their comparatively low value. The concern was that carriers might simply establish themselves outside the Exchange and draw away those looking for bargain-rate health care by providing Bronze plans only. If they are concurrently required to offer more expensive plans, their overall care framework will be sturdier than a Bronze plan.

Even for those insured in Washington, the ACA represents perhaps the nation's most significant increase in health insurance comprehensiveness; the state ranked last in a *U.S. News &World Report* ranking in 2012 for that category, with only 4% of plans earning 4 or 5 stars on a 5-star scale.[312] Health care reform pioneer Massachusetts, at 100%, ranked first.

This is a reason why one Washington carrier, which offered an individual market plan with an extremely low actuarial value, warned of a rate increase apocalypse under the ACA. A conservative blog ran a July 2012 headline screaming of "Staggering Health Insurance Premiums Right Around the Corner."[313] After killing 2013 legislation that would have allowed regulation of its surplus cash, in excess of $1 billion, the nonprofit carrier publicly moderated its alarmism.[314] When the carrier's 2014 premiums actually materialized they were not dramatically higher, as it had been allowed to game its deductibles and networks.

The Washington law further provides that catastrophic plans, as defined in the ACA, may only be sold inside the Exchange.[315] The ACA makes provision for the sale of catastrophic plans, the most bare-bones coverage available, only to those under 30.[316] Were a special market to exist for that coveted, healthy demographic outside the Exchange, the Exchange would lose that good risk.

The Democratic Legislature effectively precluded the Exchange from active purchasing by requiring it accept any qualified health plan determined by the insurance commissioner to meet the requirements of the insurance code. Insurers were also not required to offer small business products in the Exchange, which would have disastrous consequences.

Despite these substantial concessions, all House and Senate Republicans – with one exception – voted against the 2012 bill.

Yet, ironically, no-new-taxes Republicans, when they took control of the Washington State Senate in 2013 with the help of two quisling Democrats, unsuccessfully pushed to shoehorn tens of thousands of part-time school district and state employees into the Exchange beginning in 2014 for a speculative budget savings. In other words, they attempted to rely upon savings extracted through an entity they fought just the previous year.

The proposal would have stripped coverage from those workers, including up to 3,500 part-time adjunct community college instructors, saving the state $57 million over two years – part-time workers would instead receive a $2 hourly wage increase to buy their own benefits.[317] It was a way to remove collective bargaining rights over health care.

A major challenge confronting Washington, and any state setting up an exchange, is the development of an information technology infrastructure. In Washington, the federal resources dedicated to this effort were considerable. In a May 2012 report, a consultant estimated $135.6 million in Exchange development costs from 2012 through 2014—of which 71% would be dedicated toward "Systems Development & Support."[318]

Complicated information technology system designs have a way of blowing up. In the 1990s Washington spent $20 million on a new welfare computer system that was abandoned. More recently, it committed to $643 million over the life of bonds to pay off an unnecessary state data center that did not account for "cloud" computing and virtualization.[319]

As was true nationally, the outsourced Washington Healthplanfinder website malfunctioned when consumers began shopping through it in October 2013 – even miscalculating the tax credits for the first 6,000 applications for commercial insurance.[320] One upset victim of this, who had been singled out by President Obama as an ACA success story, was then featured by FOX News and other outlets as a symbol of the act's failings.[321] By the end of 2013, 90% of calls for assistance were met with automated messages to call back; only 66,700 got through compared to 617,000 turned away.[322]

By June 2014, an estimated 15% of Healthplanfinder enrollees were not having their payments processed correctly – leaving insurers, which were not billing those covered directly, unaware the affected enrollees had coverage.[323] As the *Washington Post* reported, "Premera Blue Cross, which won the largest share of Washington exchange enrollment in 2014, estimates about 10,000 of its 92,000 enrollees are having payment issues."[324] Despite these missteps, and with a budget problem looming for 2015 and beyond, the Healthplanfinder Board had voted in November 2013 – with only the single consumer representative opposed – to retroactively increase the CEO's salary to an amount well in excess of what Washington's governor makes.[325] An ostensibly progressive state that had, in 2011, fined an insurer over having denied access to IUD coverage to 984 women,[326] now had policymakers who sat by silently as thousands of residents were denied access to health care coverage despite having paid for it.

While these problems were fixed, they were among many issues that depressed the confidence of prospective enrollees. Enrollment for 2015 fell far below expectations, actually falling 2% from the 2014 level,[327] even as the Healthplanfinder sought a massive two-year appropriation from the Legislature. Its request for $147 million actually exceeded, for example, the operating budget for The Evergreen State College – a 44-year-old college with over 4,300 students.[328] Given that progressives had, in the past, dismissed insurers as costly middlemen standing between consumers and care, it is ironic that progressives were now willing to countenance such a costly new intermediary between consumers and their insurers.

As state exchanges develop their processes, they face unaccustomed pressure from consumers and carriers alike. In Washington, for example, a September 2012 letter to the Exchange, governor, insurance commissioner, and two other state agency heads—signed by 103 groups ranging from labor unions to the Washington State Hospital Association—complained "there are no opportunities for stakeholder involvement or information-sharing in a joint and coordinated setting," and opined that the Exchange's "siloed approach raises serious concerns about our state's success in health care reform implementation, and particularly the ability of consumers to succeed in using the new system."[329]

Because it is not wholly a public entity, the Healthplanfinder avoided civil service laws by outsourcing its call center, for example. It even outsourced the progress reports to measure the results of its outsourcing.

In Washington State, as was true elsewhere, the stakes were high for Exchange success. Through 2011, there were over one million uninsured Washingtonians receiving over $1 billion in uncompensated care.[330] Yet simply making consumers aware of their options would be a formidable undertaking, requiring outreach into minority and rural communities, for example. Not every state, like Massachusetts, can use the Boston Red Sox to promote their Exchange.

10

OTHER STATES MOVING
FORWARD ON EXCHANGES

WHILE THE DISTRICT of Columbia and thirty-four states accepted "level one" federal grants to begin planning for establishing exchanges,[331] only fourteen states and the District of Columbia would establish self-administered post-ACA exchanges and avoid federal intervention in their health care marketplaces for 2014.

Two states have Exchanges that predate the ACA. They are as different as can be imagined. Massachusetts was first in health care reform and has had an operational exchange, a hybrid public-private entity, since 2006.[332] Consumers compare choices and prices through what is called the Commonwealth Choice program. As of October 2013, the Massachusetts' Health Connector's board of seven voting members included faculty from Harvard and the Massachusetts Institute of Technology, as well as two business consultants, an insurance firm's CEO, and two labor leaders.[333]

Republican Utah was also well ahead of the curve, with a health care reform effort up and running prior to the ACA's passage. Utah began serving the individual market in 2009, and began fully serving the small group market in 2010.[334] A nonprofit entity within the Utah Insurance Department—the Utah Defined Contribution Risk Adjuster—was created with a governance structure stacked toward insurers.[335] Under this plan, the governor appointed up to nine voting members, with at least three, and up to five, to have actuarial experience and represent insurance carriers.[336] The only "consumer representative" worked for the governor.[337] Separately, a governing board for Utah's exchange was co-chaired by the lieutenant governor and a representative of Intermountain Healthcare, Utah's largest health care provider. Of the twelve other members named initially, insurers dominated with no official consumer voice.[338]

While Massachusetts inspired the ACA, it seemed hard to reconcile the Utah Exchange with federal health care reform. Under the ACA, if an exchange is formed through an independent state agency or state-established nonprofit, the governance structure must a "clearly-defined governing board" that cannot be "made up of a majority of voting representatives with a conflict of interest, including representatives of health insurance issuers or agents or brokers, or any other individual licensed to sell health insurance[.]" It must allow for regular public meetings announced in advance and consist of at least one consumer representative.[339]

The NAIC had even objected to federal rules ensuring voting members of an exchange governing board represent consumer interests, asserting that "[s]tates should have the flexibility to determine the categories of individuals and the types of individuals that might have conflicts of interest."[340]

In an understatement, one congressional report cited Utah as "[a]n example of a minimalist health insurance exchange[.]"[341] However, federal regulation presumed that exchanges established prior to January 1, 2010 (i.e., Massachusetts and Utah) are compliant if they covered a percentage of their citizens not less than that projected by 2016 under the ACA by the Congressional Budget Office.[342] Utah would decide to only offer a small business exchange for 2014 and let the federal government handle the individual market. And that exchange would prove to be more successful than those in states with policymakers a great deal more enthusiastic about the ACA. Indeed, as early as 2011, the head of Utah's exchange was able to tell *Governing* magazine, "There are 146 different plans on our exchange, with various prices, copays and deductible levels, so that employees can choose which plan fits best for them and their family."[343]

California was the first state to establish an exchange in response to federal health care reform, with Republican Governor Arnold Schwarzenegger signing the law in 2010.[344] A public entity, it consists of five voting members—two appointed by the governor, and one apiece by the House and Senate, along with the state's secretary of Health and Human Services or a designee.[345] Strict conflict-of-interest provisions bar board membership by those affiliated with insurers or health care providers.[346]

By the beginning of 2013, the other nine states that had legislatively established exchanges, including Washington and the District of Columbia, had followed similar paths, with some interesting features worth noting:

- Like Utah, Connecticut has a governing board chaired by the lieutenant governor.[347] In Maryland the lieutenant governor was in charge of the overall health care reform effort.[348]
- Colorado,[349] Connecticut[350] and Nevada[351] allowed direct appointments to their exchange boards by legislative leaders.
- While small in geographical size, Hawaii had what is easily the largest governing board of any state exchange, with fifteen members to "reflect geographic diversity and the diverse interests of stakeholders[.]"[352]
- Progressive Oregon's law was perhaps surprising for allowing as many members (two) who work in the health care industry, or work for insurers, to serve on its exchange board as those representing consumers – which drew consumer criticism that the law "lets the foxes into the henhouse[.]"[353]
- Connecticut,[354] the District of Columbia, and Maryland[355] barred anyone tied to the insurance industry from membership on their boards, with both Connecticut[356] and D.C.[357] barring members from taking jobs with insurers for a year after leaving their boards. Connecticut, however, was criticized for having three *former* health insurance executives on its board.[358] The D.C. conflict-of-interest law is the strictest, as it bars both board members and exchange staff from affiliation with health professional or health care facilities or clinics, and applies the prohibition on accepting employment with an insurance carrier within one year after leaving service to exchange staff as well.[359]
- Vermont stood out for having enacted a law providing for universal single-payer "Green Mountain Care," with the Vermont Health Benefit Exchange to serve as its foundation.[360] The single-payer plan would be abandoned by Vermont's governor following the 2014 election. The board is appointed by the governor, and is unique among exchange governing bodies in that its members are fully-salaried.[361]

Three states, Kentucky, New York and Rhode Island, have governors who sidestepped recalcitrant legislatures through exchange-creating executive orders,[362] while Mississippi's elected insurance commissioner, as noted earlier, had tried to create his state's exchange through an executive order.[363]

As 2013 began, states on the bubble included Idaho, Minnesota and New Mexico.

After public agonizing, and despite a Legislature that already rejected federal exchange planning money, Republican Governor "Butch" Otter of Idaho narrowly beat (by three days) a December 2012 deadline by announcing his state would run its own exchange. A rally against it was immediately scheduled the next day.[364]

Minnesota, with a Democratic governor, Mark Dayton, was stymied by Republican legislative majorities in moving forward on an exchange. With progressive majorities incoming in 2013, Minnesota worked fast to get an exchange operational with a federal blessing despite the fact that $39 million in federal monies were not applied for until after the 2012 election.[365]

The Republican governor of New Mexico, Susan Martinez, waited until after the 2012 election to announce a state-based exchange, having previously vetoed legislation to establish one, and announced it would be administered by an existing nonprofit public corporation—the New Mexico Health Insurance Alliance. This proposal was modified by Democratic legislative majorities.[366]

Both Idaho and New Mexico fell short of getting their own exchanges operational in time for 2014, and, in 2015, New Mexico abandoned plans to run an exchange of its own.

Federal policy does not favor outliers. The ACA is that rare federal law where compliance is the exception not the norm, which shifts the federal government's normative focus to accommodating the vast majority of the states where it assisted, or wholly managed, exchange markets.

The federal government lacks regulatory experience concerning health care beyond Medicare and Medicaid. It seemed highly possible that the federal government's preoccupation with its own role might, paradoxically, disadvantage states working to implement the ACA by moving ahead with their own exchanges.

Entirely unaccustomed to the state function of commercial insurance regulation, the federal government can only provide so much assistance. After two successive former state insurance regulators used their federal health care reform roles to launch lucrative private sector careers, the federal Center for Consumer Information and Insurance Oversight hired Oregon's very competent insurance commissioner, Teresa Miller.[367]

By February 2013 the nonpartisan Congressional Budget Office had expressed new pessimism about the ACA, reducing by five million the number of Americans expected to gain insurance by 2017 and voicing concern about "the readiness of exchanges to provide a broad array of new insurance options[.]"[368] The rollout catastrophe for 2014 enrollment confirmed the prescience of those worries. The Hawaii, Maryland, Minnesota and Oregon state-run exchanges experienced such problems that by December 2013 the heads of each had announced their resignations; the head of Minnesota's exchange had luxuriated in Costa Rica amidst problems.[369] The Nevada Health Link worked well initially, but began faltering in January 2014 – its executive director resigned in March 2014.[370]

After reporting revealed that the Oregon exchange's chief information officer, Carolyn Lawson, had heavily-promoted Oracle, despite the software company's troubled programming of the Cover Oregon website, Lawson resigned. As *KATU News* reported, "Lawson was also making outrageously sunny claims about her work on the online exchange that in hindsight sound like outright lies."[371] Legislative oversight meetings were held in secret, without media or public participation, for two years.[372] Finally the Cover Oregon board decided to transition to the federal website, although it was puzzlingly unclear whether the entity's state budget would go away or even be reduced. Blamed by the state for the debacle, Oracle, in turn, blamed poor state management. It filed suit in federal court, alleging Cover Oregon was still using its software without paying for it.[373]

Nevada also decided that the troubled federal exchange was a better alternative for 2015 than its own faltering system – abandoning a $75 million investment through Xerox to build its exchange. "We've seen so many broken promises from Xerox on how they're going to fix it that at some point it just becomes not credible" stated one board member in *POLITICO*.[374]

Maryland's exchange was such a mess that the state decided to junk its investment and replicate Connecticut's system instead – losing at least $47 million from its earlier technological investment.[375] The exchange operated in such secrecy that it did not even make public the conference call in which it fired its contractor – repeatedly violating open meetings laws according to the Maryland Open Meetings Compliance Board.[376]

Yet there appeared to be no accountability for the failures. In June 2014 Governor Martin O'Malley's lieutenant governor, Anthony Brown, won the Democratic gubernatorial primary despite the fact that, as the *Washington Post* noted, "Brown's premier responsibility as O'Malley's deputy — overseeing the implementation of the Affordable Health Care Act — was considered a fiasco."[377] Voters overall were not the ACA cheerleaders Democratic primary voters were; although Maryland is an overwhelmingly-Democratic state, Brown was defeated in November 2014 by a Republican, Larry Hogan, denouncing Maryland's exchange failures.

Upon transitioning into office, Hogan promptly named as his insurance commissioner the owner of an insurance brokerage firm who, ironically, had left to run a managed care company during a prior stint as Maryland's insurance commissioner.

Even health reform pioneer Massachusetts found its online Health Connector staggering in 2014 – the state faced the embarrassment of a federal takeover as the Democratic governor, Deval Patrick, had to enlist a special adviser to take a leave of absence from Blue Cross/Blue Shield.[378] As its software failures meant it could not verify eligibility, the state was forced to place enrollees in a "temporary Medicaid program" – potentially incurring a payback liability to the federal government.[379] The ubiquitous UnitedHealth Group subsidiary Optum was paid $105 million for the website for 2014 and 2015.[380] Focusing on Health Connector failures, a Republican then won the 2014 gubernatorial race to succeed Patrick.

Quantifying the success or failure of exchanges was initially made difficult by the fact that, as Sebelius confessed in a March 2014 U.S. House hearing, the federal government was somehow not equipped to track which enrollees had actually gone through with paying their premiums.[381] When solid data about state-run exchanges did come through it was not too reassuring: An April 2015 study by Avalere found such exchanges performed worse than those facilitated by the federal government – California, for example, only increased its enrollment by 1% in 2015 from its first year of enrollment, while other state-run exchanges saw enrollment plunge.[382]

11

THE FAILED PROMISE OF
MEDICAID EXPANSION

IN REJECTING MEDICAID expansion for the nation's poorest, unhealthiest state, Mississippi Governor Bryant sanctimoniously offered an alternative to the poor, in a piece in the *Washington Times*: "Living a healthy lifestyle that includes regular exercise and a proper diet can help shrink Mississippi's obesity rate and the chronic diseases such as diabetes that accompany it."[383] Presumably every *Washington Times'* subscriber in Mississippi took heed.

Nebraska's Republican Governor Jim Heineman was similarly dismissive. "The governor suggested healthy habits and private charities could help low-income people who cannot qualify for Medicaid now and cannot afford health insurance," reported the *Omaha World-Herald*.[384]

In March 2013 Mississippi's Bryant belied his rhetoric about healthy lifestyles by signing a law, sponsored by a barbecue restaurant chain owner selling sand-wiches called "L'il Piggies," to prevent mandatory restaurant disclosure of calorie contents, bans on toys with fast food meals, or regulation of food portion size.[385] Mississippi tied with West Virginia as the state with the highest rate of adult obesity: 35.1 percent.[386]

Under Mississippi law, the state's Medicaid participation must be reauthorized annually – a legislative vote that, given tax implications, requires a supermajority. Because Republican legislators were afraid the Democratic minority would hijack a reauthorization vote with an amendment to expand Medicaid, they adjourned in

April 2013 without a Medicaid budget. That forced the possibility the state might leave Medicaid July 1. Upon a special session being called in June 2013, Medicaid participation was reauthorized.

"You got to be almost dead before you can get Medicaid in Mississippi," related one impoverished resident to the *New York Times*.[387] Almost three-fifths of the state's poor, uninsured adults are African-American. And their incomes are too low to qualify for subsidies through the federally-facilitated exchange.

As 2014 approached, only half of the states were willing to take the federal government's deal to pay 100% of the costs of Medicaid expansion through 2016 – a funding proportion that by 2017 would decline, point by point, from 95% to 93%, and become 90% by 2020.

Yet, as the Congressional Budget Office (CBO) has written, "although the 10 percent share of the costs of newly eligible people that states would ultimately bear would be a small share of total additional Medicaid spending, it would nevertheless represent a large extra cost for some states."[388] State governments, after all, cannot avoid cuts by simply borrowing money from China. Many state governments are not paying *current* Medicaid bills. Through 2015, the Washington State Legislature had left nursing home cost reimbursement based upon 2007 costs.

In her 2013 State of the State Address, South Carolina Governor Haley admitted that "here in South Carolina we have one of the lowest life expectancies and highest infant mortality rates in the U.S."[389] Yet she rejected Medicaid expansion: "The federal government likes to wave around a nine dollar match like it is some silver bullet, some extraordinary benefit that we cannot pass up. But what good do the nine dollars do us when we can't come up with the one?"

That was not necessarily a dishonest perspective. Maryland's exchange was such a debacle that by March 2014 it was projecting to make over $30 million in unnecessary Medicaid payments that the state itself would be on the hook for.[390]

Medicaid expansion had held the promise of being the only single-payer aspect in the ACA, giving some economic justice hope to at least the poor, yet the ACA bungled even that in making expansion coercive by not fully funding it.

Even when it assumed all states would participate in Medicaid expansion, the CBO, as late as March 2012, projected the federal cost to be $931 billion from 2014-2022 relative to $73 billion in cost for the states. Thus, for the sake of saving $73 billion over nine years, a federal government that spent over $2 trillion waging war in Afghanistan and Iraq jeopardized access to health care for the poor in half of the states.

As a consequence, with states balking at Medicaid expansion, the CBO's March 2013 projection showed the number of Americans gaining coverage in 2014 through Medicaid would be 8 million. One study of 14 states refusing to expand Medicaid projected they would lose out on $8.4 billion from the federal government, spend an extra $1 billion on uncompensated care in 2016, and have 3.6 million fewer insured residents.[391]

Dubious math was employed by many fighting Medicaid expansion.

In Louisiana, Governor Jindal asserted "President Obama's Medicaid expansion could cost taxpayers in Louisiana $1.7 billion over the first 10 years of implementation, and the cost will continue to rise."[392] Yet a nonpartisan analysis by the state's Legislative Fiscal Office showed potential state savings of over a half-billion dollars over that period. Not only was there no possibility Louisiana would expand Medicaid, but Americans for Prosperity – a Tea Party group financed by the conservative billionaire Koch brothers – sought to get every single Louisiana legislator to publicly declare opposition to expansion prior to the 2014 session.[393] As that session unfolded, the *Baton Rouge Advocate* editorialized that "turning down the chance to return our U.S. tax dollars to the state, when the state's budget is in such bad shape, is simply irresponsible."[394]

With Jindal term-limited, Louisiana's leading Republican candidate for governor in 2015, Senator David Vitter, publicly left the door open to Medicaid expansion.[395]

Beyond being unwilling to run exchanges and expand Medicaid, some Republican governors were working actively to subvert the ACA.

One was Maine's governor, Paul LePage, who declared, "I tell Maine businesses to pay the penalty. It would be cheaper by just writing a check for the penalty and then let Obamacare fall on its own weight. In one year it would falter."[396]

Upon taking office in 2011, LePage had busily preoccupied himself with removing a 36-foot labor history mural from his Department of Labor's building and ordering the renaming of its conference rooms, including one named after Maine's Frances Perkins, the nation's first female Cabinet secretary and key architect of Social Security. His efforts were validated by his 2014 re-election.

Pennsylvania Governor Tom Corbett foresaw "the whole thing collapsing and, potentially, in the long run that may have been the plan. I'm a prosecutor. I believe in conspiracies."[397]

Unmentioned was his role in facilitating any potential collapse, including his objectively false claim that Medicaid expansion would cost the state more than $4 billion over eight years (his state government's Independent Fiscal Office found expansion would save Pennsylvania $190 million over that period — while gaining $3.2 billion in federal funding).

Corbett was the rare Republican to lose in 2014, and Medicaid expansion occurred in 2015.

Not all Republicans, even some vocal in their hostility toward the ACA, failed to see the benefits of Medicaid expansion.

In his 2013 State of the State address, Florida Governor Scott stated, "I concluded that for the three years the federal government is committed to paying 100 percent of the cost of new people in Medicaid, I cannot, in good conscience, deny the uninsured access to care."[398] He admitted that "[a]fter a long fight, we lost in the Supreme Court over the President's health care law, and we lost a presidential election along with the promise of the law's full repeal."

Yet the Republican legislature adjourned without expanding Medicaid. There was a poignant aspect to this reported by the *Miami Herald*: "Florida House Republicans last month loudly and proudly rejected billions of dollars in federal money that would have provided health insurance to 1 million poor Floridians. Quietly, they kept their own health insurance premiums staggeringly low."[399]

Thus Florida House members would pay "pay just $8.34 a month for state-subsidized health care next year, or $30 a month to cover their entire family." That $8.34 per month was a third of the $25 per visit that Republicans had discussed charging Medicaid recipients as co-pays for medical visits.

In supporting Medicaid expansion, Republican Governor John Kasich of Ohio went so far as to invoke President Ronald Reagan: "I urge those who esteem Reagan to consider the principled, big-picture perspective at the core of his decisions. When we consider what Reagan would do, let's also remember what he did do — expand Medicaid."[400] Yet his fellow Republicans in control of the Ohio Legislature would not go along. Thwarted by legislators, Kasich obtained Medicaid expansion approval in October 2013 through a state board stacked with his appointees.[401]

The most dramatic battle occurred in Arizona in 2013. Republican Governor Jan Brewer, a longtime Tea Party figure, touted before her Republican legislature "the enormous economic benefits" of Medicaid expansion that would "inject $2 billion into our economy; save and create thousands of jobs; and provide health care to hundreds of thousands of low-income Arizonans."[402]

Brewer even created a webpage dedicated to the issue, and characterized Medicaid expansion as "The Conservative Choice for Arizona." The page opened with a testament to Brewer's ACA-opposing bona fides: "First, a reality check: Nobody in

Arizona has done more to oppose the Affordable Care Act than Governor Brewer. Whether pushing Congress, leading our State's legal challenge all the way to the U.S. Supreme Court or saying 'no' to an Arizona-based health exchange, the Governor has consistently fought for health reforms with more patient choice, fewer costs and less bureaucracy."[403]

Nonetheless, Brewer – who set to vetoing unrelated bills until she got her way – was accused of "Obrewercare" by those who disfavored compromise. The far-right Foundation for Responsible Accountable Government solicited contributions to stop Medicaid expansion, accusing Republicans who sided with Brewer of being "Brewercrats" and writing angrily that "[t]he heroine of Arizona has self-inflicted a wound and it is becoming quite a natural wonder." The Maricopa County Republican chair wrote that "Arizona has a rogue Governor and a few state legislators who say they're Republicans aligning themselves with the liberal Democrats and progressive socialists." The House's budget chair stated he had "never seen a more toxic vote for Republicans than to vote yes on this expansion."[404]

When Brewer called a June 2013 special session to force the issue, the Republican Senate president and House speaker issued a joint statement: "We are disappointed and stunned that the Governor and her staff would resort to such an unnecessary, impulsive and unprecedented tactic." They accused Brewer of an "impetuous decision to intercede and collude with the democrat minority in order to force an expedited vote on her sole legislative priority of Obamacare."[405] As the special session convened, 16 anti-expansion House Republicans sat sulking in the House gallery in protest.[406] Yet Brewer managed to quickly overcome intransigence, and raised funds to defend Republican legislators who stood with her.[407]

Medicaid expansion was fraught with compromises even where Republican governors went along.

Michigan Governor Snyder pushed a Healthy Michigan Plan through his Republican Legislature. It had the typical Republican personal responsibility language – requiring expansion beneficiaries to pay 5% of the costs of their care even if they are "medically frail" – even though the federal government was on the hook for 100% of those costs.[408] As one Republican representative said, "This is a very unique opportunity for us to negotiate from a position of strength to get reforms in what have been long-held entitlement reforms, real reforms that will help people and help taxpayers."[409]

Based upon my past experience working with Medicaid-contracting long-term care providers, this will, at best, simply mean providers – whether doctors or hospitals – get saddled with bad debt. Even worse, co-pays may actually deter the poor from seeking preventative care or treatment they need, which only increases costs down the road.

In May 2014, with speculation that he would be a 2016 Republican presidential candidate, Indiana Governor Mike Pence released a Hoosier 2.0 plan for "all low-income Hoosiers" described as "grounded in the principles of personal responsibility and consumerism" – implying the poor might otherwise lack those principles. It involved a "Personal Wellness and Responsibility (POWER) account which functions like a Health Savings Account (HSA) to help pay for deductible expenses." The deductible was $2,500. Those who chose not to contribute to their POWER accounts – or, more likely, couldn't afford to – would be punished by being relegated to a plan that had "reduced benefits such as no vision and dental coverage and provides a more limited prescription drug benefit." They would also then be subject to punitive co-payments, such as $75 for inpatient services. The transactional Obama Administration agreed to Pence's design.[410]

Progressives had become so unconditional in their cheerleading for the ACA that *Washington Post* columnist Dana Milbank celebrated Pence as "a happy warrior for conservatism" and wrote that "[a]s more conservatives realize that the law they hate allows them to implement policies they like, they may have trouble recalling what all the fuss was about."[411] Was that really why Democrats passed the ACA – to allow the working poor to be treated as a social science experiment?

Wisconsin was a special case. The state already had expansive eligibility for Medicaid that predated the ACA. While Governor Walker was unwilling to implement the ACA's Medicaid expansion, his plan to roll-back Medicaid eligibility under the existing BadgerCare program, transferring Medicaid enrollees into the subsidized federally-facilitated exchange, would open up more Medicaid slots under BadgerCare – even though one nonpartisan analysis found it would cost the state's taxpayers $460 million more through 2020 than accepting expansion would have.[412] That polling showed a majority of Wisconsin voters supported expanding Medicaid made little difference to Walker's 2014 re-election, as a majority also opposed the ACA.[413]

A desperate Obama Administration had, by 2013, hit upon an idea that seemed like a grotesque parody of a single-payer system. For states reluctant to expand Medicaid, the Administration would, instead, provide funding to purchase commercial insurance for those who would otherwise be Medicaid-eligible. Some ideologically objecting to government paying health care providers for care were apparently comfortable with government paying an intermediary, a private insurer, which, in turn, would pay health care providers for care after extracting its own costs.

The plan was first implemented in Arkansas under the guise of "premium assistance." One insurance carrier's CEO exulted: "We are very capable of doing an Arkansas-type model. That's something that would be a sweet spot for us."[414] It is reasonable to say this was not a "sweet spot" contemplated by Congress, despite its general disregard for the poor. During the Senate Finance Committee debate on health care reform, Senator Rockefeller noted that "you just do not hear people talking, public officials or people, about Medicaid, because it is something they had rather not hear about, something they had rather not have in their communities." Choking up, he said, "So I like to keep poor people where they have health care benefits. I do not wish to see them handed over to the tender mercies of a private exchange, or whatever."[415]

Iowa, experiencing a second round with its seemingly-permanent Republican Governor Terry Branstad, who also served as governor from 1983 to 1999 before winning again in 2010, adopted a strange hybrid alternative to Medicaid expansion after majority Senate Democrats overcame the intransigence of Branstad and majority House Republicans.

The Iowa Health & Wellness Plan would allow those under the federal poverty line who were not already on Medicaid to go onto a state public insurance plan that would be an alternative to Medicaid. For those whose income was between 100% and 138% of the federal poverty level there would be a "premium assistance program" for commercial health insurance purchases through the exchange, similar to the Arkansas plan.[416] If the federal government's contribution were to fall below the 90% guaranteed under the ACA, hospitals agreed to bear the first 5% of expansion costs below that level.[417] The program required a federal waiver.

Thus, to secure coverage for the poor in Iowa, Democrats had to agree to further enrich the commercial insurance industry. For that industry, the ACA was a gift that would keep giving in ways wholly unimagined at the time of its passage.

In 2014, Utah Republican Governor Bob Herbert failed to win legislative support in pushing for a federal Medicaid block grant – long a conservative ideal – through which private insurance would be purchased after tagging impoverished Medicaid recipients with hefty co-payments averaging $420 annually.[418] In New Hampshire, with a Democratic governor in Maggie Hassan, the 2014 legislative session brought an expansion of Medicaid through 2016 – with money to be used to subsidize private insurance purchases.

Yet even this hybrid "free market" approach was not enough for many Republicans. In a sad farce in Montana, a bill to allow Medicaid dollars to be used to purchase commercial insurance for those who would otherwise qualify for Medicaid expansion died on the House floor in 2013 after a Democrat accidentally voted with the Republican speaker, in a 50-50 tie vote, to affirm the speaker's re-referral of the bill to the burying ground of a Republican-controlled committee.[419] The Democratic governor had favored Medicaid expansion. When the legislature reconvened in 2015, an odd hybrid passed into law with burdensome co-pay and premium components. Premiums would consume 2% of the scant household income of a beneficiary, while co-pays and premiums combined could consume up to 5 percent. Bizarre features include contracting with a third party administrator to run Medicaid.

In Virginia, Medicaid expansion was blocked when a Democratic state senator reportedly secured from Republicans appointments for himself and his daughter. His resignation in June 2014 came during a high-stakes budget showdown over expansion between Democratic Governor Terry McAuliffe and Republicans, and turned control of the Virginia Senate over to Republicans as the month-end deadline approached for adopting a budget.[420] Following the passage of a budget that did not expand Medicaid, McAuliffe announced he would work to expand it unilaterally – denouncing what he characterized as "the demagoguery, lies, fear and cowardice that have gripped this debate for too long."[421] With Republicans thwarting that effort too, McAuliffe finally, in September 2014, decided to simply expanded coverage to 25,000 Virginians using funding available to him – split between "20,000 uninsured Virginians with severe mental illnesses" and 5,000 "children of Virginia's state workforce."[422] When the legislature convened that month in a special session to fill a budget gap, the Republican House voted 65-32 to authorize the speaker to hire an attorney to sue McAuliffe in the event he expanded Medicaid without legislative approval.[423]

Even prior to "hybrid" Medicaid expansion that featured commercial insurance, Medicaid, where it involved private carriers working with governments to secure coverage for beneficiaries, was not immune from the worst excesses of the profit motive.

In Washington, D.C., the dominant Medicaid carrier, D.C. Chartered Health Plan, having been forced into receivership and sold, notified providers in April 2013 that it would not be paying their claims. One of the only private obstetrician-gynecologists in the District who took Medicaid was left roughly $100,000 in arrears for his altruism in responding to the District's call for more primary care physicians.[424]

D.C. Chartered had served over 100,000 residents. The $43 million in unpaid bills it owed included $8,355,320 for one hospital alone and even $973,223 for the District's Fire Department.[425]

In Kansas, Governor Brownback was implicated in an alleged scheme by confidantes and former campaign aides working as lobbyists to improperly steer Medicaid contracts – representing over $3 billion annually – through the state's privatized KanCare program.[426] Given this alleged impropriety, it was ironic that Brownback also signed legislation surrendering to the Legislature his authority to expand Medicaid under the ACA.[427]

By November 2014 the New York Times was able to report that Medicaid expansion had been a boon to the commercial insurance industry, with the ubiquitous UnitedHealth Group alone accounting for over one million new Medicaid enrollees.[428] With so much of Medicare and Medicaid now run by commercial insurers, the Times noted that "federal officials are eager to collaborate with an industry they once demonized."[429]

Beginning in 2011, the Obama Administration went someplace no Republican Administration dared to go since the 1965 enactment of Medicaid. It argued before the U.S. Supreme Court that Medicaid beneficiaries and providers had no legal right to challenge adequacy of state payments in court. Only the federal government itself, which routinely rubber-stamps state Medicaid cuts of any magnitude, could disapprove such cuts under this argument – not federal courts.

Democratic Congressional leaders – including Pelosi, Reid, and even Baucus – disputed the Administration's position in their own brief filed with the Court. And the Court narrowly avoided the question, in a 5-4 ruling where Justice Anthony Kennedy, a Republican appointee, joined the four Democratic appointees in punting the case back to the Ninth Circuit Court of Appeals for further argument.

In a dissent written by Chief Justice John Roberts, it was clear four justices were anxious to take the Obama Administration up on its invitation: "Nothing in the Medicaid Act allows providers or beneficiaries (or anyone else, for that matter) to sue[.]"[430]

The Obama Administration then renewed its arguments before the Ninth Circuit, arguing "[t]here is no general mandate under Medicaid to reimburse providers for all or substantially all of their costs."

It is telling the Obama Administration employed such forcefulness in arguing it is permissible to make providers operate at a loss in providing care to the poorest and

most vulnerable citizens; this was a courage the Administration lacked in controlling profits by health insurers even where government itself was the payer (such as
Medicare Advantage).

In a December 2012 decision, the Ninth Circuit admitted that "[t]he idea that a
state should consider providers' costs prior to reducing reimbursement rates seems
at first blush to be logical."[431] It then ignored logic by stating the only thing that matters is if enough providers take Medicaid. In effect, this was a freedom-of-contract
argument that ignored the Hobson's choice where Medicaid is the only game in town.

Think about state-paid in-home care, for example, in a state – like Washington –
where such care exists as an alternative to nursing home care. Home care hours had
been arbitrarily slashed 10 percent by state lawmakers. What if they were slashed 50
percent? If the Administration still rubber-stamped cuts, caregivers, who are often
no better off than those Medicaid beneficiaries they serve, could not sue.

In Washington State, for example, a trial judge awarded $95 million to home care
workers after Medicaid care hours were arbitrarily reduced by the Legislature.[432] The
state argued those caregivers had to accept whatever hours their clients were given
– even if care hours bore no relationship to care needs. Not wanting to abandon
their clients, caregivers effectively worked for free beyond hours officially allotted
to them. While cutting hours, no-new-taxes legislators had loudly proclaimed to the
public that they had "saved the safety net." The only way this could be disproven was
in court. In April 2014, the Washington Supreme Court upheld $57.1 million of the
award.

The Ninth Circuit decision, and the Administration's position, ignored a federal
statutory requirement that Medicaid payments be consistent with "quality of care." If
this language has meaning, it should be enforceable in court. Are we to believe actual
care costs bear no relationship to quality? It was as if the Administration protested
federal budget sequestration in Washington, D.C. while secretly encouraging it in
states. Not only was this position alarming to advocates for those with disabilities
and provider groups, it makes the landscape uncertain in enlisting providers under
the ACA's Medicaid expansion. It fed conservative conspiracy theories that Medicaid
expansion was a "rationing" scheme.

On March 31, 2015, the Supreme Court gave the Obama Administration what it
asked for. Writing for a 5-4 majority, Justice Scalia struck a blow against the Medicaid
poor that one Democratic appointee, Justice Stephen Breyer, joined in. In his concur-
rence, Breyer rhapsodized that no private right of action was needed as "States engage
in time-consuming efforts to obtain public input on proposed plan amendments" to

implement Medicaid cuts. This was certainly news to me, as I had, in the past as a long-term care advocate, actually had to file public disclosure requests to simply see those documents.

Neither Scalia nor Breyer remarked upon the fact that the draconian cuts made by Idaho legislators in the underlying case were contrary even to the recommendations of a Republican governor's state agency, or that court action had restored $12 million in funding in 2013.[433] In dissent, joined by Justice Kennedy and two Democratic appointees, Justice Sonia Sotomayor noted the longstanding fact "[t]hat parties may call upon the federal courts to enjoin unconstitutional government action" – writing that suing over Medicaid cuts "allegedly preempted by a federal statute falls comfortably within this doctrine."

Its posture before the Court was yet more evidence that the Obama Administration had no real regard for Medicaid. When enhanced federal Medicaid matching funds were provided to cash-strapped states as part of economic stimulus during the Administration's first two years, there was no requirement the states maintain their own commitments to Medicaid funding. Instead, many states paradoxically – and, from a purely-economic perspective, quite foolishly – slashed Medicaid funding even as they raked in the additional federal commitment toward the costs. The Administration approved every cut, no matter how egregious.

By June 2014, even with only half of the states expanding Medicaid, Roll Call reported that "[a]t least 2.9 million Americans who signed up for Medicaid coverage as part of the health care overhaul have not had their applications processed, with some paperwork sitting in queues since last fall[.]"[434]

The Obama Administration even stalled inexcusably in moving forward on an ACA provision providing extra Medicaid reimbursement for primary-care physicians to begin in 2013. A reason the American Academy of Family Physicians supported the ACA was that "for two years, it will provide funding to states to make sure Medicaid payments to primary care physicians are on par at least with Medicare payments for the same services" as part of the transition, they hoped, toward "a system eventually based on primary care."[435] Yet, by May 2013, with only four states offering the incentive due to federal delay (even though every state had applied to offer it), a letter from physicians' groups to the Obama Administration cited "confusion both by state employees responsible for administering the program and the physician community."[436]

The diffidence with which the incentive was acted upon by the federal government was unlikely to enlist new physicians in providing Medicaid care. And yet access to primary-care physicians is critical if health care reform is to succeed. Economic incentives drive physicians away from general practice; in Washington, D.C., for example, only 453 out of over 8,000 physicians were active primary-care practitioners in 2013.[437]

The federal incentive expired December 31, 2014, with the Urban Institute calculating an average 43% fee cut for primary-care physicians.[438] Even during its existence Medicaid patients had struggled to find access to care and were forced to endure long waits at best.

In the state of Washington, neither Democrats nor Republicans showed any appetite during the 2014 and 2015 legislative sessions for a doctor-led effort to permanently increase Medicaid payments for primary-care physicians. Indeed, by the end of the 2015 session, both parties were openly discussing raiding revenue that had been dedicated by voters to primary-care in health clinics with the passage of the state's recreational marijuana legalization initiative.[439]

12

THE ACA AND THE ANTI-CHOICE CRUSADE

To WIN THE votes of conservative Democrats for the ACA, Democrats favoring reproductive choice for women agreed to anti-choice language.

The ACA provides that "[a] State may elect to prohibit abortion coverage in qualified health plans offered through an Exchange in such State if such State enacts a law to provide for such prohibition." It requires insurers to segregate costs for abortion if offered, dictating that insurers "may not take into account any cost reduction estimated to result from such services, including prenatal care, delivery, or postnatal care[.]" Insurers are not allowed to "estimate such a cost at less than $1 per enrollee, per month."

In other words, an act that permits insurers to take into account the cost of tobacco use, allowing them to rate up to 50% higher for such use, disallows them from accurately rating the cost of abortions in the alternative to carrying pregnancies to term, and requires them, falsely, to suggest abortion has a net cost relative to childbirth.

The ACA also encouraged, through 2019, federal study of "the relative mental health consequences for women of resolving a pregnancy (intended and unintended) in various ways, including carrying the pregnancy to term and parenting the child, carrying the pregnancy to term and placing the child for adoption, miscarriage, and having an abortion."

Prior to enactment of the ACA, just five states had laws limiting insurance coverage for abortion.[440]

Because insurance is still state-regulated under the ACA, and with the encouragement of the ACA's anti-abortion op-out language, 25 states through December 2014 had enacted laws restricting abortion specifically in any exchange offerings – even though most of those states would not be operating their own exchanges.[441]

The *Washington Post*'s Ezra Klein predicted this in 2009:

> Stupak's amendment is a limited, though bad, policy in its current form. But it could grow into something much larger. If it sets the standards for the exchanges and the exchanges eventually become the standard for the whole insurance market, then the Stupak amendment could transform coverage for not just poor women, but all women.[442]

Prior to the ACA's passage, the state issues manager with the Guttmacher Institute noted, "This issue had been dead since the '80s at the state level."[443]

Not only were new state restrictions encouraged by a federal law enacted by the largest Democratic Congressional majority in decades, but they enjoyed some Democratic support. In Pennsylvania, for example, where Republicans controlled state government, a restriction on exchange abortion coverage passed the House 144-53 and the Senate 31-19 in 2013. Republicans only had a 109-93 majority in the House and a 27-23 Senate majority. "Never before has the state government prohibited a private insurer from providing coverage to a private customer who pays for that coverage with private money," pointed out the American Civil Liberties Union of Pennsylvania.[444]

In Virginia, two Senate Democrats were critical to the April 2013 passage of language sought by then-Governor Bob McDonnell, a Republican, to bar any insurance offered through the state's federally-run exchange, or even a policy rider to such insurance, from abortion coverage unless the mother's life was imperiled or the pregnancy resulted from incest or rape. The measure only passed the Senate 20-19 – with one Senate Republican opposed.[445]

A pro-choice group noted McDonnell's language would ban abortion coverage even "where a woman faced a severe and totally-incapacitating fetal anomaly."[446] Such a woman "would be forced to either come up with money to pay out-of-pocket for a potentially very costly procedure or carry a severely-incapacitated fetus to term and face the associated health risks and emotional and financial hardships."

Some states banned exchange coverage of the procedure altogether, while others allowed for some exceptions including incest or rape, or where the mother's life was in danger. Arizona, Kansas, Kentucky, Louisiana, Missouri, North Dakota, South Dakota and Tennessee made no exception for rape or incest.

In Louisiana, Governor Jindal had no intention of establishing an exchange but still signed into law a bill prohibiting abortions – with no exceptions – from being covered by plans in the nonexistent state exchange.

Five more states joined the five pre-ACA states that restricted the procedure in the entire health insurance market. There, too, through your regular health insurance you could only obtain an abortion in 8 of those ten states to save your life – insurance paid for entirely with your own private dollars would not obtain you the right to terminate a pregnancy resulting from incest or rape. So much for "free market" rhetoric.

Michigan was an example. There Republican legislators passed a law requiring an abortion insurance rider – which critics labeled "rape insurance" – over the opposition of a Republican governor who, like them, opposed abortion. The Abortion Insurance Opt-Out Act, applying to insurance sold both inside and outside the federally-facilitated exchange, had been vetoed by Governor Rick Snyder, but voter signatures gathered by an anti-abortion group allowed a second legislative vote to bypass his signature.[447] Oklahoma law requires similar rape insurance.

In Indiana, illustrating the bipartisan nature of such restrictions, a 2014 bill banning private insurance coverage of abortion passed the House 75-11 and the Senate 37-10 – margins well in excess of Republican majorities.[448] The Senate's "Democratic Leader Emeritus" even joined in the sponsorship.

In 2013, in progressive Washington State, an effort was made to pass a Reproductive Parity Act that would require health insurers to provide elective abortion coverage – something most Washington insurers did already. The bill passed the House and was killed by a Senate majority leader who Senate Democrats had recruited, as a House Republican, to run as a Democrat in 2006, displacing the pro-choice woman Democrat who almost beat him in 2004. In 2013 those Senate Democrats could only watch helplessly as their handpicked hero flipped again and built a ruling coalition with anti-choice Republicans.

The "Hyde Amendment" that predated the ACA will prevent those women eligible for Medicaid expansion from receiving abortions through Medicaid. As the National Institute for Reproductive Health notes:

One of the Patient Protection and Affordable Care Act's (ACA) most important provisions is a significant expansion of the Medicaid program, which is estimated to bring health coverage to millions of currently uninsured women. While this is a positive development overall, it also means that millions more women will be subject to restrictions on abortion coverage.[449]

Yet Planned Parenthood, which was – as an earlier chapter describes – apoplectic when abortion restrictions were first adopted in House debate of health care reform, never followed through on threats to oppose reform. The organization provides far too many women's health services beyond abortion to be anything but a net beneficiary under the ACA, and could not afford absolutism. Indeed, in the summer of 2013 Planned Parenthood President Cecile Richards was among those working behind closed doors with the Obama Administration and key allies on messaging strategy.[450] This has sidelined the organization as ACA-facilitated abortion restrictions pass in state after state.

In June 2014 the U.S. Supreme Court issued an opinion allowing certain closely-held corporations, such as the Hobby Lobby chain, to opt-out, for religious reasons, of a federal regulatory requirement (adopted under the ACA) to provide contraceptive coverage to employees. Expanding the concept of corporate personhood, Justice Alito, writing for the 5-4 majority, found that "[a] corporation is simply a form of organization used by human beings to achieve desired ends" – and that even corporations were entitled to religious beliefs. Democrats reacted with an outrage somewhat perplexing given their willingness to sacrifice abortion rights in the ACA, not to mention the fact that as many Senate Democrats had refused to filibuster against Alito's Supreme Court appointment as had been willing to confirm Chief Justice Roberts, who, predictably, joined Alito in his opinion.

Having used abortion as a wedge issue for decades, and accusing Republicans of imposing their own value judgments upon access to abortion, Democrats, in passing the ACA, had made a value judgment of their own: Access to abortion simply didn't matter as much as enriching health insurers.

Given their concessions, it is reasonable to conclude Democrats had made themselves implausible as defenders of choice. Colorado, a state progressive on social issues, was an excellent example. With everyday Coloradans, women and men alike, losing coverage altogether due to insurance cancellations, Colorado Senator Mark Udall focused on the contraceptive issue so much in his doomed 2014 re-election bid that he was derisively referred to as "Mark Uterus" – even by a woman journalist moderating a debate with his challenger.[451] He lost the support of the Democratic-leaning *Denver Post*, which stated Udall's "obnoxious one-issue campaign is an insult to those he seeks to convince."[452]

As Frank Bruni wrote in the *New York Times*, "Mark Udall's focus was more womb-centric than 'The Handmaid's Tale.' While I believe strongly in reproductive freedom and salute him for defending it, I also wish I could tell you, without intensive research, what sort of script he has for restoring this country's confidence."[453]

Because the contraceptive issue was all that apparently mattered to Democrats, Udall's Republican opponent, Congressman Cory Gardner, was able to artfully deflate it by simply proposing that insurers pay for prescription-free, over-the-counter, contraceptive access. As Ross Douthat wrote in the *New York Times*, "The politics of contraception turned out to be pretty easy to finesse by G.O.P. politicians with an ounce of savvy[.]"[454] In Colorado and other places, latter-day Democratic championing of reproductive choice had proved in 2014, as it had in 2010, to be a dog that would no longer hunt. Who could believe it anymore?

13

AN ACT IMPOSSIBLE
TO IMPROVE

IN A MARCH 25, 2010 *Washington Post* column, David Broder, then the face of establishment punditry, opined: "Next year, if not before, Congress will surely have to amend the new law to deal with some of the flaws its critics have noted. In fact, lawmakers will be dealing with health care every time they meet for the foreseeable future."[455]

The ACA was a unicameral law produced by a bicameral Congress. Yet, contrary to Broder's prognostication, the law was impossible to improve. Republicans, upon taking control of the House, wanted only to repeal it, while Democrats might never have the 60 votes again they conceded were necessary to accomplish anything in the Senate.

Thirty-six months after Broder's column, the *New York Times* ran an article on how, unlike previous enactments such as Medicare, Congress could not muster a majority to change anything about the ACA. As Senator McConnell stated in 2013, "I don't think it can be fixed. Everything is interconnected, 2,700 pages of statute, 20,000 pages of regulations so far. The only solution is to repeal it, root and branch."[456] And, given that Democrats had yielded veto power to McConnell's Republicans, Senator Baucus feigned helplessness: "I'm not sure we're going to get to the point where it's time to open the bill and make some changes. Once you start, it's Pandora's box."[457]

Having buried those working to comply with the ACA under an avalanche of regulations, and unable to acknowledge an objectively-imperfect law had flaws, the

Obama Administration tried to shift focus to rare instances of simplicity. As President Obama explained in a press conference:

> [W]e put together initially an application form for signing up for participation in the exchanges that was initially about 21 pages long. And immediately everybody sat around the table and said: Well, this is too long, especially, you know, in this age of the Internet. People aren't going to have the patience to sit there for hours on end. Let's streamline this thing. So we cut what was a 21-page form now down to a form that's about three pages for an individual, a little more than that for a family, well below the industry average.[458]

Form had truly been elevated over substance. The president's enthusiasm over the application form was at odds with his initial diffidence when people were unable to even access the form beginning October 1, 2013 due to glitches in the federal government's outsourced Internet enrollment portal. Obama glibly compared the flawed rollout to one for an Apple operating system, stating "I don't remember anybody suggesting Apple should stop selling iPhones or iPads or threatening to shut down the company if they didn't."[459] A critical difference, of course, was that no one was forced to buy iPhones — nor had taxpayers paid toward their manufacture.

Poignantly, three weeks later, after Obama finally acknowledged there was a website problem and urged people to call a toll-free number, POLITICO reported that "[m]inutes after Obama finished his Rose Garden remarks Monday, POLITICO reporters dialed in. 'Your call cannot be completed at this time. Please try your call again later,' an automated message told one reporter." Another reporter was referred to the malfunctioning federal exchange website.[460] Only six Americans had been able to enroll through the website on its first day.[461]

What is unfortunate is that the Obama Administration had not prepared the public for these transition problems, which were not without precedent — the rollout of Medicare Part D had also been a fraught experience. The whole concept of an ACA exchange had been sold through countless analogies to shopping websites such as Expedia. Thus, when the federal website failed to work, it was implausible for the Administration to assert that the ACA was much more than a website. While conservative Utah's pre-ACA small group exchange was often derided as inadequate by ACA supporters, the head of that exchange had, as far back as 2011, noted "it's important to beta-test your exchange before opening it up to a large-scale enrollment."[462] And while state exchanges built under the ACA floundered, Utah's continued enrolling customers.

The Administration also did not help itself when it failed to be forthcoming about the scale of the problems. Testifying before the House Ways & Means Committee on October 29, 2013, Marilyn Tavenner, the former health industry executive running the Centers for Medicare and Medicaid Services (CMS), refused to answer direct questions about how many people had enrolled. While Republicans bore down, many committee Democrats, all insured themselves through the federal government, showed no concern for their frustrated constituents. "Some Democrats didn't even ask Tavenner a question – they just used their time to make speeches," noted POLITICO.[463] The next day, the Healthcare.gov website crashed during testimony by Secretary Sebelius before the House Energy & Commerce Committee.[464]

Of an October 2013 appearance by Sebelius on "The Daily Show with John Stewart" on Comedy Central, the New York Times would later report, "Everyone knew it was a disaster. . . . At the White House, President Obama's top aides were aghast at her wooden performance."[465]

On December 31, 2013, Michelle Snyder, who oversaw development of the Healthcare.gov website as the chief operating officer for CMS, suddenly retired. Republicans had blamed Snyder for the problems, leading to her defense before a House committee by Sebelius: "Michelle Snyder is not responsible for the debacle. Hold me accountable for the debacle."[466]

In April 2014 Sebelius announced her own resignation, which the New Tork Times characterized as a "slow-motion resignation" precipitated by the president's lack of confidence in her.[467] As they noted, it was "the self-sacrificial and expected conduct of high-level officials under siege in Washington" and, upon Sebelius offering to resign, "Mr. Obama did not protest."

Sifting through the evidence, the General Accounting Office would conclude, in a July 2014 report, that "the efforts by CMS were plagued by undefined requirements, the absence [of] a required acquisition strategy, confusion in contract administration responsibilities, and ineffective use of oversight tools."[468] Rather than hold vendors accountable for poor performance CMS just kept paying them more: "Ultimately, more money was spent to get less capability."[469]

By September 2014 Bloomberg would calculate that well over twice as much had been spent on the Healthcare.gov website ($2.1 billion) as the Obama Administration had estimated in public testimony before Congress ($832 million).[470] And the tax-payer costs of ACA implementation – at least $73.5 billion through September 30, 2014 in Bloomberg's measurement, or perhaps over $90 billion with elusive Medicaid expansion costs factored in – well-exceeded the highest CBO projection of $71.2 billion.[471]

As 2015 enrollment approached, insurance expert Robert Laszewski wrote in *USA Today* that "[i]nstead of learning critical lessons from the mistakes of the first open enrollment fiasco, the Obama administration appears to be trying to silence potential critics."[472] The Administration had delayed the start of open enrollment from October 1 to November 15 in order to tamp down bad pre-election news.

Despite the ACA's objective flaws and troubled rollout, Republicans offered no substantive alternative. From a purely-political standpoint, they did not seem to need to. As one *POLITICO* article noted in June 2014, with so many Democrats refusing to defend the ACA, "GOP candidates don't feel as much pressure to do what Democrats would like them to do: spell out what their alternative to the health care law would be. As one GOP ad maker put it, Democrats aren't forcing Republicans to lay out any specifics because they're too busy 'running away from health care.'"[473]

In taking the U.S. Senate seat of retiring liberal Democratic icon Tom Harkin, Republican Joni Ernst, a far-right Iowa state senator, described her health care position simply on her website: "Joni is staunchly opposed to the Obamacare law. Joni supports immediate action to repeal Obamacare and replace it with common sense, free-market alternatives that put patients first, and health care decisions back in the hands of each of us rather than Washington bureaucrats." Nothing more needed to be said. One of her television ads showed her firing a handgun at "Obamacare."

By May 2013, the Republican House had voted 37 times to repeal or defund the ACA since January 2011 – which equated to about 15 percent of the time spent voting over that period. As Republicans prepared for their 37th vote, South Carolina Republican Congressman Mick Mulvaney was quoted saying: "The guys who've been up here the last year, we can go home and say, 'Listen, we voted 36 different times to repeal or replace Obamacare.' Tell me what the new guys are supposed to say?"[474]

What could be a more principled policy position that that?

Led by their whip and conference chair, House Republicans organized a House Obamacare Accountability Project in 2013 "to raise public awareness about Obamacare's impact on jobs, health costs and access to care."[475] Republicans went so far as to discourage the National Football League from promoting the ACA.[476] A government shutdown in October 2013 compelled by House Republicans over the ACA ended up boomeranging badly on the Republican brand, and, quite inconveniently for their message, overshadowed news of severe problems accessing exchanges. Yet even that shutdown, given the ACA challenges that followed, would still be completely forgotten in the 2014 election amidst inept Democratic messaging.

Many Republicans who called for complete ACA repeal faltered when it came to specific elements. As a *New York Times* editorial noted, "Sometimes the dissonance reaches nearly comic levels."[477] Facing a seemingly-challenging 2014 re-election campaign, Senator McConnell had even suggested that neither Kentucky's relatively successful state-run exchange, nor its Medicaid expansion enrollment, would be jeopardized by the ACA repeal he had consistently advocated. In a debate, asked to reconcile his view that Kentucky's Kynect exchange could continue absent the ACA, he only made matters more perplexing by stating that "[t]he Web site can continue. But in my view the best interests of the country would be achieved by pulling out Obamacare root and branch."[478]

Of course, given that McConnell's Democratic challenger, Kentucky Secretary of State Alison Grimes, refused to say whether she would have voted for the ACA (or even for Obama) – only resorting to the familiar, defensive, Democratic refrain that she would "fix the law" (admitting it was broken in undefined ways) – McConnell didn't need to worry. He handily romped to victory and won even among Kentucky women.

Those Republicans acknowledging the need for an alternative vision were in the minority.

The most prolific Republican thinker on health care may be Avik Roy of the Manhattan Institute for Policy Research. Roy authored a 65-page paper entitled "Transcending Obamacare."[479] Admitting he wouldn't please either side of the ideological debate, he acknowledged the "bipartisan heritage" of exchanges and suggested retaining them through a "Universal Exchange Plan" with a number of modifiers. While "the consumer-friendly system of metal tiers" would be kept, the actuarial values would be reduced (Bronze would go from paying 60% to 40% of medical costs, for example).[480] The prohibitions on health-screening and gender-rating would be retained while the 3-1 band on age-rating would be removed.[481] The medical loss ratios would be eliminated, ostensibly because they prevent "carriers from investing in customer service and other quality initiatives[.]"[482]

A conservative group called the 2017 Project had an interesting proposal, embraced by Republican Senate candidate Ed Gillespie in Virginia, to replace the

ACA with tax credits for those without employer-provided health care, impose a cap on the tax deductibility of employer-provided health insurance (to facilitate cost control), and create a federally-funded high-risk pool for those unable to secure coverage.[483] Those with existing medical conditions could not be dropped from coverage so long as they maintained it. In 2014 Gillespie came close to upsetting Democratic Senator Mark Warner. It remained to be seen whether Republicans would support a proposal like this after the 2014 election.

In January 2014, two Republican senators, Orrin Hatch of Utah and Tom Coburn of Oklahoma, proposed an ACA alternative that no other Republicans seemed to rally around. The "Patient Choice, Affordability, Responsibility and Empowerment Act" would provide a tax credit for employees of businesses with 100 or fewer employees that do not provide health care – that credit would be available to those with incomes up to 300% of the Federal Poverty Line. It borrows from the auto-enrollment trickery proposed by the Heritage Foundation during ACA debate: "In the case of individuals who have a health tax credit, but who fail to make an affirmative choice in choosing a plan within a specified timeframe, states would be allowed to utilize default enrollment."[484] However, the senators were at pains to specify that "if an individual did not like the initial default plan selected for them, they would be able to switch plans, or affirmatively opt-out of coverage altogether."[485]

The Republican politician perhaps most authoritative on health care was Louisiana Governor Jindal, himself a former state health administrator. In April 2014, Jindal issued a 23-page blueprint that acknowledged "we must also enact positive reforms to move our health system in the right direction, because the status quo of American health care and insurance is simply not defensible."[486] Among other ideas, he encouraged price transparency as a means of reducing costs incurred as a result of "due to uncompetitive pricing levels by medical providers."[487] Jindal also embraced guaranteed coverage for those with preexisting conditions, and allow states to experiment in serving their needs – he dismissed the ACA's protections by stating "patients have also found that their Obamacare plans don't include the specialists or hospitals they need; for instance, many plans do not offer access to advanced cancer centers."[488]

Yet Jindal was largely a voice in the wilderness. Beyond homages to tort reform, the only real health care reform idea pushed in an organized way by Republicans, including John McCain and Mitt Romney in their presidential campaigns, was the free market notion of selling insurance across state lines as a means of allowing new entrants into states lacking competition.

While this was but one component of Jindal's blueprint (and that of Coburn and Hatch), it is an article of faith for many Republicans that eliminating barriers to sell insurance would fix all problems.

Mike Huckabee, a former Arkansas governor and perennial presidential candidate, offers familiar Republican nostrums for what ails our health care system: "We must allow health insurance to be sold across state lines – now prohibited – in order for the insured to shop around for the most reasonable policies. We need to implement legal liability reform so that personal injury lawyers can't treat the health care system as a grab bag."[489]

Glenn Beck, the clown prince and intellectual sage of the Tea Party movement, agrees the answer is even freer markets: "Don't get me started on the ridiculous restrictions on buying across state lines. Eliminating those would go a long way toward eliminating these problems."[490] Of course, Beck also maintains that "[t]he real size of the group that is chronically uninsured is likely in the area of three percent[.]"[491]

"If you want access to low-cost health insurance, allowing people to purchase it across State lines after we defund ObamaCare would make a real difference," asserted Republican Senator Ted Cruz of Texas in a marathon September 2013 Senate floor speech against the ACA.[492]

Actually, there is no evidence insurers are even interested in selling insurance across state lines. A 2012 report from Sabrina Corlette and fellow scholars at Georgetown's Center on Health Insurance Reforms put the problem with this approach succinctly in a section heading: "It's the Network, Stupid."[493]

They noted "out-of-state insurers must build a network of local providers and negotiate competitive reimbursement rates." Those they surveyed "reported the enormous difficulty that out-of-state insurers face in building a network of local providers, and insurers identified doing so as a significant barrier to market entry that far surpasses concerns about a state's regulatory environment or benefit mandates. This difficulty is compounded in states . . . which face provider shortages in rural areas."

In fact, as mentioned before, the ACA does allow so-called multi-state plans contracted with the federal government and offered on a nationwide basis through state exchanges. And those selling a "multi-state plan" in states tended to be the very same dominant carriers already there.

Furthermore, effective in 2016 the ACA allows states to form "Health Care Choice Compacts" in which insurers can sell in any state participating in such a compact. To be sure, this is a voluntary process for states, not the involuntary yielding of state standards that Republicans have advocated.

Even assuming insurers could, and wanted to, sell across state lines as Republicans desire, allowing such practices would simply drive a disadvantaged state's domestic insurers to re-domicile in the least-restrictive regulatory state – a significant loss of economic activity and jobs for states facing an exodus. Another possibility would be for an outside carrier to simply market to the young and healthy – depriving a state's existing market of good risk. Finally, where would disputes over coverage denials be resolved?

Robert Laszweski, whose insurance industry background provided pointed ACA criticisms that often proved prescient, dismisses the notion of selling across state lines as "silly":

> It's a 1990s idea that fails to recognize the business a health plan is in in 2014. Health plans don't just cross a state line and set up their business like they did decades ago when the insurance license and an ability to play claims was all a carrier needed to do business. This idea was first suggested by the last of the insurance industry cherry pickers back in the 1990s and it has long outlasted its relevance. Building a new health plan in a market can easily cost hundreds of millions of dollars over a plan's first few years of operation.[494]

He notes that, at best, selling across state lines "is a great time tested way for a predatory insurance company to attract the healthiest consumers at the expense of the legacy carrier who is left with the sickest."[495]

Yet the idea's superficial appeal is powerful to some. In 2013 the Washington State Senate unanimously passed a bill to allow individuals to purchase insurance across state lines.[496] The bill also passed the state's House Health Care and Wellness Committee unanimously, even though the state's associations for hospitals, chiropractors, psychologists, and others strongly opposed it and noted such a bill would allow insurers to operate outside of state consumer protections.

Those concerns resulted in the bill failing to receive a House floor vote – but it came close. Its success showed how susceptible even Democrats can be to unsophisticated, article-of-faith health insurance arguments advanced by conservative ideological groups. Indeed, in 2014 Democratic Senator Mark Warner of Virginia introduced legislation directing the NAIC to facilitate selling insurance across state lines. The "Commonsense Competition and Access to Health Insurance Act of 2014" bore the signatures of seven other Democrats, including Senators Franken and Amy Klobuchar – both erstwhile Minnesota liberals. Such proposals do little to fool voters; Warner was nearly defeated in 2014 after his campaign of tepid moderation failed to turn out Democrats.

Nonetheless, in April 2015, in her first full week of openly campaigning for the 2016 Democratic presidential nomination, Hillary Clinton expressed an openness to the sale of insurance across state lines, stating, "I think it's something something we should look at" that was consistent with "a free market system[.]"[497]

14

THE SELF-DEFEATING
DEMOCRATIC PARTY

IT HAS BEEN pointed out in defense of the ACA that it is a concept identical to one offered by Senate Republicans, including Republican Leader Robert Dole of Kansas – the 1994 Republican presidential nominee – in the alternative to Clinton's Health Security Act of 1993. Is that *really* a defense, though? Is the best defense for Democrats to tacitly admit they have become 1990s-era Republicans?

The Health Equity and Access Reform Today Act of 1993 had 21 signatures, with one of two from Democrats being that of the future Democratic presidential nominee, and secretary of state, Massachusetts Senator John Kerry.

Another way of putting it, though, might be that the ACA is far less liberal than President Nixon's 1974 proposal.

The problem in getting a better product was not so much Republicans as Democrats. For example, because Senate Democrats, by maintaining the filibuster rule, elevated their sacred procedure above policy, even as the American economy reeled from its greatest crisis since the Great Depression, they had to accommodate sanctimonious egomaniac Joe Lieberman of Connecticut as a committee chairman. Lieberman had addressed the 2008 Republican Convention and traveled the country on behalf of his friend John McCain. It was impossible to imagine Republicans being so pathetic as to empower someone who betrayed them.

Yet it wasn't unforeseeable given the long trajectory Democrats had been on. As Chris Hedges has written in *Death of the Liberal Class*: "[T]he liberal class continues to speak in the prim and obsolete language of policies and issues. It refuses to defy the corporate assault. A virulent right wing, for this reason, captures the legitimate rage articulated by the disenfranchised."[498]

Ever have a job you immediately wanted to walk away from?

I did twice. Once was as a cashier for a convenience store. The first night I worked was so daunting, in learning how to simultaneously stock, watch gas pumps, look out for shoplifters, fry food, and man the cash register, that I never showed up for a second night.

Another job was as a telemarketer for some charity. In cold-calling on my first day I asked for a man only to find out from his wife, obviously elderly, that her husband had passed away. I walked out for a break and never came back.

What if the job is that of a legislator?

For six years, beginning in 2005, I was a frustrated observer of politics from the inside as a Democratic state representative in the Washington House of Representatives. I observed compromises leading up to 2008 that made the betrayal of progressive values that followed predictable. I felt like a passenger on the Titanic who could actually see the fatal iceberg getting closer.

For other progressives it was a shock to watch the promise of President Barack Obama's 2008 election deteriorate into the typical squalid morass of Washington, D.C. game-playing and elevation of process-over-policy.

After all, Obama won by the largest margin of any non-incumbent president. Furthermore, he was joined by seemingly-unassailable Democratic majorities in the U.S. House – led by a woman from San Francisco, no less – and in a U.S. Senate where even a former Saturday Night Live comedian pulled out a Minnesota victory.

Yet there had been so many harbingers of the disappointments to follow. Even when in the minority, Democrats were desperate to be liked by those opposing their values.

Examples abounded.

Eighteen Senate Democrats – including Harry Reid and the future vice president, Senator Joe Biden of Delaware – supported the so-called Bankruptcy Abuse and Consumer Protection Act of 2005 that was essentially drafted by the credit card industry and pushed through by Republicans. Many of those same Democrats, including Reid, would later feign helplessness in the face of Republican filibustering under President Obama.

Indeed, Biden, representing the state, Delaware, in which many credit card and other financial services corporations are headquartered, even opposed Democratic amendments designed to make the bill less onerous.

Despite its cynical title, the act did nothing to address late fees, over-limit fees, penalty interest rates, and other excesses of the credit card industry. It was opposed by civil rights groups, and was so egregious that President Clinton twice vetoed similar legislation. Yet the allure of campaign contributions was irresistible to too many Democrats.

The law's perverse irony became apparent just a few years later. Although its pretext was that consumers, in declaring bankruptcy, were walking away from unpaid bills, the same financial institutions making those arguments lined up before Congress in 2008 seeking taxpayer-funded bailouts to avoid their own corporate bankruptcies. And Democrats gave them those bailouts.

In contrast to the agonizing delay with which Democrats acted on their own president's health care reform initiative, they rushed through a Troubled Assets Relief Program in 2008 pushed by a Treasury secretary, Henry Paulson, who happened to be a former investment banker. In his book *Rich People Things: Real Life Secrets of the Predator Class*, Chris Lehmann describes it as "a seven-page piece of virtual draft legislation rushed through a Congress too panicked and jumpy to have any clear idea what it was doing."[499] In passing it, a Congress led by Democrats "had ceded virtually all effective leverage to make our financial infrastructure more fair and stable — let alone to prevent it from being swamped from any future meltdowns on the scale of the 2008 crisis that very nearly plunged our economy into all-but-permanent depression."

Simply put, Republicans are disciplined but can lack ideas. Democrats have ideas but lack discipline.

Consider the audacity of the so-called K Street Project, where, beginning in 1995, Republicans — under the leadership of Congressman Tom "The Hammer" Delay and anti-tax operative Grover Norquist — purified ranks of federal lobbyists by pressuring lobbying firms to hire only Republicans.

Was it improper? Perhaps. Was it successful? Yes. Could Democrats pull it off? Never.

In Washington State, even after passing the Senate, and winning the governor's support, legislation to give homeowners' rights was denied House floor votes by a Democratic super-majority in 2007 and 2008.[500] Under Washington law, homebuilders cannot be held accountable for their negligence — even though attorneys, doctors, and other professionals can be for matters far less consequential than new home construction. The homebuilders' lobby, which spent millions of dollars against Democratic candidates, and was promising to do so against the Democratic governor in her 2008 re-election campaign, opposed any warranty rights for those buying new homes.

When the economy collapsed, and people lost their homes due to upside-down mortgages and joblessness, a Democratic Congress and president would bail out . . . the banks and homebuilders. I bring this example up because a Democratic Party unwilling to stand up for the rights of those making their lives' greatest investments – the purchase of a new home – could hardly be counted upon to stand up to the health insurance industry. As one family would plaintively write me during the Washington State fight over homeowners' rights:

> We had a home built in 1999 for our new family. We had three
> small children born while living at this home. Our family was very
> ill. We discovered after living there for four years that our builder
> had left a hole in the roof and water was leaking through the walls,
> which created Stachybotrys toxic mold. . . . We only have God on
> our side, and would appreciate it if our government was too!

God didn't get any company. The family didn't have the political influence to matter.

The Washington homebuilders' organization had called Democratic Governor Chris Gregoire a "heartless, power-hungry she-wolf who would eat her own young to get ahead," previously accused women of eradicating "manly jobs," and then, in March 2008, compared environmentalists to Nazis in an article that the Anti-Defamation League denounced for its "deplorable lack of judgment" that "serve[d] to trivialize the history of the Holocaust."[501] After the Democratic House killed the legislation they opposed, builders financed the 2008 Republican victories for three House Democratic seats.

Such "punish our friends, reward our enemies" lapses in discipline would never occur with Republicans.

In the years leading up to the 2008 election, I heard frequently that Democrats just simply needed to be more conservative to preserve their majorities. Yet, in a sign of what was to come, Washington – with perhaps the nation's most conservative "blue state" Democratic legislative super-majorities – was one of the only states in

2008 to see its Democratic legislative margins diminished in what was otherwise a Democratic electoral romp.

The pattern of appeasing conservative interests continued following the 2008 election.

In Washington, the 2009 legislative session included an attempt by Democratic leaders to have a labor lobbyist arrested by the state patrol for his impertinent suggestion, in an e-mail circulated among labor supporters, that Democrats who broke their campaign to vote for labor's top priority bill might not receive future contributions. While law enforcement quickly exonerated the advocate, this police state pretext killed the bill.[502]

The bill, which would have forbidden employers from browbeating their workers about their political and religious views in closed-door meetings, was most prominently opposed by Boeing and Wal-Mart. During the 2008 presidential campaign Wal-Mart, for example, summoned thousands of employees to mandatory meetings about the importance of defeating Barack Obama.[503]

At what point will Democrats realize voting like Republicans will never fool Republicans into voting for Democrats?

The ACA can be looked at as part of a continuum of Democratic appeasements that please no one. Thomas Frank has noted that "Democrats threw themselves into the arms of their corporate allies. They jettisoned the simpler, more popular, but more government-centric idea under consideration and settled on the 'individual mandate,' which required that everyone in the land sign up with a private insurance company. This solution would be more intrusive than the other one, more complicated, more regulatory."[504]

In 2014, the self-proclaimed architect of the ACA, economist Jonathan Gruber of the Massachusetts Institute of Technology, only added to the perception that the ACA was a conspiracy of the elites when it was revealed he had told an audience that its passage was predicated upon "the stupidity of the American voter" and stated that the ACA's complicated nature was by design: "Lack of transparency is a huge political advantage."[505]

During the ACA debate, liberal groups had the temerity to push against the compromises made. Rahm Emmanuel, yet to further make his name as Chicago's union-fighting mayor, scoffed at their efforts. In an August 2009 White House meeting with liberal activists, The *Wall Street Journal* reported he called such liberals "f---ing retarded" for running ads on health care reform cajoling conservative Democrats to do the right thing.[506] There was no place for idealism in pursuing an idealistic agenda.

It is common to the narrative of Democratic victimhood to blame every setback on irrational Republicans. Yet what was irrational was for Democrats to ever predicate ACA success in any way upon Republican cooperation. Having adopted a health care model designed to appeal to Republicans, Democrats seemed crestfallen when Republicans rejected it. Like Charlie Brown falling for the same trick each time Lucy held the football for a kick, they were dumbfounded the football wasn't there to drive through the goalposts.

Further, President Obama was conciliatory by nature. E.J. Dionne would note that "Obama is a tempered sort of progressive who repeatedly annoys his party's left with an incessant pursuit of Republican support for 'grand bargains' — one reason his health-care plan is so state-oriented and gives Republican governors and legislatures so much opportunity to undermine it."[507]

Democrats set the terms of their own defeat. Perhaps it was traceable to 1999, when they joined Republicans, including then-Texas Senator Phil Gramm, in repealing the Glass-Steagall Act. "We are here today to repeal Glass-Steagall because we have learned that government is not the answer," declared a triumphant Gramm at the White House signing ceremony.[508]

"It is true that the Glass-Steagall law is no longer appropriate to the economy in which we live," agreed President Clinton. He crowed that "today what we are doing is modernizing the financial services industry, tearing down these antiquated laws and granting banks significant new authority. This will, first of all, save consumers billions of dollars a year through enhanced competition." Perhaps most tellingly, Clinton hailed "what can happen when Republicans and Democrats work together in a spirit of genuine cooperation."

Why does every heralded instance of "bipartisanship" signal defeat of Democratic values?

Just nine years later, in 2008, the largely-unregulated financial industry collapsed and Democrats joined Republicans in bailing out Wall Street. They even gave retroactive tax breaks worth billions to giant homebuilding companies. On March 23, 2010, Democrats turned over health care to Wall Street insurers. Was it a surprise that in November 2010 Republicans were successful in portraying *Democrats* as the party of the moneyed elites?

Democrats only added to their ideological incoherence by running away from the ACA during the 2010 mid-term election, when they lost control of the U.S. House, lost even Obama's former Senate seat, and were swept out of statehouses around the country. In part one could not blame them: The ACA was irreducible to positive sound-bites because of its mind-numbing complexity.

Yet, as the signature accomplishment of the first two years of the Obama presidency, what did it say about Democrats that they could not even explain, let alone stand by, their work? This incoherence was only slightly eased when President Obama, too belatedly but necessarily, had to stand by the ACA in the 2012 presidential election, even claiming the pejorative "Obamacare" as a badge of honor. Yet, following the president's re-election, Republicans were predicting that, without him on the ballot to defend it, they would return to their winning formula of 2010 and use the ACA in the 2014 mid-term election to beat up on hapless, inarticulate Democrats.[509]

In a harbinger, a March 2014 special election for an open U.S. House seat in a Florida district carried by President Obama was won by a Republican lobbyist who was vastly outspent by his Democratic opponent, a former statewide officeholder. The lobbyist had made his message almost entirely about the ACA's failings.

Even having opposed the ACA was no inoculation against public ire. Of the 36 House Democrats to vote against the ACA, by the 2014 election only four were left on the ballot – and one of those four, Stephen Lynch of Massachusetts, had voted against it from the left.[510]

The effects of one of the most lasting Democratic appeasements, John Roberts' confirmation as chief justice of the U.S. Supreme Court, have a real chance to merge with the Democratic concessions made on the ACA.

In September 2005 half of the Senate Democrats joined all Senate Republicans in voting for the confirmation of John Roberts. Prior to his nomination by President George Bush, Jr., the then-50-year-old Roberts had been virtually incubated by Republicans for the position.

Senator Patrick Leahy of Vermont, the ranking Democrat on the Senate Judiciary Committee, encouraged Roberts' confirmation: "Judge Roberts is a man of integrity. I take him at his word that he does not have an ideological agenda."[511] Leahy would not learn his lesson – as the Senate Judiciary chairman he would refuse to consider any Obama judicial appointees opposed by their home state Republican senators.

The confirmation of Roberts came at the same time that only 25 Senate Democrats were willing to filibuster against archconservative Samuel Alito's nomination as an associate justice, making a filibuster impossible.[512]

Roberts, of course, would lead a Court that, in the 2010 *Citizens United* decision, overturned a century of precedents and unleashed unfettered corporate contributions into politics. The majority would find that "[n]o sufficient governmental interest justifies limits on the political speech of nonprofit or for-profit corporations." In fact, they determined, corporations are "the best equipped to point out errors or fallacies in speech of all sorts, including the speech of candidates and elected officials." Concurring, Justice Scalia exulted that "to exclude or impede corporate speech is to muzzle the principal agents of the modern free economy."

The toxicity of the mixture of the *Citizens United* opinion and an ACA that pushes Americans into the arms of huge corporations is a fusion yet to be measured. Yet it was Democrats that made both elements possible. It can be anticipated that health insurers and the pharmaceutical industry will use their limitless political contributions to maintain the status quo and keep the "affordable" out of the ACA's title.

Following a June 2013 dinner with K Street lobbyists at posh Charlie Palmer Steak on Capitol Hill, it was learned that Congressional Democrats were looking for $125 million for their own "Super PACs" to spend in 2014.[513] It was unimaginable that this goal, which was exceeded, would be achieved without heavy reliance upon the health care industry. Yet Democrats still experienced disastrous 2014 results despite having actually outraised, and outspent, Republicans in direct money. Their attacks upon the conservative billionaire Koch brothers failed given that Democrats themselves had wealthy benefactors they relied upon. Warning of "muddled moderation," Richard Trumka, the president of the AFL-CIO, had presciently warned that "for Democrats the rising tide of money in politics has pushed them further away from the issues that working class voters care about."[514]

There is plenty of money to play both sides. In September 2014, an inadvertent disclosure revealed that the Republican Governors Public Policy Committee, allowed as a tax-exempt entity to keep its donors secret, had sponsors for a 2013 retreat that included, at the top-level of $250,000 donations apiece, Aetna and UnitedHealth Group; Blue Cross Blue Shield gave $100,000.[515] In a *New York Times* article on this, Aetna defensively noted it had separately given the same public donations, of $300,000, to both the Democratic and Republican governors' groups.

Upon President Obama nominating billionaire, union-fighting hotel heiress Penny Pritzker as commerce secretary, Dana Milbank of the *Washington Post* noted that it "[t]urns out the wealthy didn't lose the 2012 election; rather, the Republican rich lost to the Democratic rich."[516]

It was common to the Democratic narrative of victimhood to portray their 2013 capitulation on extending the Bush tax cuts as forced by Republicans. In truth, that ignores facts like Democrats choosing Congressman Steve Israel of New York to run their House campaign committee. Israel's website bragged that in 2001 he voted with Bush to end "the Death Tax."[517] With Bush's tax breaks expiring at the end of 2012, *The Hill* quoted Israel encouraging President Obama to break his re-election promise to set the high-earners' income threshold at $250,000: "I would hope that he would not go back to 250. . . . $250,000 may sound like it's a lavish income in Louisiana. Not on Long Island."[518]

The threshold was set at $400,000. This tax surrender would starve the federal government of future revenue for social programs and even ACA implementation. And Israel's efforts were not unappreciated: J.P. Morgan Chase forgave him $93,000 he owed on his house.[519]

Democratic chair Debbie Wasserman Schultz may have been dismissive about health care costs when citizens' health plans were cancelled, but *POLITICO* reported that she repeatedly implored the DNC to cover her own clothing costs.[520] Cullen Murphy has noted Washington, D.C.'s "professional classes are largely insulated from economic conditions in the rest of the country."[521] That was apparent when, in April 2013 on the cusp of a congressional recess, Democrats joined Republicans in exempting air travel from "sequestration" budget cuts. The major effect of the Reducing Flight Delays Act of 2013 was to make it easier for members of Congress to travel back to their districts.

As Congressman Dingell asked, "Mr. Speaker, is there no one in this chamber who is embarrassed? Or perhaps the question should be: Is no one in this chamber not embarrassed?" As Dingell noted, "Many other perils to our society, to our safety, and to the wellbeing of our people are quietly ignored as we sneak out of Washington to go home for speeches, campaigning and schmoozing with our people."[522]

Yet only 28 House Democrats joined Dingell is voting no; 159, including Minority Leader Pelosi, voted with Republicans. Was it possible that the House's longest-serving member was nearly alone in feeling a sense of shame? Cuts not rescinded included devastating reductions to education, Medicare provider payments, and other programs. And in 2014, both parties agreed in a secret meeting of the House Ethics Committee to rescind the decades-old requirement that members of Congress report lobbyist-paid trips on their financial disclosure forms – only reversing that decision after public blowback when the secret agreement came to light.[523] Undeterred, the two parties worked together on a December 2014 budget "deal" that effectively rescinded what remained of campaign finance limitations.

In a telling sign of how little confidence either party truly had in the ACA, congressional members and staff flew into a panic by mid-2013 as the effective date for one of the ACA's provisions – the so-called Grassley Amendment – loomed. Designed to score political points, the Grassley Amendment required all members of Congress and their staffs obtain health care coverage through exchanges beginning in 2014. In the face of uncertainty over out-of-pocket costs, staff began quitting – and even members of Congress questioned whether they would stay.[524] The Obama Administration averted this "crisis" through rulemaking that spared members of Congress and allowed them to opt their staffs out. Yet, for those not opted out, one *POLITICO* article noted, "Veteran House Democratic aides are sick over the insurance prices they'll pay under Obamacare, and they're scrambling to find a cure."[525] Members of Congress floated above the problem – special websites and dedicated phone lines were set up by insurers for them.[526]

As if their 2014 rate shock was not enough, congressional staff faced 12.7% increases for 2015 through the dominant carrier in the D.C. Health Link exchange: CareFirst BlueCross BlueShield.[527]

Indeed, following the ACA's adoption, everyday federal workers saw what Federal Employees Health Benefits Program (FEHBP) officials described as the first "four-year stretch of premium increases in the 4 percent range since the early 1990s."[528] As the nation's largest employer-sponsored plan, the FEHBP serves roughly 8 million Americans in total – even its massive purchasing power had not been enough to avoid the rate increases the ACA was supposed to prevent. Meanwhile, federal workers had gone years without pay increases.

Chris Hedges is unsparingly critical of what Democrats wrought: "The so-called health-care reform bill will force citizens to buy a predatory and defective product, while taxpayers provide health-related corporations with hundreds of billions of dollars in subsidies."[529] Of President Obama, he wrote, "He shoved a health-care bill down our throats that will mean ever-rising co-pays, deductibles, and premiums and leave most of the seriously ill bankrupt and unable to afford medical care."[530]

Whereupon they will, of course, be penalized by the Internal Revenue Service.

If the idea was to appeal to "moderates," it failed. As Ezra Klein has written, in our polarized society there really are no moderates – "the idea of the moderate middle is bullshit: it's a rhetorical device meant to marginalize some policy positions at the expense of others."[531] It is a myth employed to compromise and raise campaign contributions at the expense of party ideals. Unlike politicians, voters can handle honesty. They would rather see a party position in its unadulterated form than in some disguise meant to trick them.

Where's the passion and idealism? During the 2012 presidential campaign, as Mark Halperin and John Heileman document in *Double Down: Game Change 2012*, when President Obama was "[a]sked about health care, he didn't tout the benefits of the Affordable Care Act or hit Romney for wanting to voucherize Medicare. Rather, he disgorged a skull-numbing explanation of the ACA's Independent Payment Advisory Board (IPAB), the entity Sarah Palin once decried as a 'death panel.'"[532]

Only in 2014 did Democrats, responding to grassroots advocacy and public protests, start making an issue out of "income inequality" and focus on a federal minimum wage that they had not tried to raise since 2007 – even with their supermajorities following the 2008 election. Of course, the convenience of delaying such a focus until 2014 was that it was impossible by then to get a minimum wage increase through a Republican U.S. House.

Lehmann refers to the "hostage to adverse political circumstance" defense as the "ignore-the-potbellied-plutocrat-behind-the-curtain feint" that "spineless Democrats" have used to rationalize "giveaways to the privileged class since the age of Reagan[.]"[533] As Republicans move the goalposts, Democrats always follow. It is a learned helplessness. And it is hard to see how Democrats have moral high ground over those they assail and then consistently vote with.

15

The Lure of Lucre

Shackling health care policy to the private insurance and pharmaceutical markets would also create the potential for seduction. The amounts of money involved are fantastical.

When Angela Braley, the chief executive officer of the nation's second-largest health insurer, WellPoint, stepped down under shareholder pressure in August 2012, her compensation had not reflected any performance concerns – at $20.6 million it was up 55% from the previous year.[534]

With $110.6 billion in revenue in 2012, and earnings-per-share 11.6% higher than the previous year despite the minor inconvenience of the ACA's medical loss ratio, UnitedHealth Group's CEO, Stephen Hemsley, saw his bonus rise 7.3% – taking home $34.7 million in 2012.[535] In 2014, the year ACA tax subsidies began rolling in, his income exploded – he took home $66.1 million in total compensation.[536] His company's revenue of $130 billion in 2014 was projected to rise to $141.5 billion in 2015 and $151.6 in 2016.[537]

And to think that some suggest the American Dream is dead.

In November 2011, I shared a stage in the venerable Willard Hotel in Washington, D.C. with Joel Ario, the Obama Administration's first head of the Office of Insurance Exchanges spearheading state exchange efforts.

In the labyrinth of the federal bureaucracy, the Office of Insurance Exchanges was part of the new Center for Consumer Information and Insurance Oversight (CCIIO) created under the ACA. CCIO reports to the Centers for Medicare and Medicaid Services which, in turn, reports to the Department of Health and Human

Services. If this is confusing to the layperson, he or she can be comforted to know it is no less confusing to regulators.

Ario was the insurance commissioner for Pennsylvania for three years and Oregon's top insurance regulator prior to that. At the time of his speech, it had been announced in August by CCIIO Director Steve Larsen that Ario was leaving his post in September to be closer to his family in Hershey, Pennyslvania.[538] Ario had only been in the job since August 30, 2010.

The Willard is where the term "lobbying" originated after patronage-seekers lined up in its ornate lobby to beseech President-elect Ulysses S. Grant for opportunities. And thus it was that a few weeks after Ario spoke at the Willard, the national lobbying firm Mannat, Phelps and Phillips announced Ario would be the managing director of Manatt Health Solutions.

As his biography would tout, Ario was "the Administration's point person for standing up health insurance exchanges, a role that required engagement with key stakeholders to develop the regulatory framework for exchanges[.]" His practice's clients included pharmaceutical and biotechnology companies and the health insurance giant Aetna – the nation's third-largest health insurer.

In the fourth quarter alone of 2011, Aetna's earnings rose 73%. In December of that year, the Washington Office of the Insurance Commissioner levied the biggest fine in the agency's history – $1 million – against Aetna for consumer protection violations.[539] Yet Aetna had support where it really mattered. From 2007 through 2012, the company and its executives contributed $70,750 to Senator Max Baucus.[540]

And Aetna knew how to make itself needed. As the *Washington Post* reported, in an April 2013 "conference call with investor analysts . . . Aetna officials said they might pull their products from the online marketplaces at the last minute."[541]

Having announced Ario's departure, his boss Larsen, Maryland's former insurance commissioner, was next to go.

To the Obama Administration's credit, there was no artifice about Larsen having left to be closer to his family. Instead, he left in July 2012 to be closer to our nation's largest health insurer, UnitedHealth Group, which he served as executive vice president at Optum, a wholly-owned subsidiary.[542]

In 2012, UnitedHealth Group spent $3.6 million on campaign contributions – including $106,536 to Obama.[543]

The Obama Administration outsourced its federally-run Preexisting Condition Insurance Program (PCIP) to UnitedHealth. As the federal brochure to prospective enrollees stated:

> We have entered into an arrangement with UnitedHealthcare
> Options PPO, the Preferred Provider network of hospitals and/
> or doctors. The doctors and hospitals participating in this network
> have agreed to provide services to Plan enrollees. You always have
> the right to choose a PPO provider or a non-PPO provider for
> medical treatment. However, if you use a non-PPO provider, your
> cost-sharing will be higher.[544]

The federal government spent billions of dollars on PCIP.

Furthermore, health care reform, already outsourced to private insurers, has been further outsourced to vendors working to make it operational through, for example, information technology development. One such vendor working with the Obama Administration was Quality Software Services, Inc. (QSSI), which Optum acquired.

As *The Hill* reported in 2012, "One critic familiar with the business rivalries of the insurance industry compared UnitedHealth Group's purchase of QSSI to the New York Yankees hiring the American League's umpires." A spokesman for UnitedHealth stated the company was not required to disclose the purchase of QSSI because it was a small transaction compared to UnitedHealth earnings.

QSSI was one of two companies to which the Obama Administration outsourced the development of the Healthcare.gov exchange portal for the states where the federal government was handling exchange transactions. The portal proved to be a frustrating, almost completely-inaccessible, experience for prospective enrolees when open enrolment began October 1, 2013.[545] The *New York Times* reported that "[t]he identity management system from Q.S.S.I., which also taps into government databases to retrieve users' personal information, was a particular source of trouble when the exchange opened."[546]

On October 25 the Administration announced the company that it was tasking as the general contractor to fix the mistakes made by QSSI and other vendors: QSSI.[547] Being a government contractor means never needing to say you are sorry. The same company was hired to fix Maryland's exchange, despite the fact that its parent company – UnitedHealth – was one of four insurers selling through the exchange.[548]

In June 2014, the new secretary of Health and Human Services, Sylvia Burwell, named an Optum executive, Andrew Slavitt, to oversee the work performed by Optum and its QSSI subsidiary.[549] By now such stories were so common as to attract little notice in the new era of Democratic defense of insurers. Optum's ambidexterity was such that it even had a unit, Executive Health, "helping hospitals exploit what they describe as a gray area in Medicare payments for hospital stays" as the *New York Times* described it.[550] In his new government role, Slavitt would be tasked with overseeing Medicare payments too. Slavitt became acting CMS administrator upon Marilyn Tavenner's surprise resignation in early 2015; in July 2015 it was revealed that Tavenner was to become the new face of the nation's health insurance industry as head of America's Health Insurance Plans.

One can only imagine many problems would have been avoided if those tasked with leading the effort had stayed on their jobs. Yet Administration figures like Ario and Larsen had traded up. Who, really, could blame them? Just as children grow up dreaming of being astronauts, regulators dream of someday working for the industries they regulate. For all regulators stuck in boring jobs and living on civil servant salaries, Ario and Larsen proved something good could come from the ACA after all.

In July 2013, Robert Gibbs, President Obama's close 2008 campaign aide who went on to be White House press secretary, enlisted, along with Obama for America spokesman Ben LaBolt, pharmaceutical giant Eli Lilly as a client. At the time of this hire, *POLITICO* noted the company had spent $4.5 million on lobbying in 2013.[551] In June 2014 Gibbs and La Bolt announced a new crusade to combat teachers' unions.[552] Gibbs also became a prominent proponent of eliminating the ACA's employer mandate (one of its only popular elements). In a sign of how far the party had shifted, MSNBC used Gibbs as its election night "Democratic strategist" commentator for 2014.

After helping as White House deputy chief of staff to give away meaningful reforms on health care reform, the protégé of Max Baucus, Jim Messina, ran President Obama's 2012 re-election campaign. Two years later, while also running a "Super PAC" promoting Hillary Clinton, Messina was advising the British Conservative Party in its successful efforts to retain control – with an anti-immigrant, anti-social services platform – against the Labour Party.[553]

Nancy-Ann DeParle, who so artfully steered President Obama away from standing up to pharmaceutical companies or addressing other health care cost drivers, became a partner in a new private equity firm, Consonance Capital, guiding health care investments made all the more lucrative by her past government decisions.[554] A longtime top adviser to Secretary Sebelius, Dr. Dora Hughes, became a "strategic adviser" for Sidley Austin – representing insurance, medical device, and pharmaceutical companies affected by the ACA.

Even prior to leaving the Obama Administration for pharmaceutical giant Johnson & Johnson, Elizabeth Fowler, who had helped shape the ACA for Max Baucus after leaving an insurer's employ, would arrange meetings with Wall Street investors hungry to know which direction ACA implementation was going.[555] She was not alone. Andrew Shin, who was the acting director of stakeholder engagement for the Obama Administration's Center for Medicare and Medicaid Innovation, also spoke with investors before leaving to join a firm that advertised itself as "a rapidly growing independent research firm that provides Washington policy analysis to institutional investors and private equity firms."[556]

In a sign of this interconnection, in 2013 Secretary Sebelius was forced to go "hat in hand to health industry executives" – as the *Washington Post* described it – to implore them to contribute large donations toward raising awareness of the ACA.[557] Congress was denying additional funding for outreach.

Another sign of how the Administration had miscalculated in prefunding its ACA costs, the solicitation raised the unprecedented specter of a groveling regulatory agency begging assistance from those it ostensibly regulated. It was reasonable to ask who was in charge. Even insurers felt embarrassed. The *New York Times* reported that "several executives said they were uncomfortable with the discussions because the federal government has the power to approve or reject the health plans they want to sell in insurance markets that will be run by federal officials in more than 30 states."[558]

One might naively think regulators would be less susceptible to the charms of lobbyists than check-cashing politicians, but that's not true. For example, the Dodd-Frank Act that passed in 2010 and purported, following Wall Street's excesses crashing the American economy in 2008, to re-regulate Wall Street, was insubstantial to begin with – it was made even less substantial when Wall Street lobbyists swarmed regulatory agencies and watered down implementation to be accomplished through rulemaking.[559]

"ObamaCare's architects reap windfall as Washington lobbyists" noted a headline in *The Hill*. The article cited experts who observed that those in highest demand came from either the Department of Health and Human Services or congressional committees overseeing ACA implementation. The law had singlehandedly reinvigorated K Street: "While lobbying revenue at major firms has been flat or declining in recent years, the healthcare law has generated steady work[.]"[560] The money at stake is almost incomprehensible. After Fowler went to work for Johnson & Johnson the company paid a $2.2 billion fine for health care fraud.[561]

Amazingly, the ACA was even a new boon for the defense industry. Military contractor General Dynamics was among those getting in on the action, with $815 million paid to it in 2014 to answer the Healthcare.gov phones; doing it on the cheap by hiring temporary workers made the profits even richer.[562]

Not only are apparatchiks in the federal government lured by lucre, but state insurance regulators are as well — as described in a previous chapter. Indeed, only nine months after open enrollment began, the head of Connect for Health Colorado, Patty Fontneau, left to join Cigna as its new president for private exchange business.[563]

16

MEDICARE ADVANTAGE AND THE BIRTH OF GOVERNMENT SUBSIDIZATION OF INSURERS

THE MASSACHUSETTS' HEALTH care reform enacted under then-Republican Governor Mitt Romney is often looked at as the antecedent of Obamacare.

As former House Speaker Newt Gingrich stated of Romney during the 2012 Republican presidential nomination process: "As governor, when he signed RomneyCare, who did he say was his No. 1 collaborator? Ted Kennedy."

Yet, at the time of that law's 2006 enactment Gingrich trumpeted it: "The health bill that Governor Romney signed into law this month has tremendous potential to effect major change in the American health system." Of the individual mandate, he wrote approvingly that it "requires those who earn enough to afford insurance to purchase coverage, and subsidies will be made available to those individuals who cannot afford insurance on their own. We agree strongly with this principle."

When Romney signed health care reform in 2006, he did so in a place that stands out in Revolutionary history: Boston's Faneuil Hall. He was led in by a fife-and-drum corps with enormous signs by the stage stating "Making History in Health Care."[564]

Later that day, Romney would be full of smug triumphalism: "It's a Republican way of reforming the market. Because, let me tell you, having thirty million people in this country without health insurance and having those people show up when they get sick, and expect someone else to pay, that's a Democratic approach."

Having overcome a Democratic legislature, Romney couldn't foresee a Democratic Congress four years later capitulating to his "free market" ideology. The paradox made him incoherent on the issue. As late as a September 2012 "Meet the Press" interview, he said, "Of course, there are a number of things that I like in health-care reform that I'm going to put in place. One is to make sure that those with pre-existing conditions can get coverage."[565] Yet that was only feasible through spreading risk through an individual mandate.

Bitterness persisted in Republican circles. In September 2013, the ACA-opposing *Wall Street Journal* editorialized it didn't "need any lectures about principle from the Heritage Foundation that promoted RomneyCare and the individual mandate that is part of ObamaCare. Or from cable TV pundits who sold Republicans on Mitt Romney despite RomneyCare."[566]

Yet, in fact, the truest antecedent of the ACA may have been a program signed into law under President Clinton when Gingrich was speaker. At a time when Clinton was famously "triangulating" with the advice of Republican adviser Dick Morris, the Balanced Budget Act of 1997 created what were called Medicare + Choice or Part C plans offered through private insurers with payments higher than fee-for-service Medicare.

Originally this was a gambit to attract more providers to Medicare, particularly in under-served rural areas. These became Medicare Advantage plans under the Medicare Prescription Drug, Improvement, and Modernization Act of 2003 that Senator Baucus famously broke with his party in supporting. This act increased Medicare Advantage payments beyond traditional Medicare payments in every county in the nation.

In a 2008 study, the Commonwealth Fund estimated Medicare Advantage plans offered through insurance company intermediaries were 12% more expensive than care paid for directly by the federal government by traditional fee-for-service (FFS) Medicare, for an average extra payment $986 a year higher. It noted that "overpayment of private plans presents a threat to Medicare's efficiency—contravening the original reason for including a private plan option in Medicare." Instead, "These extra payments, which represent a drain on the federal budget, could otherwise be used to reduce the nation's deficit or to offset the costs of Medicare policy improvements."[567]

By 2011 a full quarter of Medicare beneficiaries were enrolled in Advantage plans. The annual report of the Medicare Payment Advisory Commission in 2012 noted "such plans often restrict the choice of provider. By contrast, traditional FFS Medicare has lower administrative costs while offering beneficiaries an unconstrained choice of health care providers."[568] As the 2013 report explained, "Because bench-marks are often set well above what it costs Medicare to provide benefits to similar beneficiaries in the FFS program, MA payment rates usually exceed FFS spending."[569]

Payments for 2013 were projected to be up to 8% higher than FFS Medicare. That meant "the Medicare program will pay approximately $6 billion more for MA enrollees than it would have paid to cover the same enrollees in FFS Medicare." There was a billing incentive to code Advantage beneficiaries as more complex than those in the traditional Medicare system, and insurers are more sophisticated than indi-vidual providers: "Experience supports the contention that MA plan enrollees have higher risk scores than otherwise similar FFS beneficiaries because of more complete coding."

Yet, a 2011 report by the National Bureau of Economic Research, found "indi-viduals who are more expensive than the average person to insure are less likely to enroll in Medicare Advantage plans."[570] Thus, the federal government ended up paying a higher cost "for people who, had they stayed in fee-for-service Medicare, would have cost the government much less." Consequently, the study concluded "the Medicare Advantage program both increased total Medicare spending and transferred Medicare resources from the relatively sick to the relatively healthy, and that risk-adjustment was not able to address either of these problems."

To quote Mitt Romney: "I like Medicare Advantage."[571]

In his 2009 health care speech to Congress, the president stated that "[t]he only thing this plan would eliminate is the hundreds of billions of dollars in waste and fraud, as well as unwarranted subsidies in Medicare that go to insurance companies – subsi-dies that do everything to pad their profits and nothing to improve your care."

At last, there would be an effort to reign in Medicare Advantage.

The issue was discussed early on before the Senate Finance Committee. Ron Pollack, the executive director of Families USA, testified on May 5, 2009 before the Finance Committee about the perverse incentives of Medicare Advantage:

> We keep on talking about a level playing field, but we have seen something exactly the opposite with respect to the Medicare pro-gram. We do not have a level playing field. As we have learned from MedPAC, the payments to the private plans in Medicare Advantage are considerably larger than it would be for somebody who stayed in traditional Medicare.[572]

A "Medi-Scare" effort began immediately, some of it facilitated by the government's own vendor Humana in mailings to Medicare Advantage enrollees. The Centers for Medicare and Medicaid Services ordered Humana to desist such communications, given that they could be understood by beneficiaries "as official communications about the Medicare Advantage program[.]"[573] An angry Mitch McConnell took to the Senate floor to denounce what he called a "gag rule" – and the Obama Administration backed down. Kentucky-based Humana and its founder, David Jones Sr., were major campaign benefactors for McConnell, and millions in donations from Humana and Jones have gone toward the McConnell Center at the University of Louisville.[574]

According to a fiscal analysis provided to House Speaker John Boehner of Ohio in July 2012, the reduction in Medicare Advantage rates would save the federal budget $156 billion from 2014 through 2022.[575] In evaluating the ACA just prior to its being signed in to law, the Congressional Budget Office estimated "enrollment in Medicare Advantage plans in 2019 would be 4.8 million lower than we project under current law[.]"[576]

Contrary to Republican hysteria, that was hardly tantamount to the elimination of this option for seniors. Traditional fee-for-service Medicare, the promise made in 1965, would always be available as the alternative.

In the 2012 presidential election, the issue of whether insurers would feel any pain under the ACA became the subject of a Medi-Scare debate accompanying any presidential election.

In the first 2012 debate between Obama and his challenger Mitt Romney, in which the president was famously listless, Obama fended off charges that the ACA cut Medicare. Romney stated that "the idea of cutting $716 billion from Medicare to be able to balance the additional cost of 'Obamacare' is, in my opinion, a mistake." Obama characterized it as "$716 billion we were able to save from the Medicare program by no longer overpaying insurance companies, by making sure that we weren't overpaying providers."[577]

Romney kept on the attack, asserting "we have 4 million people on Medicare Advantage that will lose Medicare Advantage because of those $716 billion in cuts. I can't understand how you can cut Medicare $716 billion for current recipients of Medicare."

Obama sought to change the subject, and deflect the attack, by assailing Romney for wanting to offer a private voucher alternative to compete with Medicare, which would allow insurers to target "the younger and healthier seniors. . . . leaving the older, sicker seniors in Medicare." Obama was referencing the so-called "Ryan Plan" offered by Romney's running mate, Congressman Paul Ryan of Ohio.

Later, Obama asserted that, were the ACA repealed, "the primary beneficiary of that repeal are insurance companies that are estimated to gain billions of dollars back when they aren't making seniors any healthier."

The point the president was seeking to make was that Medicare Advantage plans skim vast sums of money from seniors. In fact, relative to Romney's voucher proposal, he did make that point: "Medicare has lower administrative cost than private insurance does, which is why seniors are generally pretty happy with it. And private insurers have to make a profit. Nothing wrong with that; that's what they do."

The president was palpably suffering cognitive dissonance. It was hard for him to defend cuts to Medicare Advantage, advancing the argument that private insurers were price-gouging, when he had turned over the lives of so many Americans under age 65 to private insurers.

In fact, a major supporter of the ACA, the American Association of Retired Persons, is basically a giant insurer itself – offering its own Medicare Advantage plan through UnitedHealth Group. The AARP, which had incurred progressive blowback for having backed Bush's Medicare Part D gift to the pharmaceutical industry, also sells Part D insurance through United.

Obama won re-election. Yet he won a battle only to concede the war. On April 1, 2013 – April Fool's Day – it was learned that the Obama Administration blinked in following through on its plan to squeeze Medicare Advantage for savings. As *POLITICO* described it, "The insurance industry chalked up one of its greatest political victories in recent memory . . . as the Obama administration reversed course on a proposal to cut Medicare Advantage rates."[578]

Instead of a 2.3% cut the Administration planned a 3.3% increase. The difference meant billions of dollars. Insurer stocks soared on the news. As the *Washington Post* reported: "Monday afternoon was a really great time to be a health insurance plan."[579] Indeed, the Securities and Exchange Commission (SEC) would subpoena a K Street lobbyist for Humana, whose stock jumped 9.2% that day, over the leak of this hot political intelligence just 20 minutes before the end of the trading day.[580] The formal announcement by the federal government occurred post-trading. The lobbyist, Mark Hayes, had worked for the Senate Finance Committee's Republicans, under Senator Grassley, as their health policy director and chief health counsel.

One poignant explanation for this gift to insurers surfaced in a chronology of the leak reported by the New York Times: "Mark Hayes sends an email to an analyst at

Height Securities, indicating a deal has been hatched to increase Medicare Advantage rates in order to smooth the confirmation of Marilyn Tavenner as the new head of Medicare."[581] Yet, despite their enthusiasm for investigating the Administration, House Republicans refused to comply with a SEC subpoena for a staff member accused of having leaked the rate information to Hayes.[582]

It was Grassley's old friend, and the insurance industry's faithful ally, Max Baucus, who helped pressure the Administration to abandon a cost savings flowing from a law that Baucus had drafted.

In a March 15, 2013 letter to the Centers for Medicare and Medicaid Services (CMS) that was, that same day, posted on the website for America's Health Insurance Plans (AHIP), Baucus and Republican Senator Orrin Hatch of Utah asked that the payment rate for Medicare Advantage plans be recalculated to assume no cost savings from physicians – despite existing law requiring such savings.[583]

That same day a letter was sent to CMS (and AHIP) by 98 House members, with Democrats joining Republicans in lauding Medicare Advantage: "Medicare Advantage (MA) plans have a proven track record when it comes to coordinating care for chronically ill individuals and this proposal will reduce their ability to continue to do so."[584]

In an editorial on this lobbying – "The Liberal Medicare Advantage Revolt" – published prior to the Administration's decision to reverse course, the *Wall Street Journal* had written, "A big political story this year is likely to be Democrats turning on their White House minders as the harmful and unpopular parts of the Affordable Care Act ramp up."[585]

Chortling, the editorial concluded, "we thought it would be a cold day in The Villages of central Florida before Democrats came out for a private version of Medicare. Paul Ryan, call the White House."

Following the capitulation, a *Journal* editorial exulted over "the spectacle of Democrats beseeching HHS not to nuke a program they voted to nuke as part of ObamaCare."[586] Wryly, the editorial observed that "[t]he political options under ObamaCare usually come down to change for the worse or change for the much worse, so be thankful for small mercies."

The year 2014 was supposed to ease the way into larger Medicare Advantage cuts. Based on the Administration's retreat, reacting to a Congress panicked by AHIP television ads entitled "Drastic" and "Too Much" that ran in a few places, it seemed clear there would not be the political will to accomplish this.

Indeed, the cycle repeated itself in April 2014. As a *USA Today* editorial opened, "Here we go again. Insurance companies and members of Congress are trying to scare seniors[.]" The editorial noted that "[f]orcing Medicare Advantage plans to live with little or no subsidy over government Medicare is entirely fair, but you wouldn't know it from the howling by Congress, where 273 members of the House and Senate from both parties have signed letters demanding that upcoming cuts for 2015 be suspended."[587]

With Democrats on the run, AHIP had begun pressing its advantage in areas beyond Medicare Advantage. In May 20, 2013 congressional testimony, an AHIP lobbyist rued premium increases to result from the ACA – a law the AHIP supported – and suggested an answer was to repeal the ACA's modest tax on health plans.[588] A bill to do so had 182 House co-sponsors.

An October 2014 *New York Times* article highlighted significant deficiencies uncovered in Medicare Advantage plans, including failures in half of all audited cases to adequately or correctly explain denials of service to beneficiaries or providers.[589] In 61% of audited cases insurers improperly denied prescription drug claims.[590] Although the federal government imposed fines, they were laughably-low ("more than $500,000" for Aetna's "widespread and systemic" mismanagement of drug claims) and no deterrent – any insurer could easily absorb them as the cost of doing business.[591] Small wonder "[f]ederal officials expressed frustration that they were seeing the same kinds of deficiencies year after year."[592] Needless to say, none of the members of Congress who had run to the defense of Medicare Advantage's rates were quoted criticizing its practices.

But this is the same as it ever was. A May 2013 *Washington Post* story reported that Medicare Part D prescribing practices were going unregulated because "officials at the Centers for Medicare and Medicaid Services say the job of monitoring prescribing falls to the private health plans that administer the program, not the government." The *Post* noted that "Congress, under heavy lobbying by the drug industry, opted for a payment pipeline for drugs, not another layer of bureaucracy."[593] The federal government simply pays private insurers a fixed amount per enrollee and then lets insurers run the program.

Sound familiar?

17

EMPLOYMENT AND THE ACA

A JULY 3, 2013 headline on the *Washington Post* website said it all: "Big business continues its winning streak in health reform."[594]

The Obama Administration had decided to not enforce, for 2014, the requirement that businesses with 50 employees or more buy insurance or pay a penalty.
While President Clinton's health care reform proposal would have had employers pay
80% of the cost of insurance for employees, and even President Nixon's would have
required they pay 75%, the ACA only forces large employers to pay a small penalty
if they do not offer insurance. And now even that penalty would not be enforced.

Max Baucus would pen a *POLITICO* column bragging that "[t]he administration
listened to my concerns. And more important, it listened to the concerns of the business community."[595] Yet, when House Republicans sought to force a vote "authorizing"
the delay, only 35 House Democrats voted for it.[596] Contrary to the Administration's
actions, requiring large employers to provide health insurance, or pay a penalty, is
one of the *only* popular parts of the ACA – a November 2013 *Washington Post/ABC
News* poll showed 57% of voters support it.[597]

In February 2014 the Administration announced a further delay of the penalty
through 2015 for employers with between 50 and 99 full-time employees. In May
2014, the Urban Institute, a leading ACA defender, published a paper asking, "Why
Not Just Eliminate the Employer Mandate?"[598]

Prior to the announced delays, a commonly-expressed fear about the ACA
was that employers would drop health care coverage in the face of greater expense,

reduce the hours of employees to avoid the employer penalty, or simply pay the pen-alty rather than add coverage.

For employers to drop coverage would not be new. In fact, the Robert Wood Johnson Foundation found the percentage of the nonelderly population with employer-sponsored insurance dropped from 69.7% to 59.5% in the decade between 1999-2000 and 2010-11.[599] The only demographic that saw an increase in such coverage were dependent adults ages 19 to 25, from 30.7% to 36.5%, as a result of the ACA provision allowing them to stay on their parents' insurance until 26.

In part, declining employer coverage rates were due to employees not taking up employer-offered insurance where they had the option, likely due to price. Take-up rates had fallen from 81.8% to 76.3% over the studied period. Further, there was a significant decline in the number of small employers, those with 50 or fewer employ-ees, offering coverage. That proportion dropped from 47.2% to 37.5% over the decade.

In other cases, the economy and recession was clearly a factor – manufacturing state Michigan saw the nation's biggest decline in employer health insurance coverage (15.2%).

In advance of 2014, a number of service industry employers, particularly, were publicly making plans to drop full-time employees. In 2012 the company that owns the Carl's Jr. and Hardee's fast food chains began hiring part-time employees to replace departing full-time employees.[600] A study conducted by the University of California—Berkeley Labor Center – no conservative think tank – estimated up to 2.3 million workers nationwide risked being reduced to part-time status – 1.8% of the nation's total workforce.[601] Restaurant workers were easily most at risk, 16.2% of all workers in that setting, followed by those working in hotels (8.3%). Regal Entertainment and SeaWorld were among those reducing part-time employees' hours to avoid the mandate.[602]

Even workers who were already part-time were feeling the pinch. For 2014, grocery chain Trader Joe's stripped part-time workers of their preexisting health care coverage – informing them they would instead be given $500 checks and direc-tions to buy insurance through exchanges.[603] As taxable income, $500 would hardly cover health care costs even for workers eligible for subsidies. Retail giant Target followed suit in a January 2014 announcement to its part-time workers, along with one-time $500 payouts for yanking their coverage effective April 1, 2014.[604] Thus, taxpayers were to foot the bill for companies' existing health care costs – allowing those companies to further maximize profits. Ironically, dumping full-time workers into exchanges under these sorts of "employer payment plans" is expressly forbidden under the ACA, which creates a further incentive to reduce hours.[605]

So many employers used the ACA as an excuse to terminate health care coverage, where they could, that Republicans could easily juxtapose such instances against the ACA's promises, as Senator Cruz did in a marathon Senate floor speech in September 2013: "A few weeks ago UPS sent a letter to 15,000 employees and it said: We are terminating spousal health insurance because of ObamaCare. Their husbands and wives were told: Sorry, your health insurance is gone. Remember, the promise was: If you like your health insurance, you can keep it."[606]

Another way of addressing the employer mandate that ran contrary to the ACA's stated objective of affordable health care would be to raise employee contribution rates for covered employees.

The law deems coverage affordable where the employee pays no more than 9.5% of family income toward the employee's premiums alone. This entirely ignores costs for the employee's family. Sacrificing one-tenth of household income is a huge burden for many cash-strapped families, but other family coverage costs may be well in excess of that proportion; a 2013 Kaiser Family Foundation study showed an average employee's annual premium cost alone for family coverage was $4,456 (and that was apart from a deductible that might be $12,700 in 2014).[607]

The ACA will further penalize even employers who offer health care by fining them if the health care is too generous. The so-called "Cadillac tax" penalizes high-end health insurance benefits by 2018 as part of an ostensible effort to equalize health care coverage. The tax would be 40% of whatever employer cost exceeded $10,200 for an individual and $27,500 for a family.

This has given an excuse to employers for many family-wage union workers to squeeze workers into high-deductible plans that can be medically-bankrupting. For many union workers, benefits are the best part of their compensation package. Unlike wages, they are tax-free. At my local hospital, management's cited desire to avoid ACA costs led to hard bargaining by the hospital, which insisted upon health savings accounts, leading to a 2013 strike by the nurses' union.[608]

Former Labor Secretary Robert Reich had worried that the Cadillac tax was "a blunt instrument that could too easily become a bargaining chit for cutting back benefits of workers."[609] After seeing how it was being used by employers in bargaining, his fears were confirmed.

After commissioning an actuarial study, the nation's leading teachers' union – the National Education Association (NEA) – called for the repeal of the Cadillac tax in a press release: "We believe that it's more accurate to call the excise tax on high-cost plans an 'Age-Sex-Geography Tax.'"[610] Their study found that variations between regions and by gender and age could be dramatic and that such factors, as opposed to excessive employer generosity, could explain higher premiums. As the NEA reported, "The actuaries concluded that, compared to their benchmark, geography had a potential 69.3 percent impact on premiums, meaning that area-specific health care costs alone could boost a $9,189 premium in 2018 to $15,556."[611]

Contrary to what Republican conspiracy theories suggest, ACA support from organized labor – which bargains predominantly with large employers for employer-provided health care – was always altruistic and perhaps even self-defeating. First, it could be cynically argued that accessible health care, especially Medicaid expansion for low-wage workers, destroys a major incentive to organize into a union in the first place. Second, the ACA could undermine Taft-Hartley plans through which many union members already obtain health care.

Somewhat ironically, these plans bear the name of an anti-labor law passed by a Republican Congress over President Truman's veto in 1947. Employers contribute toward these nonprofit plans in amounts determined by collective bargaining, and the plans are administered by boards of trustees comprised of employer and labor representatives.

These are efficient nonprofit arrangements. In Massachusetts, for example, there is a Massachusetts Coalition of Taft-Hartley Trust Funds that represents over 150,000 lives and pools its purchasing power. Joseph Hansen, the president of the United Food and Commercial Workers International Union (UFCW) and chairman of the national Change to Win coalition of unions, has noted that the medical loss ratios for Taft-Hartley plans often exceed 90% — greater efficiency than what the ACA required of private insurers. For a union like the UFCW, which represents grocery store clerks, the multi-employer nature of a Taft-Hartley benefit plan is the perfect configuration.

While efficient, such plans could be more expensive. And the mandates of the ACA would add costs, without providing any tax credit offsets for the over 20 million workers on them whose wages would otherwise qualify them for tax credits through exchanges. One union official declared, "We're concerned that employers will be increasingly tempted to drop coverage through our plans and let our members fend for themselves on the health exchanges."[612] Were such a thing to occur, a principal reason for being in a union would be lost.

In a September 15, 2009 speech to the AFL-CIO, President Obama made a promise: "If you already have health insurance through your job — and because many of you are members of unions, you do — nothing in this plan will require you or your employer to change your coverage or your doctor. Let me repeat: Nothing in this plan will require you to change your coverage or your doctor."

Yet, in May 2013, Hansen pointed out this wasn't true for Taft-Hartley plans:

> [T]he ACA would block these plans from the law's benefits (such as the subsidy for lower-income individuals and families) while subjecting them to the law's penalties (like the $63 per insured person to subsidize Big Insurance). This creates unstoppable incentives for employers to reduce weekly hours for workers currently on our plans and push them onto the exchanges where many will pay higher costs for poorer insurance with a more limited network of providers.[613]

Realistically, with Congress intransigent, Hansen noted the only fix on the Taft-Hartley issue was regulatory: "We'd be open to a legislative fix, but ultimately this is the administration's responsibility. They are leading the regulatory process. It's their signature law."

As the *Northwest Labor Press* would note, "Organized labor — entirely left out of the legislation that became known as Obamacare — has spent years behind the scenes patiently pleading with the Obama Administration to be allowed to benefit from the law's implementation."[614] Instead, "Union health trusts will actually have to pay a temporary tax to subsidize private insurance companies selling individual coverage on the exchanges."

It is no exaggeration to imagine the ACA having the effect of destroying unions by destroying the incentive to be in them. By July 2013, Hansen had joined with the presidents of the Teamsters and UNITE HERE in an ardent letter to Senate Majority Leader Reid and House Minority Leader Pelosi: "Right now, unless you and the Obama Administration enact an equitable fix, the ACA will shatter not only our hard-earned health benefits, but destroy the foundation of the 40 hour work week that is the backbone of the American middle class."[615]

In September 2013, the AFL-CIO adopted a resolution at its annual convention calling for changes to the ACA.[616] While Resolution 54 reaffirmed organized labor's commitment to covering the uninsured, it noted "current negotiation of collective bargaining agreements setting the terms of health insurance coverage for plan participants are already demonstrating the adverse impact of the application of the Affordable Care Act to multiemployer plans[.]" It warned that "unless changes are made, the ACA will effectively use taxpayer dollars to subsidize employers that refuse to take responsibility for providing their employees health care, placing more responsible employers at a competitive disadvantage, and destabilizing the employment-based health care system."

While the resolution was amended to take out references to the ACA's repeal unless labor's concerns were addressed, many union presidents at the convention were very critical. "We've had our asses kicked on retirement security and we know our health funds are under siege" said Terrence O'Sullivan, president of the Laborers International Union, in the *New York Times*.[617]

Within two days of succeeding in having the resolution watered down, the Obama Administration informed labor leaders it would do nothing to address their concerns.[618] It did, however, exempt corporations from 2014 enforcement of an ACA provision prohibiting them from offering better health care coverage to their top executives than to everyday workers.[619]

In March 2014 UNITE HERE published a report entitled "The Irony of ObamaCare: Making Inequality Worse" that detailed the burdens imposed by ACA costs upon working class families. A May 2014 Wall Street Journal article noted that "[d]isputes between unions and employers over paying for new costs associated with the Affordable Care Act are roiling labor talks nationwide" – with the Laborers International Union attributing cost increases of 5-10% to the ACA and the UFCW having "agreed to eliminate existing coverage for thousands of newer part-time workers at New England supermarkets, in order to preserve benefits for full-time workers."[620]

The union most resolute in supporting the ACA, the Service Employees International Union, has seen its biggest membership growth among low-wage service industry workers who lack bargained-for health care benefits. For those workers the ACA could only be a gain, and the defense of it a potent organizing tool.

Those who work for, and own, small businesses fare little better than organized labor.

Most businesses are too small to be affected by employer penalties. However, if they have fewer than 25 employees, they could benefit from ACA subsidies that are up to half of an employer's contribution toward health care premiums. Yet the value of the ACA to small businesses is greatly exaggerated relative to its burden.

The concept of Small Business Health Option Program (SHOP) exchanges showed little understanding of health care economics, and seemed more designed to put a friendly face on the ACA. Carriers, already making considerable money, were under no obligation to participate in SHOP exchanges even if they might gain additional small business customers interested in obtaining the federal tax credits available to them only through those exchanges.

An insurer can make the cold-eyed calculation that, rather than assuming risk by playing in a small business exchange, it will get small businesses' employees anyway through the individual market – with employees financing their own health care and getting their own tax deductions. While a far worse deal for those individual consumers than employer-subsidized health care, the equities were not a matter insurers were required to consider.

The Obama Administration's promises were oversold, including the proposition that "SHOP Exchanges will reduce the burden and costs of enrolling employees in small group plans, and give small businesses many of the cost advantages and choices that large businesses already have."[621] What magic would compel insurers to treat small businesses like large businesses?

Congressional Democrats demonstrated indifference to this aspect of the ACA by leaving it exposed to cuts from Congress's self-inflicted 2013 "sequestration" for unprotected parts of the federal budget. As a result, small business tax credits were reduced 7.2% – hardly an option that small businesses could reliably budget for. In November 2013 the Administration further undermined SHOP exchanges it was administering by announcing online enrollment for small businesses through Healthcare.gov would not be available until November 2014.[622] "Sometimes to save the patient, you have to chop off a limb" noted a *Roll Call* article.[623]

In many places insurers blew up state SHOP exchanges on their launch pads by not participating.

As a consequence, small businesses faced being far worse off than they were prior to the ACA, as those small businesses already offering insurance below the newly-mandated Bronze actuarial value would see the value of the insurance available for purchase rise to that level – raising premiums with no corresponding opportunity to use their tax offset.

Prior to Washington State's SHOP imploding for 2014, Small Business Administration regional administrators had published a newspaper column encouraging Washington small businesses to buy insurance through it. "By making the health insurance market work better for Washington's small businesses, the law is letting them focus on what they do best: delivering great products and services, creating jobs, and growing our economy," they effused.[624]

Instead, Washington's SHOP exchange became a "pilot" offered through one insurer doing business in two counties out of 39. That meant only small businesses in those two counties could use their ACA tax credits. By May 2014 only eight businesses had signed up. Democratic U.S. Senator Patty Murray of Washington was able to get the Obama Administration to agree to allow Washington small businesses in the other 37 counties to use their tax credits outside the SHOP exchange for 2014.[625] Similar meltdowns occurred in other states.

For 2015, the Washington SHOP was to finally operate statewide, but with only a single option in 37 out of 39 counties.[626] By June 2015 the *Seattle Times* reported that 100 small businesses, covering only 535 lives, were using the SHOP.[627] Compare that enrollment to the fact that, according to the Small Business Administration's most recent data, there were 127,600 small businesses in Washington employing 1-19 employees.[628] In total, 506,300 Washingtonians worked for such businesses.[629] Many Washingtonians get health coverage through small business association plans, and, in 2015, the insurance commissioner's efforts to deny the continuity of that coverage were overturned by one of his own administrative law judges.[630]

Even those state-run exchanges that were "functional" had issues: Covered California took its enrollment offline in 2014, and made it impossible for small businesses to even get real-time quotes online. Its website tersely explained that the "SHOP enrollment portal is projected to return online in the fall of 2014."

As was true with the individual market, the value of the ACA to small businesses was sold using the image of one-stop comparison shopping. Absent that user-friendliness, in California, for example, only 1,200 small businesses had enrolled by May 2014 through the SHOP exchange – despite an estimate that as many as 350,000 small businesses might be eligible for the tax credit.[631]

Using the data most recently-available, and with the federal government refusing to reveal its own SHOP enrollment, a U.S. General Accounting Office report issued in November 2014 found that 76,000 Americans were enrolled through state-based SHOP exchanges—compared to a projection that 2 million would be enrolled in 2014.[632] Almost half of that enrollment was in tiny Vermont (33,696 covered lives versus, say, 9,563 in California).

One analysis suggested that small business premiums might dramatically rise nationwide toward the end of 2014, as new requirements took effect—with the bad news, including discontinuations of non-compliant policies, coming just after the 2014 election (and breaking, again, the "you can keep your insurance" promise).[633]

The law actually punishes small businesses relative to larger ones by requiring of the small group market protections, including the ten essential health benefits, not required of the large group market. It was small wonder that hardly any small businesses enrolled in SHOP exchanges.

This was foreseeable. After Kentucky tried health care reform in 1994, a 1997 report on its failure noted

> Kentucky failed to recognize the uniqueness of the small group segment. This segment has traditionally subsidized the large group segment which has the numbers to negotiate large discounts. Carriers would spread the cost over small groups to ensure some margin of return for bigger groups. . . . *To combine this segment with the individual market only increased its exposure for high rates.*[634]

(Emphasis added).

Under the ACA, the tax credit can only be claimed for two years. And even without the complication of sequestration the formulas for claiming this credit would be utterly baffling to the average small business owner or, frankly, anyone who is not a statistician. Consider this helpful example from the IRS:

> **Example:** For the 2014 taxable year, Employer has four FTEs with average annual wages of $23,000. Employer offers one plan under a list billing system with different tiers of coverage. Employer receives a list billing quote for each of the four employees. For Employee A, the employee-only premium is $3,000 per year, and the family premium is $8,000. For Employees B, C and D, the employee-only premium is $5,000 per year and the family premium is $10,000. Employer computes an employer-computed composite employee-only rate of $4,500 ($18,000 / 4). Employer offers to make contributions such that each employee would need to pay $2,000 of the premium for employee-only coverage. Under this arrangement, Employer would contribute $1,000 toward employee-only coverage for Employee A and

$3,000 for employee-only coverage for Employees B, C and D. The total employee-only premium for the four employees is $18,000 ($3,000 + (3 x $5,000). In the event an employee elects family coverage, Employer would make the same contribution ($1,000 for Employee A or $3,000 for Employees B, C and D) toward the family premium and satisfy the uniform percentage requirement.

No human being could possibly understand this.

President Clinton's Health Security Act was more pragmatic about the insurance marketplace for small businesses, and would have been better for them. As his proposal noted, "Today, a major insurance carrier doesn't have to give any kind of deal to the Mom and Pop store in Peoria. But they will not be able to ignore 5000 Mom and Pop stores brought together in an alliance from Central Illinois." Only giving small businesses the opportunity to do group purchasing will address their health care costs. Yet existing arrangements to do that were imperiled in some states by ACA implementation.

The January 2014 proposal from Senators Coburn and Hatch was on the right track when it stated "[s]mall businesses would be free under our proposal to band together to negotiate small business health plans, similar to how large employers are able to leverage purchasing power through their size. This step could help some businesses expand access to coverage and lower health care costs for these smaller firms."[635] However, the senators did not reduce their proposal to bill language so that one could see how it would actually work.

In April 2014, both parties, in a little-noticed section of a perennial bill to "fix" Medicare reimbursement for doctors, agreed to remove ACA language that had arbitrarily limited small group plans to $2,000 deductibles for those plans covering single individuals and $4,000 for any other plans. Because the limitation upon out-of-pocket expenses already otherwise limited deductibles, it is unclear why the ACA had ever precluded small businesses from buying the high-deductible plans allowed in the individual and large group markets – plans that had, indeed, become common in a 2014 individual market where insurers often sought to make the deductible the entire 2014 out-of-pocket limit of $6,350 for an individual.

For both 2014, and then 2015, the Obama Administration delayed the clear statutory requirement that small business employees have choices in purchasing through SHOP exchanges, even though the Administration's May 2014 rulemaking acknowledged that "[c]ommenters expressed concern that the deferral of employee choice could go on for years, and could possibly be permanent." Instead, the Administration was happy to defer to those state insurance commissioners who paternalistically felt "that not implementing employee choice in 2015 would be in the best interest of small employers and their employees and dependents[.]"

California, often cited by ACA supporters as an exemplar of ACA implementation, chose to delay the inevitable for its small group market. With the state's SHOP exchange floundering, Democratic Governor Jerry Brown signed legislation in July 2014 delaying the application of the ACA's market reforms to small group offerings until 2016.[636] It was not clear how this tacit acknowledgement of how disastrous the ACA could be for small businesses was actually reconcilable with ACA support.

Giant corporations were much better off than small businesses under the ACA in another respect. Call it the Wal-Mart Loophole: A retail giant like Wal-Mart could easily employ a workforce of part-timers and then have states provide health care to them through Medicaid expansion. Medicaid was already a significant source of Wal-Mart employee health coverage even prior to the ACA's enactment.

And that was just fine with the Obama Administration.

When President Obama named Jason Furman as his chief economic adviser in June 2013, the corporate-funded American Enterprise Institute was ecstatic: "He has written on the importance of fiscal discipline, the need to undertake entitlement reform sooner rather than later, the role of international trade in improving living standards, and the benefits of Wal-Mart in boosting living standards for low-income Americans."[637]

Indeed, in 2005 Furman had written a piece defending Wal-Mart: "For some Wal-Mart employees, Medicaid is the sensible choice. A family policy costs $1,800 annually for a Wal-Mart worker, similar to the cost for other retailers. . . . The beneficiary of choosing Medicaid is the worker – who gets to keep an additional $1,800 – not Wal-Mart[.]"[638] He effused that "[t]he overall fiscal impact of Wal-Mart is overwhelmingly positive." Rather than criticize Wal-Mart, he opined, we should "recognize that Wal-Mart is a progressive success story."

As Ron Suskind has written, Furman was a protégé of Larry Summers – the insufferably arrogant Clinton Administration Treasury secretary who helped push the repeal of Glass-Steagall in 1999. It was Furman, in fact, who brought Summers into Obama's inner circle.[639]

In October 2014 Wal-Mart rewarded Furman's loyalty by announcing that in 2015 it would end access to health care coverage for 30,000 part-time employees.[640] While Wal-Mart may not have been willing to cover its own employees, that is not to say it did not find opportunity in the ACA, as the *New York Times* reported in November 2014: "Aetna recently teamed with Sam's Club, a unit of Walmart Stores, to also offer a private exchange for small businesses."[641] In other words, a law creating more challenges for small businesses had created more opportunity for Wal-Mart.

With the employer penalty suspended for 2014, there was not even a modest deterrent for major employers like Wal-Mart to steer full-time employees to Medicaid or exchanges. The Congressional Budget Office had calculated that in 2014 there would be $5 billion in employer penalty payments – revenue that was surrendered.[642]

The more things change, the more they remain the same. In June 2013, the *New York Times* could not get a straight answer from the Obama Administration as to why the employer penalty was set so low, and concluded that "[w]hatever the reason, the government is about to conduct a huge experiment in corporate decision-making."[643] When the Administration decided, in July 2013, to suspend the penalty for 2014, it was just as enigmatic. It did not announce this major policy change in a press conference – it did so in a blog posting while the president was on Air Force One returning from Africa.[644] In February 2014, the Administration used the distraction of the Winter Olympics to announce it would further delay – through 2015 – the mandate for employers with fewer than 100 employees.

18

UNAFFORDABLE CARE

As a December 2012 report by the Commonwealth Fund, a ACA supporter, noted, "If trends continue at their historical rate, the average premium for family coverage will reach nearly $25,000 by 2020"—under the ACA.[645] In other words, "with private insurance costs projected to increase faster than incomes over the next decade" too many working families "have effectively traded away wage increases to hold unto health benefits." By 2011, more than 25 states had average health insurance premiums that equaled 20% more of income. Even under the ACA, "[t]he U.S. health insurance system remains highly fragmented, marked by elevated spending on administration and an inability or unwillingness to combat high health care costs in private insurance markets."

Not only does the medical loss ratio construct give insurers ample room for profit, it gives them little incentive to control health care costs. Why control costs when you can pass them on to consumers? For example, hospitals, with enormous bargaining power, can actually profit off of their own mistakes under insurance billing. One study showed hospitals ended up with about $17,000 of profit for privately-insured patients without post-surgical complications – compared to roughly $56,000 in profit for privately-insured patients with complications.[646]

"Prices also rise steeply in some markets because insurance companies lack sufficient impetus or bargaining power to negotiate for lower prices when they can usually pass on the costs to their enrollees in the form of higher premiums," explained a *New York Times* editorial.[647]

Hospitals are providers that can hold even insurers hostage – contracts with them are essential to network adequacy. The problem is particularly acute in rural areas, as a *New York Times* article noted: "Often a single hospital dominates an area, giving insurers little leverage when negotiating reimbursement rates."[648]

In New Hampshire, Anthem Blue Cross and Blue Shield, the only insurer offering insurance through the federally-facilitated exchange, avoided this problem by simply failing to include 10 of the state's 26 hospitals in its network – which meant some residents would have to drive an hour for care by a doctor or hospital.[649] The penalty for going out-of-network could be limitless. Again, as the Obama Administration made clear, "A plan *may*, but is not required to, count out-of-pocket spending for out-of-network items and services towards the plan's annual maximum out-of-pocket limit."[650] (Emphasis added). At the NAIC's urging the Administration abandoned plans to set minimal federal standards for network adequacy.

As 2014 approached, monopolistic practices by hospitals threatened cost control objectives. In Washington State, for example, two Catholic nonprofits were busy snatching up hospitals or forging "strategic affiliations" with them – even the University of Washington's public hospital system – and pushing insurers for higher reimbursements.

Hospital charges could vary in ways that defied rational explanation, as a 2013 federal study showed with amounts charged Medicare.[651] At least on cost, one would appear to be better-advised paying inpatient charges of $5,300 for a joint replacement at a hospital in Adna, Oklahoma than $223,000 at a hospital in Monterrey, California. In one of the nation's capitols of obesity – Jackson, Mississipi – average inpatient charges for heart failure ranged from $9,000 to $51,000 in the same hospital market. It was a deal that Max Baucus struck to win the support of hospitals for health care reform that as much as anything sunk a public option – hospitals opposed a public option for fear it would lead to cost controls.

In the medical arms race, the incentive for many hospitals – even the majority that are ostensibly nonprofit – is to build shinier facilities packed with the latest technology. Many states do not have certificate of need laws that restrict competition and the opening of new hospitals. Large states without such laws include California, Pennsylvania, and Texas.[652] Even where state certificate of need processes restrict new players from entering into the hospital field, hospitals are generally unrestricted in renovating excessively or building ancillary kingdoms – such as hospital-owned MRI facilities.

A *Kaiser Health News* article that examined hospital compensation around the country found it tied to expansion. "In a story matched at hospitals across the country, the institution has repeatedly added space, programs, amenities and technology once reserved for top teaching hospitals to become Renton's second-biggest employer, after Boeing," it wrote of one Washington State hospital. It noted:

> Patient revenue doubled over the decade ending in 2012, to $406 million, as Valley added a new surgery center; a $115 million tower that included an expanded emergency department and a joint and spine center; a birthing center with whirlpool tubs and reclining chairs for dads; and a "soothing, light-filled lobby" with pyramid skylights and waterfalls.[653]

For 2012, the CEO's salary of $1.2 million included a $213,000 bonus tied to financial goals and expansion – past years had also included compensation tied to patient volume. Salary-based goals for 2011, for example, included increasing angio-plasties (an overprescribed artery-clearing procedure), and increasing surgeries using its da Vinci robot – a fantastically-expensive device (up to $2.6 million apiece) hospitals have begun stockpiling. Each robot can add up to $4,800 to the cost of a prostate surgery, according to another article.[654] One Washington State hospital alone had seven. Even a rural 25-bed hospital bought one that cost twice as much as what the hospital netted in 2010. "Robotic assisted surgery is clearly part of the 'medical arms race,' as hospitals struggle to keep market share," observed one surgeon in the *Seattle Times*.

In Houston, Texas – a city where one-in-three residents were uninsured as of 2013 according to the Texas Hospital Association – a wave of hospital building and renovation began in 2009 on the Texas Medical Center campus that, at the time, was projected to cost $3.3 billion.[655]

Maryland was among states seeking, prior to the ACA, to control health care costs. The state treats hospitals as utilities by setting insurance rates for individual procedures at all hospitals in the state. While, through an agreement with the federal government, this led to higher federal Medicare payments of as much as $1 billion a year, it eliminated haggling that would result in disparate commercial insurance payment rates between hospitals. Yet the higher Medicare payments incentivized hospitals to admit more patients, defeating the logic of cost control.[656]

In 2014, Maryland changed its approach. Subject to regulatory oversight, hospitals agreed that their payments, from both private and public sources, would rise no higher than the rate of growth in the state's economy.[657] Per an agreement with the federal government, Medicare payments would grow slower than elsewhere in the country.

In a celebrated 2013 *TIME* article, Stephen Brill examined cost-drivers for the health care system, and concluded that "insurers are increasingly losing leverage because hospitals are consolidating by buying doctors' practices and even rival hospitals." This creates situations "in which the insurer needs the hospital more than the hospital needs the insurer" – in such situations lowering government payments, like Medicare or Medicaid, to control costs will not work because hospitals will simply shift costs to insured patients.[658]

A Robert Wood Johnson report showed that the consolidation encouraged under the ACA could drive costs higher. Increased hospital market concentration following mergers drove "significant price increases" and actually lowered quality too – as competition was an incentive to quality. It found "the prospect that the ACA could encourage greater physician-hospital consolidation gives some cause for concern."[659]

One pre-ACA 2006 study found hospital consolidation, driving costs, actually caused a significant decrease in those with private health insurance – as many as 695,000 lives in 2003 alone.[660] An economic analysis in the *Journal of Law & Economics* of hospital merger data from 1989 through 1996 found hospitals increasing prices roughly 40% following the merger of rival hospitals.[661]

In 2002 doctors had owned about 75% of physician practices. Hospitals owned more than half of those practices by 2008.[662] All evidence suggests the pace of acquisitions has quickened since then, particularly following the ACA's passage. In fact, a 2013 PricewaterhouseCoopers' Health Research Institute study of health care costs found "[h]ealth industry consolidation has increased more than 50% since 2009 – activity that is expected to continue through 2014."[663]

A November 2014 *New York Times* article noted oncologists were giving up independent practices and going to work for hospitals.[664] Hospitals command higher profits from insurers for chemotherapy drugs; furthermore, "patients end up paying, out of pocket, an average $134 more per dose[.]" Of 1447 private oncology practices existing nationwide as of 2008, over a third (544) had been acquired by hospitals, while 313 had closed and another 395 were reputedly teetering.

Reflecting "growing concerns that the wave of consolidation may be increasing prices" a June 2014 *New York Times* article reported that "[c]harges for some of the most common inpatient procedures surged at hospitals across the country in 2012 from a year earlier, some at more than four times the national rate of inflation[.]"⁶⁶⁵ Upon acquisition by a hospital chain, charges at one 300-bed Florida hospital featured in the story had soared over a year's time, with charges for a case of pneumonia going up 25%, charges for severe irregular heartbeat admissions doubling, and charges for intestinal procedures going up "168 percent to $152,047 in 2012 from $56,704 in 2011."⁶⁶⁶

Hospital contract demands made of insurers could appear less related to care costs and more related to subsidizing acquisitions, with, for example, a profitable hospital subsidizing a less-profitable one elsewhere at the expense of local patients. Even conservative economist Avik Roy is among those alarmed by hospital consolidations, although he suggests the solution is to eliminate CON laws that prevent "new entrants from competing against incumbent hospitals" (a thesis that ignores the states that don't even have such laws) while at the same time "*discouraging* more hospital consolidation" by increasing the Federal Trade Commission's (FTC) hospital industry staff, "so that the agency could do more to challenge anticompetitive hospital mergers."⁶⁶⁷ He notes that the FTC presently "challenges a very small number of hospital mergers, despite the large amount of anticompetitive and rent-seeking activity among large hospital systems."⁶⁶⁸

Not every conservative was displeased, to be sure. Betting on consolidation has proved alluring to even the biggest "Obamacare" opponents. As one account by Josh Barro in the *New York Times* noted, former Florida Governor Jeb Bush, the 2016 Republican presidential candidate, realized an enormous profit from his stock in Tenet, a health care concern: "Mr. Bush's tax returns reflect a gain of 105 percent on Tenet stock he acquired in May 2011 and sold in October 2013."⁶⁶⁹ Tenet had gobbled up a rival.

There were other implications to hospital consolidation. Progressive advocates were so concerned by the trends in hospital control in Washington State that in May 2013 the American Civil Liberties Union of Washington led a coalition of groups, including Pro-Choice Washington and Planned Parenthood, asking Governor Inslee to impose a six-month moratorium on hospital mergers. They noted:

National expert group MergerWatch reports that the number of pending, simultaneous religious hospital mergers in Washington is unprecedented in the 15 years it has tracked the issue. While 26% of hospital beds were in religious hospitals in April 2010, today that figure is 40% and could rise to 45% by year's end.

The concerned groups cited the Washington Constitution's prohibition on public property and tax dollars being used to support religious institutions. Danny Westneat, a columnist in the Seattle Times, wrote a column asking if the Catholic Church was "taking over health care" in the state.[670] With "nonprofit" hospital executives making millions – at the same time they, ironically, sought to squeeze nurses for health care concessions – something less noble than Christian charity was motivating hospital mergers.

After a major hospital in Orange County, California, entered into a "corporate partnership" in 2013 with St. Joseph Health System – a Catholic chain that already owned five Orange County hospitals – it abruptly stopped performing elective abortions due to its partner's "sensitivity" about the issue. California's Attorney General Kamala Harris, a Democrat, approved the transaction, though the denial of access to abortions was a reason under California law that she could have disapproved it.

Reporting on the issue, Michael Hiltzik, a *Los Angeles Times* columnist, noted "faith-based hospitals receive billions of dollars in taxpayer support — reimbursements from Medicare and Medicaid and legal status that allows them to operate tax free and their donors to take a tax deduction."[671] He observed that "Catholic hospitals now account for 15% of the nation's total hospital beds, serving 1 in 6 patients. Their reach is expanding, as they enter into management affiliations with non-Catholic hospitals and move to impose their doctrinal rules on their partners."

In 2014, as the *Boston Globe* reported, "Attorney General Martha Coakley made an important political decision this week: She will not go to war with the state's largest health care company and its largest private employer while running for governor."[672]

The Partners HealthCare System hospital merger approved by Coakley, the Democrat who had so improbably lost the 2010 race for the late Ted Kennedy's U.S. Senate seat to Scott Brown, brought "attack from candidates and critics on the left who contended it did not go far enough to rein in Partners' market clout, which has been blamed for driving up health costs." While it tied future price increases to the rate-of-inflation until 2020, it did nothing to reel back already-exorbitant prices.

The new merger would only add to damage created by an older one. As the *New York Times* wrote in an editorial, "In retrospect, it looks as if Massachusetts made a serious mistake in 1994 when it let its two most prestigious (and costly) hospitals — Massachusetts General Hospital and Brigham and Women's Hospital, both affiliated with Harvard — merge into a single system known as Partners HealthCare."[673] An effect of that 1994 merger "was to take away the ability of insurance companies to demand lower prices from one hospital with the threat that they could just send patients to the other. After the merger, insurers had to take both of them or neither."

Of Coakley's effort with respect to Partners' latest merger, the *Times* deemed it "a dubious bargain" and noted that "[l]arge-scale mergers almost always lead to higher prices, reputable research shows." Simply put, "Mergers are hard to undo after the fact." Apart from the harms it would inflict upon patients, Coakley's appeasement brought no political reward. Voters in overwhelmingly-Democratic Massachusetts rejected her a second time in the 2014 election and chose Republican Charlie Baker for governor. Baker was a former health insurance executive who, in the very state that had served as the inspiration for the ACA, had championed reducing health care mandates – even prescription drug coverage.[674] He criticized Coakley's approval of the latest merger while expressing contrition over his own role, while working for then-Governor William Weld, in approving the 1994 merger.

In January 2015, Superior Court Judge Janet Sanders rejected the deal Coakley had approved – finding the purported consumer protections worthless.[675] Coakley's successor as attorney general, Democrat Maura Healey, pledged an antitrust lawsuit if Partners attempted to resurrect the acquisition following the judge's ruling.

Even with a state certificate of need (CON) process, everything short of a hospital can be allowed – one Washington hospital system escaped review in 2013 by opening a three-story, 45,000-square-foot self-styled "medical pavilion" that provided seven-day-a-week urgent care; employed specialists including cardiologists, gastroenterologists and oncologists; and offered on-site laboratory, diagnostic imaging, x-rays, and pharmacy services. This non-hospital had a 200-space parking garage.[676]

Citing a 2002 Journal of the American Medical Association study that showed a 22% lower risk of death in CON states as opposed to non-CON states, one California report suggested "a relationship between CON laws and quality of care. This is because CON regulations limit the number of hospitals offering specialized medical services, concentrating expertise."[677] Unconstrained competition could exacerbate malpractice risks.

As a consequence of CON, and likely the comparative good health of residents, Washington State and Oregon are tied for the fewest hospital beds – 1.7 – per 1,000 residents.[678] The national average is 2.6. Unhealthy Mississippi has 4.4, while the District of Columbia, with financially-struggling hospitals, led the nation with 5.7. Extra beds could drive unnecessary utilization.

For example, one scholar studying the relationship between empty hospital beds and neonatal intensive care units (NICU) found "that on average, more empty beds on the day prior to an infant's birth does increase the probability of NICU admission." Admitting "marginal infants to the NICU may provide an opportunity for hospitals to 'upcode' the infants in order to receive a higher reimbursement."[679]

A major study reported in the Journal of the American Medical Association in 2011 examined surgery data from January 2006 to June 30, 2009 for procedures for implantable cardioverter-defibrillators – a type of pacemaker. Of 111,707 patients, almost a quarter – 25,145 – received implants that did not meet evidence-based criteria.[680] Government was the primary payer for 66% of these patients.

An October 2013 Washington Post investigation found that perhaps half of all spinal fusions performed were medically unnecessary – including roughly half of 125,000 patient records the Post had examined in Florida. A whistleblower lawsuit against one Florida hospital found its neurosurgeons generating over $2 million apiece in profit for the hospital on procedures costing an average of $80,000; medical equipment companies selling hardware, such as braces and screws, were earning $7,000 per procedure and often had a representative situated in the operating room.[681]

"Strategic affiliations" short of merger, such as those seen in Washington State, would also allow hospitals to circumvent the Stark Law that prohibits physicians from making "self-referrals" for certain health services – ranging from lab services to imaging – to entities the referring physicians, or their family members, either own or receive compensation from. If a provider works for Hospital A, he or she could refer to Hospital B or its ancillary businesses even if Hospital A received a stream of income from an "affiliation" with Hospital B – Hospital B, after all, is not directly paying that doctor.

Outpatient surgical centers have become another part of the cost-driving medical arms race, though the idea behind them was to reduce expensive hospital utilization for procedures – like once-rare colonoscopies – that could be performed on an outpatient basis. Gastroenterologists earn an average of $433,000 a year, and, increasingly, involve high-paid anesthesiologists in colonoscopies.[682] That is, in part, because anesthesiologists have successfully lobbied administrations from President Ronald Reagan's to Barack Obama's to keep an unnecessary warning on a drug commonly used in the procedure.

As Elizabeth Rosenthal reported in the New York Times, "minor procedures typically offer the best return on investment" – salaries for volume-generating "dermatologists, gastroenterologists and oncologists rose 50 percent or more between 1995 and 2012, even when adjusted for inflation, while those for primary care physicians rose only 10 percent and lag far behind, since insurers pay far less for traditional doc-toring tasks[.]"[683] She noted that dermatology, which is already especially lucrative, will become even more so under an ACA that requires 100% dermatology screening for an aging population – guaranteeing more biopsies and treatments. Lobbyists for the interests of medical specialists can easily overpower those for primary care physicians.

As a direct result, wait times for primary care appointments can be measured in days or even months – among the worst of all countries with advanced health care systems. As Rosenthal noted:

> In our market-based system, patients can get lucrative procedures rapidly, even when there is no urgent medical need: Need a new knee, or an M.R.I., or a Botox injection? You'll probably be on the schedule within days. But what if you're an asthmatic whose breathing is deteriorating, or a diabetic whose medicines need adjustment, or an elderly patient who has unusual chest pain and needs a cardiology consultation? In much of the country, you can wait a week or weeks for such office appointments — or longer if you need to find a doctor who accepts your insurance plan or Medicare.[684]

Atul Gawade, a surgeon who has written on medical cost-inflation in The New Yorker, notes that "[n]o one has yet invented a payment system that cannot be gamed."[685] Not only are more-expensive procedures favored, they are also priced higher than they should be. A Washington Post investigation revealed an American Medical Association committee that values procedures doctors perform exaggerated – "sometimes by as much as 100 percent" – the time involved for purposes of pricing for Medicare and private insurers.[686] For example, the AMA estimated a basic colo-noscopy took up 75 minutes of a physician's time – the reality is closer to a half-hour. The result led to some incongruities: "Florida records show 78 doctors — gastroen-terologists, ophthalmologists, orthopedic surgeons and others — who performed at least 24 hours worth of procedures on an average workday."

Because these estimations were the basis for Medicare (in addition to private insurance) billing, the federal government had, in effect, delegated price-fixing power to a trade group. The Post reported that "even though the AMA figures shape billions in federal Medicare spending and billions more in spending from private insurers, the government is ill-positioned to judge their accuracy." Resources were a big issue: "The government has about six to eight people reviewing the estimates provided by the AMA, government officials said, but none of them do it full time."

As 2014 approached, the Obama Administration busied itself cutting one-fifth of the staff from the watchdog inspector general branch of the Department of Health and Human Services that polices Medicare expenditures.[687]

The defense of the status quo makes for a clash of the moneyed titans. In 2012, Blue Cross/Blue Shield spent $13.5 million on lobbying,[688] while America's Health Insurance Plans spent $9.3 million.[689] Meanwhile, the American Hospital Association spent $19.2 million,[690] with other hospital groups and individual hospitals spending millions more.

And let's not even get started on the pharmaceutical industry.

In 2011, the average price of brand name prescriptions jumped 17.7% – with an average price per prescription of $268.[691] Thanks Nancy-Ann DeParle! Given the general congressional subservience to the pharmaceutical industry there was little chance this issue would ever be revisited.

This is nothing new. In 1991 a *New York Times* piece on U.S. drug prices relative to other countries noted: "According to one study, Americans paid an average of 54 percent more than Europeans for 25 commonly prescribed drugs. Some essential drugs are especially costly in the United States. A month's supply of Eldepryl, a Parkinson's disease medication from Somerset Labs Inc., costs about $28 in Italy, $48 in Austria and $240 in the United States."[692] Americans subsidize drug companies' low prices elsewhere.

It is quaint, over two decades later, to look back at the article's assertion that "[r]egulators and insurers who have been trying for years to limit hospital costs and doctors' fees are now trying to rein in drug expenses as well."

Enactment of Medicare Part D in 2003 was an enormous gift to the pharmaceutical industry, thanks to President George Bush, his fellow Republicans, and Democrats like Max Baucus. Bruce Bartlett, a policy advisor to President Reagan and the first President Bush, notes that "Republicans enacted the largest expansion to the welfare state since the creation of Medicare in 1965 by adding a huge unfunded program providing prescription drugs to the Medicare program."[693] He has predicted that the program's costs would be over $1 trillion over its first two decades.

In 2007 a prescription drug safety bill was before Congress. A Senate amendment was offered to block reimportation of drugs; it passed 49-40. The 49 senators voting for it had received roughly $5 million from drug companies since 2001 according to USA Today.[694] Among the top-10 recipients of those contributions were four senators from the Democratic caucus voting with the pharmaceutical industry: Connecticut Senator Joe Lieberman (then a Democrat), Massachusetts Senator John Kerry, Delaware Senator Tom Carper, and the ubiquitous Montana Senator Max Baucus.

Notwithstanding President Obama having broken his campaign promise to support reimportation, an effort to allow it in the ACA was offered by Democratic Senator Byron Dorgan of North Dakota, who, in a December 9, 2009 floor speech, noted that "[t]he biggest argument against reimportation is safety. What everyone has conveniently forgotten to tell you is that in Europe reimportation has been in place for 20 years."[695] Dorgan argued that "it is unfair to the American people to be paying double, triple or quadruple or 10 times the cost of prescription drugs that are being paid for by people in the rest of the world."

Dorgan's amendment had the support of Republican senators Grassley, McCain and Snowe. During floor debate, in which McCain actively bolstered Dorgan, McCain posed a question: "I wish to ask the Senator, what is the basis of the argument against the Senator's amendment? What possible reason, frankly, except for the influence of a special interest in this, our Nation's Capitol?" Yet it was Dorgan's fellow Democrats who joined forces with Republicans to defeat it.

Wearing a mantle of pro-consumer piety, Democratic Senator Robert Menendez of New Jersey derisively stated that "[t]his amendment, however well-intentioned, reminds me of a time when the lack of sufficient regulation allowed people to sell snake oil and magic elixirs."[696] The sincerity of that position was belied by a federal corruption indictment on April 1, 2015 for an alleged bribery scheme involving documented attempts to procure millions of dollars in higher Medicare reimbursement for a Florida eye doctor who subsidized Menendez's campaigns and vacations. In just one year, 2012, the doctor had billed Medicare for $21 million – more than any doctor in the United States.[697]

Menendez's New Jersey hosts headquarters for Pfizer and Merck. Pfizer spreads its love around by contributing heavily to both the Democratic and Republican national organizations for state attorneys general – the very officials who might otherwise prosecute fraudulent drug marketing.[698]

The secretive Trans-Pacific Partnership trade agreement that President Obama pushed in 2015 also bore pharmaceutical industry fingerprints, by making it harder to bring generic drugs to market. To fund remediation for the many job losses such an agreement would produce, a Senate entirely unwilling to reign in the pharmaceutical industry voted to cut Medicare by $700 million – with 13 Senate Democrats voting for the agreement along with most Republicans.

The influence of the pharmaceutical industry is no less pervasive at the state level. In 2008, in an uncontested state House race, I raised $9,150 from pharmaceutical concerns on my way to raising $138,181. Most of what I raised was then turned over to the Washington House Democratic Campaign Committee.

In 2010, per capita drug spending on prescription drugs was higher in the U.S. than in any other nation – more than twice what was spent in the United Kingdom. In one study, over a decade's time, drug manufacturer prices for brand-name drugs were between 5% to 198% higher in the U.S. than in six other countries that included Canada and Western Europe. One factor is that American consumers take up name-brand medications faster than any nation.[699]

Yet as *TIME* pointed out in 2013, for the price of one Lipitor pill in the U.S. three could be bought in Argentina; the cost of one Nexium pill in the U.S. was that of eight in France. Pharmaceutical companies were charging what they thought the market could bear. And this is not new.

An AARP Public Policy Institute study of Lipitor, the cholesterol-lowering prescription drug (and all-time best-seller), found its maker Pfizer – as time ran out on its patent – jacked up the price, paid another manufacturer to delay a generic version, offered consumer and insurance discounts to discourage a generic alternative, and finally "authorized" a generic version from which Pfizer would reap 70% of the proceeds. While its sales dropped from $9.6 billion in 2011 to $3.9 billion in 2012 this was still an incredible boon for a patentless drug.[700] And such a drug could largely be avoided if Americans ate better.

The *Washington Post* reported that, given a choice between two drugs made by the same company, Genentech, physicians chose the one that cost roughly $2,000 per injection over the one that cost about $50 – even though both drugs, which prevent age-related blindness, are substantially the same.[701] When doctors administer drugs they are reimbursed by Medicare for the drug's price plus 6 percent. The incentive to use the more expensive drug, coupled with Genentech very actively discouraging doctors from using its own less-expensive drug, cost Medicare over $1 billion a year.

In 2013 John Hammergren, the CEO of health care supply company McKesson, was making over $50 million annually at the age of 54 while in line for a $159 million pension.[702] In 2012, the company paid a $190 million settlement to the federal government for charges that it had inflated Medicaid drug prices; compared to $122 billion in annual revenue the possibility of such settlements is a risk worth taking.[703] The pay-to-play cost of being among the top-10 donors for House Minority Leader Pelosi was only $11,000.[704]

In the face of all of this money, who would champion the consumers anyway? The Cystic Fibrosis Foundation gave a pharmaceutical company $75 million to develop a drug that treats cystic fibrosis for roughly 4% of those suffering from it. After the product, heavily promoted by the Foundation, was on the market for a year, the Foundation sold future royalties for $150 million. Meanwhile, the drug's cost per patient was $841 a day, or $307,000 per year. When doctors and scientists accused the manufacturer of "unconscionable" profiting and "leveraging pain and suffering into huge financial gain for speculators," the company's response was merely to raise the drug's price another $13,000.[705] Interconnectedness between "disease groups" and PhRMA is quite common.

An October 2013 *Washington Post* report found the Food and Drug Administration received advice on the effectiveness, and safety, of painkiller prescription practices from a scientific panel that required pharmaceutical companies to pay-to-play; companies paid up to $25,000 apiece to attend the panel's meetings and pay the academics who were its conveners.[706] It was another example of how, even before the ACA fully took hold in 2014, the line between government regulators and the health care industry was blurry.

As was true with narrowing networks to exclude hospitals and other providers, the risk was that insurers would simply exclude from their formularies drugs that were efficacious but expensive. Pharmacy benefits managers, in concert with insurers, were starting to squeeze pharmaceutical companies, and a June 2014 *New York Times* editorial noted this "trend holds both promise and peril for patients who depend on the drugs to control their illnesses."[707] It warned that "[r]egulators need to watch out that insurers, in their zeal to curb drug costs, don't block patients from medicines they need when an alternative is not adequate." The odds of regulators doing so are not great, although a more patently-discriminatory effort by insurers in the state of Washington to offer generic-only policies was rebuffed by the insurance commissioner in 2012.[708]

Even generics might not always offer price-relief. A July 2014 *New York Times* story documented an inexplicable rise in generic drug prices, with the price of "one of the oldest known heart medicines" tripling in less than a year's time.[709] Such increases could go unchallenged by insurers. As the article noted, "With cheaper drugs, insurers use simpler tools to discourage use and prod doctors to think about other options: They require physicians to fill out forms . . . and move the drug to a category that requires larger patient co-pays."

Nor are generics always available even where patens have expired. An April 2015 *Wall Street Journal* article chronicled a practice by pharmaceutical companies of buying rivals' old drugs then raising prices astronomically. As it noted, "On Feb. 10, Valeant Pharmaceuticals International Inc. bought the rights to a pair of life-saving heart drugs. The same day, their list prices rose by 525% and 212%."[710] In another case, a company called Horizon Pharma bought rights to a pain medication, Vimovo, from AstraZeneca, and then, on its first day of selling Vimovo, raised the list price for a bottle of 60 tablets by 597% to $954.04. A year later, in January 2015, the price was raised again to $1,678.32.[711] The *Journal* reported that since 2008, the year of President Obama's election, branded-drug prices had increased 127 percent.[712]

Where hospital and drug costs are out of their control, short of excluding hospitals from networks or drugs from formularies, insurers tend to control costs at the margins.

In Washington State in 2014, for example, some insurers were paying chiropractors less than their patient-copays, despite Washington law requiring insurers to enlist every category of provider in their networks. Insurers were denying certain therapies for children with autism, which prompted litigation under mental health parity laws. On behalf of those with autism, courts were forcing compliance with a state law regulators refused to enforce. An insurer was also reimbursing advanced registered nurse practitioners, who have prescribing authority in Washington under their scope of practice, 85% of what it paid physicians for the same care, even though the ACA was supposed to encourage access to the primary care such nurse practitioners provide.

There has been considerable speculation about slowing health care spending trends since the passage of the ACA, with the ACA's defenders happy to take credit. For example, in October 2014 economist Paul Krugman trumpeted in *Rolling Stone* that "overall health spending has slowed substantially, with the cost-control features of the ACA probably deserving some of the credit."[713]

No one really believes this. As I noted at the outset of this book, one 2014 nationwide poll showed only 14% of liberals believed the ACA lowers health care costs.[714]

The reality is the spending decline was likely linked to the most severe economic crisis since the Great Depression. Despite happy talk from ACA proponents, an analysis in 2013 by Victor Fuchs in the *New England Journal of Medicine* found a long-time correlation between Gross Domestic Product and health care spending, noting that "[i]t seems premature to dismiss the sluggish economy as the major explanation for the spending slowdown of recent years." Fuchs wrote: "Some observers place great emphasis on the particularly slow growth of national health care expenditures in 2010 and 2011. How useful is the experience of growth over a period of 2 years in predicting the growth rate over the next 20 years? The answer seems to be not at all."[715]

That analysis seems borne out by subsequent years' experience. An October 2014 *New York Times* article noted that "[t]he spending slowdown began before the law was even written."[716] Furthermore, "the growth in health spending has been slowing down around the world, suggesting that the cause may not be something special happening in this country."[717]

A team led by Andrea Sisko, which included Sisko's fellow economists and actuaries in the Office of the Actuary at the Centers for Medicare and Medicaid Services (CMS), reported, in a September 2014 analysis in *Health Affairs*, that the "four-year historically low rate of health spending growth . . . was primarily attributable to the sluggish economic recovery and constrained state and local government budgets following the 2007–09 recession."[718] If one could not trust the Obama Administration's own experts in repudiating the mythos of ACA cost control, who could one trust?

The 2013 report on health care spending by PricewaterhouseCooper's Health Research Institute had also found that "[t]he tepid economic recovery continues to affect healthcare spending growth."[719] It also reported another factor slowing health care spending that belied ACA supporters' rose-colored views: The increasing trend of employers to push employees into high-deductible health plans. Deductibles had shot up from $680 for in-network visits and $1,000 for out-of-network to $1,230 and $2,110 respectively in 2013.[720]

According to their employer survey, "44% of employers are considering offering high-deductible health plans as the only benefit option in 2014. Already, 17% of employers offer high deductible plans as the only options, a 31% increase over 2012."[721]

A Kaiser Family Foundation survey of employer-sponsored health coverage for 2013 found that premium costs for health care increased by 5% for individuals and

4% for families – over double the 1.8% growth in wages – with workers increasingly in high-deductible plans to boot.[722] For 2014, the accounting firm Milliman found that costs had risen 5.4 percent – with the employee paying an average of $9,695 a year. Since the ACA's passage, "total employee cost (payroll deductions plus out-of-pocket expenses) increased by approximately 32% from 2010 to 2014, while employer costs (premium contributions) increased by 26%."[723]

Employers forcing employees into high-deductible plans would seem to belie the ACA's claims of "affordable care." Notwithstanding this particular disincentive toward care, if health care becomes more accessible, there is reason to suppose spending will increase. Economists refer to this as "moral hazard." The theory, as described in one 2013 article in the *American Economic Review*, is "greater coverage would be more attractive for individuals whose health care utilization would increase more sharply in response to this coverage, thus generating greater cost to the insurance company."[724]

If this is true, insurance rates would either shoot through the roof in the years ahead or insurers would continue to drastically pare down consumer options and/or increase out-of-pocket burdens. The 2014 analysis by CMS economists and actuaries predicted the latter. While forecasting "faster rates of health spending growth, particularly for private health insurance" it stated "these rates of increase are expected to be dampened somewhat by the . . . the ongoing trend toward higher cost-sharing requirements for the privately insured."[725] That hardly sounded like something consumers could celebrate.

A May 2015 *POLITICO* analysis found that, unencumbered by meaningful rate review in most states, many health insurers were looking to raise rates astronomically in 2016 – on top of narrow networks and high-deductibles.[726] It was a smart play: Democrats would be tongue-tied about the rate increases given their need to defend the ACA in an election year with the presidency on the line.

The president weakly argued that exacting review by state regulators could make these rate increases disappear (""stay on your insurance commissioner, pay attention to what they're doing"),[727] without acknowledging the lack of such authority in many states. And where that authority existed, to use Oregon as an example, consumers might still be out of luck. For 2016, Oregon's insurance commissioner approved a 25% premium increase for the largest plan, and a 33% increase for the second-largest plan.[728] When one insurer asked for a 9% premium increase she gave them a 34.8% increase instead.

Matters had not been helped by the president's improvident promise that people could keep their health plans; where states had allowed them to do so the healthy stayed put, funneling unmitigated adverse risk into exchange plans. As I wrote in *The Hill*, "If premiums go up, it's a failure attributable to the architecture of the ACA, not the foreseeable failures of state regulation."[729]

19

MOVING FORWARD

In MOVING FORWARD it is important to understand those we yoked our future to.

When Michael Moore released his documentary "SiCKO" in 2007 on the failings of America's health care system, America's Health Insurance Plans (AHIP) sprang to action. Their game plan included briefing centrist Democratic organizations like the Democratic Leadership Council, of which then-Congressman Rahm Emanuel of Illinois was a key part, and encouraging "select Democratic pundits" to spread the word about the insurance industry's virtues.[730] One "metric" was to "Portray SiCKO as a Threat to the Democrats' Larger Agenda." A strategy was to "[h]ighlight horror stories of government-run systems."[731] It was proposed they "[c]reate an ad that would show Democrats the likely response to a single-payer proposal" and float it on conservative websites, and enlist a "Democratic polling firm" to poll on Moore's views – targeting his regrettable affection for Cuba.

Any meaningful pro-consumer reforms will face similar attacks. As Senator Rockefeller had warned during the ACA debate, "the insurance industry does not know how to stop itself. They are a train which just gathers speed, and with no impediments." That is where regulators must play a role. One can hardly begrudge insurers for trying to realize the best possible return for their shareholders. For all of my criticism of the unchecked faults of some health insurers, they are a vital part of the economy and are here to stay.

The marriage between government and the health insurance industry may pressure insurers into demonstrating some more social accountability: In January 2015

Aetna, for example, announced it was increasing its wage floor for workers to $16 an hour — a well-received gesture from a company profiting greatly from the ACA. But such gestures arguably pale compared to, say, a health insurer CEO making $66 million a year.

With the federal government now effectively a subsidiary of this industry, it is unrealistic to expect positive change at the federal level. Changes to the ACA that have been proposed by Democrats tend to further profit the insurance industry. One example is the "Expanded Consumer Choice Act" introduced in 2013 by Democratic U.S. Senator Mark Begich of Alaska, with five six-sponsors, that would allow insurers to sell "Copper plans" (50% actuarial value) with even higher deductibles.

Given that a huge concern over plans sold under the ACA was their high deductibles, it is unfathomable how even higher deductibles would be appealing. As Ramesh Ponnuru, a conservative columnist, wrote, such plans would "appeal to a small number of people who foresee themselves being pretty healthy. Their low premiums would entitle them to the preventative care that Obamacare requires all insurance plans to cover, but in the event of a major problem would leave them with big bills to pay. This is more or less the opposite of the way insurance should work."[732]

Begich, in any event, was defeated following the approval of huge Alaska rate increases for 2015. Immediately following his departure from office he took a job with a health care trade association that, among other unprogressive positions, called for increasing the ACA's definition of what constitutes full-time work to 40 hours a week, so as to lift the requirement that those working 30 hours a week receive health care benefits, and was also suing to prevent home care workers from receiving overtime benefits.

In May 2014, with the congressional elections approaching, the New York Times had reported that with new direct financial assistance to insurers "Administration officials hope the payments will stabilize premiums and prevent rate increases that could embarrass Democrats in this year's midterm elections."[733] Insurers could set lower rates and know that the federal government would bail them out through the "risk corridor" program. Not only did this taxpayer investment fail to avert electoral disaster for Democrats, it could not be sustainable in the long-term — not only because it is wrong, but because Republicans would not vote for appropriations to prop up the ACA in that way.

In a poignant irony, in at least one case the insurance industry used the ACA itself to attack a vulnerable Democrat facing re-election in 2014. A July 2014 New York

Times article revealed that an anti-ACA ad being run to attack Senator Mark Pryor of Arkansas was secretly funded by AHIP – which had given $1.6 million toward the "Voice of Free Enterprise" messaging.[734] Pryor went down in defeat.

Where to go from here? How do we fix a unicameral law passed by a bicameral Congress?

Within our current political system, a single-payer system clearly will never happen. One might hope Congress someday will enact a public option to compete with commercial insurers. Given the lobbying of insurers, it is extremely improbable that will happen. Indeed, no serious Democratic effort has been made since 2010 to augment the ACA in this fashion.

One might hope Congress someday will require real rate review by insurance regulators. Yet such a bill could not even get a committee *hearing* in a Democratic Senate.

One might hope that Congress someday will reign in pharmaceutical costs. Yet when Congressman Henry Waxman introduced a bill in 2013 to do so – the Medicare Drug Savings Act – he began with just four co-sponsors . . . out of 435 House members.[735] Many members of Congress in both parties own pharmaceutical stock.

Let's be realistic. What are we left with?

While I have been very critical about the ACA, it has, however clumsily, established an important principle: Some level of health care should be a universal right. Republicans have offered no principled alternative that would cover those lacking insurance. Opposition to the ACA is not in itself a plan.

I believe single-payer should have at least been debated, and that, at a minimum, a national public option – accomplishing many of the same aims – should have been offered. However, I am not confident that a pure single-payer system could have been pulled off in the United States despite the simple appeal of a "Medicare for All" concept. The 2014 scandal over neglect by the United States Department of Veteran's Affairs, which prompted the resignation of Veterans Affairs Secretary Eric Shinseki, raised questions as to whether our government can even properly care for those most venerated for their service to our country. The agency was tens of thousands of medical practitioners short of being adequately-staffed.

I also question whether in a complex society with deeply-entrenched medical practices we could bring about a transformative system change like Britain's National Health Service, which dates back to the post-World War II rebuilding era (1948) when all things were possible. Medicare is single-payer, but only for those 65-and-older in a country where life expectancy is roughly 79 years – and it largely fails to cover long-term care.[736] Nor is even Medicare "pure" single-payer, due to the fact that the private insurance industry – through Medicare Advantage – has a very profitable stake in this Great Society program. Medicaid for our nation's long-term care population is functionally akin to a single-payer system, but it has long been woefully underfunded with little accountability or public outcry.

That latter example makes me wary about proclaiming Medicaid expansion under the ACA a success beyond the near-term, even if it had bipartisan acceptance in many places and had already reduced the burden of uninsured patients upon hospitals. For example, the *Seattle Times* was able to report in May 2014, "At Seattle's largest safety-net hospital, the proportion of uninsured patients fell from 12 percent last year to an unprecedented low of 2 percent this spring."[737] The example extended elsewhere, as the *Washington Post* reported: "LifePoint Hospitals, a Brentwood, Tenn.-based company that owns 60 hospitals nationwide, said the Medicaid expansion led to an average 26 percent reduction in uninsured patients at its facilities."[738]

These are good trends, but hospitals are a special case – federal law already required them to admit all patients. Thus their alternative to a Medicaid payment was to receive *nothing at all*. The bigger question was whether Medicaid enrollees would be able to access the primary care that would help keep them out of hospitals in the first place. That seemed doubtful, given the bipartisan unwillingness to incentivize providers to focus on primary care. Even in states that enthusiastically expanded Medicaid, like Washington, payment rates are so low – whether $21.73 for a child's dental exam, or $33.64 for a half-hour of family psychotherapy – as to be a deterrent to providers.

The unpopularity of the ACA posed the danger of collateral damage in other policy areas. Consider the cost of pushing Americans into the embrace of the insurance industry. Although President Obama won re-election in 2012, exit polls showed a majority of Americans wanted government to do less – the reverse of the finding following the 2008 election.[739] If the ACA eliminates the policy space for government to right inequities, including the greatest income disparities since the Gilded Age, how has this helped the progressive cause? The experiment must work, or trust in government's ability to address problems will be shattered.

Nor had President Obama improved trust in government by acting unilaterally in picking and choosing which ACA elements to implement – a role that properly resides with the legislative branch of government. As U.S. Senator Ron Johnson of Wisconsin, a conservative Republican, and George Washington University law professor Jonathan Turley, a liberal, wrote in the *Washington Post*: "Democrats who objected to actions by George W. Bush are silent in the face of the circumvention of Congress by Barack Obama. Republicans who were silent during the Bush years decry such actions by Obama."[740]

However flawed its conception, and execution, surrendering altogether on the ACA would betray the sacrifice of so many progressive activists who had fought for universal health care, not to mention those House Democrats who lost their seats based largely on their votes to do *something* about climate change and health care access. Both parties agree that at least those with preexisting conditions should be able to access health care. Democrats need the courage of their convictions. If the ACA is to be at all fiscally-tenable, they cannot turn and run every time AHIP flogs them about Medicare Advantage cuts, nor can they – as they started to do in 2013 – ingratiate themselves with the medical device lobby by signing bills to repeal, without any offsetting revenue, a tax that helps fund the ACA. Change is not easy.

Democrats could learn something from Republicans. Republicans figured out how to stymie the ACA through state action. Democrats could help the state-centric law succeed through state action. Health insurance, after all, is still regulated at the state level.

If the commercial insurance market is to be utilized, its excesses must be controlled in exchange for the government-facilitated bounty of newly-insured. Rather than be passive clearinghouses for insurance purchases, exchanges should be active purchasers of insurance to use their leverage to drive better prices for consumers. And citizens can advocate that this happen in each state.

Vermont is an exemplar. The state has described its work as recognizing "that health care is a public good, much like electricity." Laura Grubb, a medical doctor, studied the system for the *New England Journal of Medicine*. She touted the degree to which Vermont had involved the public and stakeholders in its reform process, and its having "created one board to consider all the variables" – with "jurisdiction over payment reform, insurance exchanges, rate setting, hospital-budget authorization, resource and workforce allocation, state formulary establishment, regulation of insurance carriers, and maintenance of a statewide quality-assurance program."[741] She found compelling the fact that "a central board can coordinate all implementation efforts, reduce redundancy and bureaucracy, and improve transparency."

Of an exchange, Governor Peter Shumlin stated: "We feel strongly that the exchange is not the answer to all of Vermont's health care problems. If we just passed the exchange, we would not contain costs adequately and be able to provide universal access."[742] Instead, the exchange would be a means to elicit federal dollars to achieve a single-payer system.

Yet even progressive Vermont shows the path forward is difficult. Shumlin nearly lost his 2014 re-election after his opponents outpolled him. Vermont allows independent candidates, and an October 2014 gubernatorial debate featured all seven candidates – some decidedly odd. As the *Burlington Free Press* related, voters were upset that Shumlin "failed to deliver on promises of a financing plan for government-funded health coverage" and "failed to fix technical problems with the state's version of the federal health care exchange[.]"[743]

Following the 2014 election, Shumlin, the chair of the Democratic Governors Association, abandoned Vermont's single-payer plan. Even had it gone forward, the state is so tiny, with just over 626,000 residents, that almost anything it does can be dismissed as having occurred in a microcosm.

Thus the probability of other states following Vermont is very slim. John McDonough, a former Massachusetts legislator and doctor who had advocated for single-payer in the 1990s, wrote in *The New England Journal of Medicine* that he had "[a]fter years of failure, I reluctantly concluded that single payer is too heavy a lift for a state."[744] Short of a single-payer system, though, states could also capitalize and introduce public options – akin to the ill-fated ACA CO-OPs – to compete with commercial insurers and give options to consumers, particularly those in rural areas or states underserved by the commercial market.

Having insured almost all of its residents, Massachusetts was also taking the next step. In 2012 Governor Patrick signed a law designed to control health care costs. A Health Policy Commission, governed by an 11-member board, would establish statewide health care cost growth benchmarks – to be no greater than the state's economic growth rate. The goal was to save $200 billion over fifteen years, beginning in 2013. For five years, from 2018 through 2022, the benchmark for health care cost inflation would actually be a half-point less than that of the state's Gross State Product economic growth factor.[745]

Maryland, having gotten hospitals to agree to a new revenue cap in addition to an existing, nation-leading system where regulators oversaw hospital rates, had the chance to go even further than Massachusetts. As described before, the existing hospital price-control system in Maryland had allowed higher Medicare rates – which facilitated a displacement of costs to Medicare. There also existed some perverse incentives to schedule more procedures as a way of beating the price-controls. By including Medicare payments as part of a cap on spending growth under the new system, Maryland, as Sarah Kliff wrote in the *Washington Post*, might look "more like

Germany and Switzerland, which aggressively regulate prices, than its neighboring states."[746]

Whether this will work remains to be seen. For 2015, the Maryland Insurance Administration approved rate increases of 10-16% in the individual market for dominant CareFirst BlueCross BlueShield; while those increases were lower than the 23-30% increases the carrier sought, Maryland consumers likely did not feel too celebratory.

Longtime Oregon Governor John Kitzhaber, a Democrat and emergency room physician, was a critic of volume-rewarding fee-for-service medicine. In an effort to control costs, Oregon has adopted a pioneering approach where the state is split into fifteen regions served by Coordinated Care Organizations (CCOs) that have their own fixed budgets for Medicaid services.[747] The objective is to hold the annual growth rate in Medicaid costs to 3.4 percent, as opposed to the projected federal growth rate of 5.4 percent. If this approach were adopted nationally in cases where government is the health care payer, Kitzhaber has estimated it could save the federal budget $1.5 trillion over a decade's time.[748] The reforms are overseen at the state level by a nine-member Oregon Health Policy Board.[749] Each of the CCOs has its own governing board to tie into the area it serves.[750]

Rhode Island is the only state with a health insurance commissioner. Beginning in 2009, Christopher Koller required health insurers to increase their spending on primary care by a percentage point each year for five years.[751] Having concluded hospital consolidation was thwarting cost containment objectives, he also attempted, in 2010, to cap the growth in hospital expenditures at the Medicare consumer price index rate. In a contract extension with Blue Cross and Blue Shield entered into for 2011, the state's largest hospital system, Lifespan, agreed to meet those terms.[752] There was some worry Koller's innovative efforts might not continue when, in 2013, he was replaced as the state's health insurance regulator by a former hospital chief executive officer.[753]

Citizens otherwise unconditionally being fed to the health insurance industry can also fight for their states to have meaningful health insurance rate review. As the ACA example reveals, it is almost impossible to beat the insurance industry within the political process. They can, however, be beaten at the ballot.

I had the experience of battling industry excess three times on the Washington State ballot.

In 2005 they referred an egregious medical malpractice initiative, Initiative 330, to the Legislature. While the Legislature did not pass it, it was unable to coalesce around an alternative to place on the ballot alongside I-330 – patient advocates had to fund an alternative themselves in order to distract the insurance industry. Yet voters rejected I-330 by a 57% margin.

In 2007, the insurance industry sought to repeal a Legislature-passed law that subjected acts of bad faith by property and casualty insurers to up to treble damages. Voters rejected the repeal by a 57% margin.

Finally, in 2010 the insurance industry sought to be able to provide workers' compensation insurance. Sixty percent of voters rejected the privatization effort.

Simply put, voters, unlike politicians, do not unconditionally love the insurance industry. Even after the Obama Administration touted the final ACA open enrollment period figures for 2014 – enrollment that had been prompted by considerable insurer advertising – an April 2014 *NBC News/Wall Street Journal* poll showed only 13% of Americans had either a "great deal" or "quite a bit" of confidence in health insurance companies (more felt positively about the Tea Party and even the Internal Revenue Service).[754] In contrast, 51% described themselves as having "very little" or no confidence in health insurers.

What has changed, however, is the vast stake insurers have in keeping the ACA gravy train rolling. It is not clear that anything can stop them.

Consumers in California took the matter into their own hands. With a Democratic legislature having killed efforts to give their insurance commissioner the ability to reject rate increases, signatures were gathered for **The Insurance Rate Public Justification and Accountability Act**. Signatures were submitted in May 2012, but state election officials were somehow unable to validate them in time for the 2012 ballot – which meant the measure qualified for the 2014 ballot.

Even before signatures were submitted, insurers busily contributed $67,440 checks to fight the initiative.[755] By the end of the campaign over $57 million was spent to defeat the measure.[756] In an era of taxpayer subsidies for health insurers there was no way for consumers to fight a misinformation campaign effectively funded, in part, by their own tax dollars.

Nor were establishment Democrats warm to a reform they had killed in the legislature. In reporting on this, a gleeful *Wall Street Journal* account noted, "Thanks to ObamaCare, liberals are beholden to insurance companies as well as vice versa (talk about ironies!)."[757] In a parody of almost laughable cruelty, insurers formed a front group entitled "Californians Against Higher Health Care Costs." On their behalf, and using the ACA as a sword and a shield, a consultant to exchanges issued a May 2014 report blasting the measure for its alleged potential to jeopardize the Covered

California exchange and create "chaos . . . for opponents of health reform to use in proving 'Obamacare' unworkable."[758] Obligingly, the Covered California executive director warned of "uncertainty" the measure would create.[759]

By August 2014, a point at which almost 70% of Californians polled supported Proposition 45, a panicked Covered California board was making its opposition clear – and considering taking a formal vote to oppose it if individual members were unable to use their titles in opposition. A Sacramento Bee account quoted the president of Consumer Watchdog urging them not to take that step, particularly given the hundreds of millions of dollars in taxpayer support the exchange had received: "Only diehard friends of the insurance companies would dare to put the credibility (of the agency) at risk."[760] Still, the Covered California chair, Diana Dooley – also the state's Health and Human Services secretary for Democratic Governor Jerry Brown – dismissed the measure as "a solution for an old problem — a solution for a time that doesn't exist now."[761] The insurer-disseminated criticisms from ostensible Democrats began taking their toll upon the measure's popularity.

Undaunted by campaign criticism – and with billions of dollars in unregulated surplus cash – Covered California's friends at two nonprofit health insurers, Blue Shield of California and Dignity Health, each purchased luxury skyboxes at Levi's Stadium, the new San Francisco 49ers home, that required a commitment of no less than $2.5 million apiece.[762] The optics did not matter; voters defeated the measure in a result that could not necessarily even be blamed on campaign dollars given the complicity of so many Democratic "leaders" in the Democratic state. Indeed, after the election Nancy Pelosi was even credited with killing Proposition 45 – having been featured in ads with a sound-bite in which she said of the measure, "If I wanted to kill the Affordable Care Act, I would do this."[763]

The necessity of rate review could hardly be clearer. The Kaiser Family Foundation is a strong supporter of the ACA, and yet its own June 2014 poll showed that two-fifths of those with exchange policies found it difficult to afford even subsidized premiums – over three-fifths were concerned those premiums would be unaffordable in the future.[764] Had Florida not surrendered its rate review authority, one could not help but wonder if insurers would have shot for the moon in 2015 with an average rate increase of 13.2% in the individual market – on top of massive 2014 increases.[765]

However, active-purchasing and rate review will not be enough if the costs that drive health insurance prices are unchecked. At a minimum, state legislatures can reign in health care industry empire-building through certificate of need laws. How is it that a society that will not even pay to maintain its roads or public infrastructure any longer can indulge the runaway, passed-along costs of new medical facilities popping up everywhere? Do we need a radiology center on every corner? Where certificate of need laws exist, they should be tightened to encompass entrepreneurial developments in health care – such as "affiliations" between hospitals and image center proliferation – un-contemplated when the laws were enacted.

State legislatures, or insurance commissioners where possible, must also require insurers selling individual market insurance in state-run exchanges to sell small group insurance. The health insurance market was already bad for small businesses prior to the ACA. Their market lacks the economies of scale of large group plans. If small businesses are beset with ACA-driven higher prices, but no opportunity to use their ACA tax credits, the act will not only be unpopular with this vital economic sector but actually harmful to it.

Congress could amend the ACA to allow use of those tax credits in the purchasing of health insurance through employer organizations representing small businesses. As most small businesses did not purchase health insurance prior to the ACA's passage, it would be quite a paradox if imposing upon the small group market expectations that do not exist for say, Wal-Mart's health plan (such as providing the ten "essential health benefits"), actually made small businesses *less likely* to buy insurance. Those expectations should be revisited, especially given that delays to a full transition in many small group markets means that the real pain is yet to be revealed.

I recommend state action with no great optimism. While Democrats at the state level are perhaps not as compromised by lobbying as those in Congress, there is no shortage of health industry money to combat reforms. As the Moreland Commission to Investigate Public Corruption in New York reported:

> Legislative committee chairs often draw much or most of their campaign funds from the very industries they are supposed to oversee. For example, between 2011 and 2012, the Republican Chair of the Senate Health Committee received 56% of his campaign funds from the health industry and another 8% from the insurance industry. The Democratic chair of the Assembly Health Committee similarly received 52% of his funds from the health industry. And the ranking minority members of the two committees collected between 33% and 40% of their funds from those industries.[766]

The example of the Covered California exchange fighting rate review shows how very cozy policymakers in even Democratic states have gotten with insurers now that the ACA has wedded them together. There are more subtle iterations of this problem, such as the refusal of regulators to enforce laws that, by guaranteeing coverage of certain conditions, might raise prices for others.

In Washington State, mental health advocates wrote an August 2014 *Seattle Times* column accusing the elected insurance commissioner, a Democrat, of ignoring a mental health parity law, "allowing millions of Washington residents with insurance to suffer unfair and illegal insurance discrimination."[767] Absent enforcement, "private attorneys have filled the void, winning on an insurer-by-insurer, exclusion-by-exclusion basis. Such litigation is time-consuming and piecemeal." The newspaper itself had made a similar editorial accusation of the commissioner regarding protection of those with autism, and pointed out that his office had not "pursued a single mental-health parity case in the nine years since the state law took effect."[768]

In October 2014 the Washington Supreme Court unanimously rejected an insurer's argument that the insurance commissioner's inaction had effective blessed the insurer's blanket exclusions on neurodevelopmental therapies for those with autism.[769] The court noted "we afford the agency interpretation deference only if the interpretation is not contrary to the plain language of the statute."[770] As the *Seattle Times* editorialized, "It took the Supreme Court justices, not the insurance commissioner, to bring the muscle."[771]

If such discrimination against those who are most vulnerable could be tolerated in a "progressive" state, what hope do health insurance policyholders have elsewhere? Indeed, even in the liberal bastion of the District of Columbia, the exchange's board was left to complain in a September 2014 press release about the failure of the District's insurance regulator to lower 2015 rates. According to the D.C. Health Link press release, independent actuarial analysis had shown most of the approved rates were well beyond what was warranted – a 12.7% small group market increase that affected members of Congress and their staffs, for example, should have been 8.2 percent.[772] Emboldened, the dominant carrier sought a 17.7% increase for its small group Silver plan in 2016.

With a rapidly aging society, one huge health care issue Congress could take up, perhaps without the possibility of bungling, is long-term care. Long-term care insurers are not an entrenched interest like health insurers. Because so many under-priced their products upon entering the market they have closed their books of business to new enrollees, jacking up rates on those still enrolled, and created a classic death spiral for a number of long-term care insurance lines. Where once around 100 companies offered long-term care insurance, there are now a dozen or so that sell significant numbers of policies. Genworth Financial, which controls about one-third of the market, announced premium increases of more than 50% in May 2013.[773]

As the payer of "last resort" the federal government – along with the states – ends up paying for over three-fifths of the skilled nursing care in nursing homes through Medicaid, and pays considerably for long-term care in other settings in those states that have received Medicaid waivers allowing alternatives to nursing home care – over 40% of all costs for long-term care services and supports.[774] Further, the federal government pays for nursing home patients, post hospital-discharge, through Medicare for up to 100 days (although only 20 in full). In contrast, long-term care insurance has become a delay-and-deny product. "With all of the hurdles, trying to get a claim paid can be like an Olympic event" noted one consumer advocate in a *New York Times* article.[775] Washington, D.C. was proposing to make matters worse by further taxing all insurance, including long-term care, to pay for its expensive D.C. Health Link exchange.[776]

As an aging society continues to put funding pressure upon Medicare, a July 2014 report from the Medicare actuary forecasted that providers "may have to withdraw from providing services to Medicare beneficiaries, merge with other provider groups, or shift substantial portions of Medicare costs to their non-Medicare, non-Medicaid payers."[777] In other words, Medicare underfunding would place an even greater burden upon private insurance. It would force "[f]urther consolidation by hospitals, physician practices, and other providers" so that they "can increase their ability to negotiate favorable prices with private health insurance plans."

The elderly are among the most cynical about the ACA, in no small part because there is nothing really in it for them following the repeal of the defined benefit Community Living Assistance Services and Supports (CLASS) long-term care program that was originally a part of the ACA. It is a gaping oversight. Addressing the issue of long-term care would be a way of bolstering support from this demographic.

Left to their own devices on long-term care, states will flounder. New York is among states that will try to shift nursing home patients on Medicaid to managed care – with patient advocates fearing the result. "Managed care isn't going to help — it's just more money going off the top," stated one advocate quoted in the New York Times.[778] To save money, the state started approving politically-connected home care firms that had been previously accused of fraud.[779] Advocates for seniors and those with disabilities were shocked. A report in the Times noted that bribes were allegedly being offered for patient placements, while "[m]any frail people with greater needs were dropped, and providers jockeying for business bought, sold or steered cases according to the new system's calculus: the more enrollees, and the less spent on services, the more money the companies can keep."[780]

The ACA's shortcomings have the real potential to merge with long-term care shortcomings. Imagine the plight of home care workers who are themselves providing Medicaid care but are unable to obtain any coverage themselves in a state like Texas without Medicaid expansion. Facility-based care is also imperiled. Because most costs of skilled nursing care are paid through Medicaid, if Medicaid reimbursement fails to keep pace with costs – costs that will now include health care coverage for caregivers – nursing homes will feel pressured to reduce caregivers and support staff to part-time status to avoid the penalty. This is a fatal trajectory for our most vulnerable citizens. Even a state like Washington, with a state government that is rhetorically pro-ACA, still refuses to pay its Medicaid share of health care costs for its vendors. With the U.S. Supreme Court having validated the Obama Administration's argument that there is no private right of action to enforce Medicaid payment adequacy, a race-to-the-bottom among states may occur unchecked in what is, functionally, our nation's biggest single-payer medical system.

The CLASS concept was not completely off the mark. I believe there would be receptiveness to a guaranteed, defined, long-term care benefit. It could not, however, be funded voluntarily and still be actuarially-sound – that was what doomed CLASS. Some involuntary revenue mechanism, likely a nominal payroll tax (as is true for Medicare), would be required to guarantee a long-term care safety net for all. This is one area where single-payer advocates could at least get their wish.

In conclusion, given the massive infrastructural changes incurred by health care providers and insurers as a result of the ACA, quite apart from the political capital expended, full retreat is unfeasible. At a minimum the ACA is a bridge to a changed health care world, if not a world that looks exactly as is envisioned by the ACA. "Right now we are beginning to enter what is all but certain to be a period of major reconsideration of the whole mess," wrote economist Gar Alperovitz in his 2013 book *What Then Must We Do?*[781]

Exchanges, whether state-run or federally-facilitated, represent an unprecedented experiment, and investment, in reshaping a vital part of our economy. The inauspicious start to the 2014 reforms created the specter of consumers beset with an unpopular mandate while being unable to fully enjoy the benefits promised them.

Further confusion or delays would only add to conservative criticism that government lacks the competence to play this new role in the health care market.

Even the best-case scenario is not entirely rosy. By 2025, the Congressional Budget Office estimates that as many as 31 million Americans, or one-tenth of the population, will still be uninsured, some of whom will be the 9-10 million who will have lost employment-based health insurance.[782] Just a few huge variables that loom include the effects of the Cadillac tax, long-overdue non-discrimination rules, Congressional appetite for assumed Medicare Advantage cost savings, and the future of risk-corridor subsidies for those carriers assuming disproportionate risk.

The merging of health insurance giants into even more massive behemoths just further undermines the premise of state regulation being able to corral insurer excesses. Absent a public option to afford competition, we are already approaching de facto "single payer" in much of the country as there simply is no real choice.

Given the uncertain battlefield of insurance regulators and state politics it is impossible to imagine how this state-centric law in its current form can possibly succeed unaltered in the long-term. If Democrats are not committed to meaningful cost controls, and they certainly do not appear to be, perhaps they should just effectively call what may be a Republican bluff. They can agree to the "free market" approach of a proposal like that put forth by the conservative 2017 Project – give consumers tax credits (at least means-testing them, which the 2017 Project wouldn't do) to purchase insurance, create a federal high-risk pool for those without affordable options, augment what the 2017 Project has proposed by continuing Medicaid expansion for the working poor, and call it a day. This would be far more explicable to voters, and would represent progress that could perhaps be sustained. Furthermore, states could still improve on the model through public options and rate review.

Is the ACA too big to fail, to borrow the popular expression from the 2008 banking crisis? The well-being of millions of Americans, quite apart from the federal budget and the U.S. economy, hangs in the balance.

NOTES

1) INTRODUCTION

1 http://www.pnhp.org/news/2008/june/barack_obama_on_sing.php

2 http://www.commonwealthfund.org/Publications/Fund-Reports/2013/Apr/Insuring-the-Future.aspx

3 http://www.commonwealthfund.org/News/News-Releases/2012/Aug/Potentially-Preventable-Deaths.aspx

4 http://www.savethechildrenweb.org/SOWM-2013/files/assets/common/downloads/State%20of%20the%20WorldOWM-2013.pdf

5 https://www.cia.gov/library/publications/the-world-factbook/rankorder/2091rank.html

6 http://healthland.time.com/2013/02/20/what-makes-health-care-so-expensive/

7 http://blog.seattlepi.com/brendanwilliams/2009/12/21/health-care-deform/

8 http://www.nytimes.com/2013/05/07/us/politics/gop-is-readying-a-new-offensive-over-health-law.html?pagewanted=all&_r=0

9 http://www.washingtonpost.com/blogs/fact-checker/post/bachmanns-absurd-claim-of-a-vast-irs-health-database-of-sensitive-intimate-information/2013/05/23/7f2953c2-c3f8-11e2-8c3b-0b5e9247e8ca_blog.html

10 http://thehill.com/blogs/healthwatch/health-reform-implementation/328133-to-bachmann-obamacare-is-deathcare-

11 http://www.msnbc.com/msnbc/dem-thinks-he-can-win-the-anti-obama

12 http://www.washingtonpost.com/page/2010-2019/WashingtonPost/2014/04/29/National-Politics/Polling/question_13961.xml?uuid=tnco4s9TEeOnFL5-fxQghQ

13 Bob Woodward, *The Price of Politics* (Simon & Schuster, 2013), 56.

14 http://www.washingtonpost.com/blogs/wonkblog/wp/2014/01/05/the-group-that-got-health-reform-passed-is-declaring-victory-and-going-home/?tid=hpModule_ba0d-4c2a-86a2-11e2-9d71-f0feafdd1394

15   http://www.washingtonpost.com/blogs/wonkblog/wp/2013/12/24/shopping-for-health-insurance-is-hard-understanding-it-is-even-harder/

16   http://kaiserhealthnews.org/news/beyond-repeal-and-replace-ideas-emerge-to-improve-simplify-health-law/

17   http://www.washingtonpost.com/politics/liberal-groups-launch-campaigns-to-boost-turnout-based-on-obamacare-support/2014/05/09/6f791808-d6c2-11e3-8a78-8fe50322a72c_story.html

18   http://www.politico.com/story/2014/10/colorado-health-care-cancellation-111991.html#ixzz3GR0CymfM

19   http://www.washingtonpost.com/page/2010-2019/WashingtonPost/2014/10/15/National-Politics/Polling/question_14764.xml?uuid=XeZmgFRZEeS4bRhKwoE4jQ

20   http://www.washingtonpost.com/blogs/plum-line/wp/2014/04/22/morning-plum-what-does-running-on-obamacare-look-like/

21   http://primarycolors.net/pagov-obamacare-frenemy-allyson-schwartz-running-on-obamacare-now/

22   http://blogs.rollcall.com/wgdb/sen-charles-schumer-health-care-distracted-democrats-middle-class/?dcz

23   http://seattletimes.com/html/nationworld/2024766672_apxappollhealthcareinsecurity.html

24   http://workforces.aflac.com/download/pdf/overview/2014_Executive_Summary.pdf

25   http://www.nytimes.com/2014/06/09/opinion/shifts-in-charity-health-care.html?hp&rref=opinion

26   http://seattletimes.com/html/nationworld/2024766672_apxappollhealthcareinsecurity.html

27   http://www.nytimes.com/2014/10/26/us/insurers-consumer-data-isnt-ready-for-enrollees.html?rref=us&module=Ribbon&version=origin&region=Header&action=click&contentCollection=U.S.&pgtype=article

2) THE COMPROMISER-IN-CHIEF

28   http://docs.fdrlibrary.marist.edu/odssast.html

29   http://www.trumanlibrary.org/publicpapers/index.php?pid=483

30   http://www.pnhp.org/facts/a-brief-history-universal-health-care-efforts-in-the-us

31   http://www.presidency.ucsb.edu/ws/?pid=4337.#axzz2hZE22sIa

32   http://www.clintonlibrary.gov/assets/storage/Research%20%20Digital%20Library/formerlywithheld/batch5/2006-0885-F.pdf

33 http://www.clintonlibrary.gov/assets/storage/Research%20%20Digital%20Library/for-merlywithheld/batch5/2006-0885-F.pdf

34 Bill Clinton, *My Life* (Vintage Books, 2005), 555.

35 http://www.nytimes.com/1994/06/16/us/moynihan-health-bill-a-political-enigma.html

36 G. Galvin Mackenzie and Robert Weisbrot, *The Liberal Hour: Washington and the Politics of Change in the 1960s* (Penguin Books, 2009), 79.

37 http://mobile.nytimes.com/2013/10/23/us/politics/sebelius-thrust-into-firestorm-on-exchanges.html

38 Ron Suskind, *Confidence Men: Wall Street, Washington, and the Education of a President* (Harper Perennial, 2011), 270-72.

39 Suskind, *Confidence Men*, 322.

40 http://www.nytimes.com/2012/06/09/us/politics/e-mails-reveal-extent-of-obamas-deal-with-industry-on-health-care.html?pagewanted=all&_r=0

41 http://phrma.org/media/releases/phrma-statement-health-care-reform-agreement

42 http://www.whitehouse.gov/the_press_office/Remarks-by-the-President-to-a-Joint-Session-of-Congress-on-Health-Care

43 Jonathan Alter, *The Center Holds: Obama and his Enemies* (Simon & Schuster 2013), 160.

3) THE DEAN OF THE HOUSE

44 http://swampland.time.com/2009/09/09/john-dingell-sr-a-legacy/

45 http://www.politico.com/blogs/thecrypt/0908/Dingell_prophet_of_doom.html

46 http://money.cnn.com/2009/09/11/news/economy/dingell_health_care.fortune/

47 Id.

48 http://www.politifact.com/truth-o-meter/statements/2009/aug/10/sarah-palin/sarah-palin-barack-obama-death-panel/

49 http://www.huffingtonpost.com/2009/08/12/grassley-endorses-death-p_n_257677.html

50 http://www.newrepublic.com/article/75077/how-they-did-it

51 Thomas Frank, *Pity the Billionaire: The Hard-Times Swindle and the Unlikely Comeback of the Right* (Picador, 2012), 172.

52 Ibid., 173.

53 http://www.nytimes.com/2013/06/13/nyregion/weiners-record-in-house-intensity-publicity-and-limited-results.html?pagewanted=1&_r=0&hp

54 http://democrats.energycommerce.house.gov/Press_111/20090731/hr3200_weiner_1.pdf

55 http://democrats.energycommerce.house.gov/index.php?q=news/statement-of-admin-istration-policy-on-hr-3962

56 http://democrats.energycommerce.house.gov/sites/default/files/documents/Statement-Waxman-Floor-HR-3962-Affordable-Health-Care-America-Act-2009-11-7.pdf

57 http://www.gpo.gov/fdsys/pkg/CREC-2009-11-07/pdf/CREC-2009-11-07-pt1-PgH12623-3.pdf#page=299

58 Ibid.

59 http://www.plannedparenthood.org/about-us/newsroom/press-releases/planned-par-enthood-condemns-passage-stupak-pitts-amendment-30821.htm

60 http://www.nrlc.org/press_releases_new/Release110709b.html

61 http://www.washingtonpost.com/wp-dyn/content/article/2010/03/26/AR2010032602921.html

62 http://opinionator.blogs.nytimes.com/2013/07/03/obamas-insurance-delay-wont-affect-many/?hp

63 http://online.wsj.com/article/SB10001424052702303901504577458741425317930.html

64 http://www.washingtonpost.com/politics/challenges-have-dogged-obamas-health-plan-since-2010/2013/11/02/453fba42-426b-11e3-a624-41d661b0bb78_story.html?hpid=z1

4) SENATOR SELLOUT

65 http://www.huffingtonpost.com/2012/12/05/liz-fowler-johnson-johnson_n_2245367.html

66 http://www.opensecrets.org/politicians/summary.php?type=C&cid=N00004643&newMem=N&cycle=2010

67 http://www.opensecrets.org/politicians/summary.php?cycle=2010&type=I&cid=N00027605&newMem=N

68 http://articles.washingtonpost.com/2009-11-20/news/36815997_1_max-baucus-white-house-staff-rahm-emanuel

69 http://www.politico.com/news/stories/1209/30478.html

70 http://voices.washingtonpost.com/ezra-klein/2009/05/ted_kennedys_coming_health_car.html

71 Ibid.

72 http://www.finance.senate.gov/issue/?id=32be19bd-491e-4192-812f-f65215c1ba65

73 http://www.kaiserhealthnews.org/stories/2009/june/03/baucus-single-payer.aspx

74 http://www.finance.senate.gov/library/hearings/index.cfm?PageNum_rs=4&c=111

75 http://www.finance.senate.gov/issue/?id=32be19bd-491e-4192-812f-f65215c1ba65

76   http://www.clintonlibrary.gov/assets/storage/Research%20%20Digital%20Library/formerlywithheld/batch5/2008-0308-F.pdf

77   http://www.washingtonpost.com/wp-dyn/content/article/2010/12/09/AR2010120906436.html

78   http://www.washingtonpost.com/blogs/wonkblog/wp/2014/01/05/the-group-that-got-health-reform-passed-is-declaring-victory-and-going-home/?tid=hpModule_ba0d-4c2a-86a2-11e2-9d71-f0feafdd1394

79   http://www.collins.senate.gov/public/index.cfm/press-releases?ID=ad910728-802a-23ad-4ea9-87b3a4b5f4e1

80   http://www.huffingtonpost.com/2009/08/05/rockefeller-stalling-repu_n_252147.html

81   http://www.finance.senate.gov/hearings/hearing/?id=d7f3a956-9ef2-b6c0-6486-3755d1b722a6

82   http://www.finance.senate.gov/hearings/hearing/?id=d7c648b3-085d-2602-c486-64625ea39e88

83   http://mediamatters.org/research/2012/03/29/foxs-bream-falsely-suggests-cornhusker-kickback/186037

84   Jacob S. Hacker & Paul Pierson, *Winner-Take-All Politics: How Washington Made the Rich Richer – and Turned its Back on the Middle Class* (Simon & Schuster, 2011), 268

85   http://thehill.com/blogs/healthwatch/health-reform-implementation/294501-baucus-warns-of-huge-train-wreck-in-obamacare-implementation

86   http://hoh.rollcall.com/sold-baucus-million-dollar-plus-home-set-to-close/

87   http://www.washingtontimes.com/news/2013/apr/10/obamacare-creator-jay-rockefeller-now-says-law-bey/

88   http://www.harkin.senate.gov/documents/pdf/4d24b42007d71.pdf

89   Mike Lofgren, *The Party's Over: How Republicans Went Crazy, Democrats Became Useless, and the Middle Class Got Shafted* (Viking Adult, 2012), 187

5) THE SUPREME COURT

90   http://media.npr.org/assets/blogs/health/images/2011/01/vinsonruling.pdf

91   http://www.motherjones.com/mojo/2012/03/obamacare-supreme-court-disaster

92   http://www.washingtonpost.com/blogs/wonkblog/post/sympathy-for-don-verrilli/2012/03/28/gIQAtEE6gS_blog.html

93   http://www.pbs.org/newshour/bb/health/jan-june12/scotusday2_03-27.html

94   Michael J. Graetz & Jerry L. Mashaw, *Constitutional Uncertainty and the Design of Social Insurance: Reflections on the Obamacare Case*, HARV. L. & POL. REV. 343, 348 (2013).

95   *Id.*

96   Kirstin Downey, *The Woman Behind the New Deal: The Life and Legacy of Frances Perkins – Social Security, Unemployment Insurance, and the Minimum Wage* (Anchor Books, 2010), 235-36.

97   http://law.ga.gov/press-releases/2012-06-28/deal-olens-disappointed-ruling-obamacare

98   http://www.paul.senate.gov/?p=press_release&id=562

99   http://www.theatlantic.com/politics/archive/2013/06/all-those-people-who-were-supposed-to-get-insurance-probably-wont/276752/

6) THE PATIENT PROTECTION AND AFFORDABLE CARE ACT

100 Joseph Stiglitz, *The Price of Inequality: How Today's Divided Society Endangers Our Future* (W.W. Norton & Co., 2013), 346.

101 http://healthpolicyandmarket.blogspot.com/2007/10/analysis-of-senator-john-mccains-health.html

102 http://www.clubforgrowth.org/projects/?subsec=35&chamber=house&year=2013&alert=16120

103 http://www.freedomworks.org/blog/jwithrow/coalition-letter-in-support-of-the-helping-sick-am

104 http://thehill.com/blogs/healthwatch/health-reform-implementation/295743-white-house-threatens-to-veto-gop-bill-on-high-risk-pools

105 http://www.finance.senate.gov/imo/media/doc/04152013%20Tavenner%20QFRs1.pdf

106 http://www.nytimes.com/2013/08/13/us/a-limit-on-consumer-costs-is-delayed-in-health-care-law.html?hpw&_r=0

107 http://www.alec.org/publications/the-state-legislators-guide-to-repealing-obamacare/

108 http://www.foxnews.com/us/2013/05/13/cancer-patients-could-face-high-costs-for-medications-under-obamacare-critics/

109 http://www.washingtonpost.com/national/health-science/aids-advocates-say-drug-coverage-in-some-marketplace-plans-is-inadequate/2013/12/09/0fca0fd0-5d18-11e3-9 5c2-13623eb2b0e1_story.html?hpid=z1

110 http://www.nytimes.com/2014/05/30/business/four-insurers-accused-of-discriminating-against-people-with-hiv.html?hp

111 http://www.kaiserhealthnews.org/Stories/2014/July/08/Some-Plans-Skew-Drug-Benefits-To-Drive-Away-Patients-Advocates-Warn.aspx?utm_source=khn&utm_medium=internal&utm_campaign=viewed

112 http://www.vanityfair.com/politics/2014/10/obamacare-health-care-reform

113 Id.

114 Id.

115 Id.

116 *See* Jon R. Gabel et al., *More Than Half Of Individual Health Plans Offer Coverage That Falls Short Of What Can Be Sold Through Exchanges As Of 2014*, 31 Health Aff. 1339, 1343 (2012).

117 http://www.oregonlive.com/health/index.ssf/2013/05/two_oregon_insurers_reconsider.html

118 http://www.pwc.com/en_US/us/health-industries/health-insurance-exchanges/assets/pwc-hri-health-insurance-premium.pdf

119 http://www.naic.org/documents/committees_b_related_wp_rate_review.pdf

120 http://www.floir.com/siteDocuments/SenatePPACA_2-18-13.pdf

121 http://www.floir.com/sections/mrtu/docs/13-15901BronzeSG.pdf

122 http://docs.house.gov/meetings/IF/IF02/20130520/100868/HHRG-113-IF02-Wstate-DurhamD-20130520.pdf

123 http://www.nytimes.com/2012/11/21/us/politics/administration-defines-benefits-under-health-law.html?_r=0

124 http://cciio.cms.gov/resources/files/Files2/12162011/essential_health_benefits_bulletin.pdf

125 http://www.iom.edu/~/media/Files/Report%20Files/2011/Essential-Health-Benefits-Balancing-Coverage-and-Cost/Essential%20Health%20Benefits%20RB_FINAL.pdf

126 http://www.pewstates.org/projects/stateline/headlines/qa-how-aca-will-affect-people-with-autism-85899496217

127 http://www.iom.edu/~/media/Files/Report%20Files/2011/Essential-Health-Benefits-Balancing-Coverage-and-Cost/EHBslides.pdf

128 http://www.healthaffairs.org/healthpolicybriefs/brief.php?brief_id=91

129 http://democrats.energycommerce.house.gov/sites/default/files/documents/Sebelius-PPACA-Essential-Health-Benefits-2012-2-6.pdf

130 http://www.naic.org/documents/index_health_reform_comments_121219_ehb.pdf

131 http://www.nidcd.nih.gov/health/statistics/pages/quick.aspx

132 https://www.congress.gov/bill/114th-congress/house-bill/1653

133 http://www.finance.senate.gov/imo/media/doc/04152013%20Tavenner%20QFRs1.pdf

134 http://usatoday30.usatoday.com/money/industries/health/2002-12-18-hca-settlement-_x.htm

135 http://www.cms.gov/CCIIO/Resources/Data-Resources/Downloads/2012-mlr-issuer-rebates-06042013.pdf

136 http://www.cbo.gov/sites/default/files/cbofiles/attachments/43472-07-24-2012-Coverage Estimates.pdf

137 http://www.unitedhealthgroup.com/investors/~/media/D6237677FB704A47B3F09D00 5A6A4C16.asx

138 http://www.naic.org/documents/committees_e_hrsi_hhs_response_mlr_100601.pdf

139 http://www.alec.org/publications/the-state-legislators-guide-to-repealing-obamacare/

140 http://www.cms.gov/CCIIO/Programs-and-Initiatives/Health-Insurance-Market-Reforms/mlr_adj_maine.html

141 http://www.cms.gov/CCIIO/Programs-and-Initiatives/Health-Insurance-Market-Reforms/mlr_adj_texas.html

142 http://www.cms.gov/CCIIO/Programs-and-Initiatives/Health-Insurance-Market-Reforms/mlr_adj_wisconsin.html

143 http://www.cms.gov/CCIIO/Programs-and-Initiatives/Health-Insurance-Market-Reforms/Downloads/2011-1215-FL-MLR-Adj-Determination-Letter.pdf

144 http://www.naic.org/documents/committees_ex_phip_resolution_11_22.pdf

145 http://www.washingtonpost.com/national/health-science/co-ops-gear-up-to-compete-with-major-insurers-under-new-health-law/2013/06/01/384e8b40-ca31-11e2-9245-773c0123c027_story.html

146 http://www.modernhealthcare.com/article/20140226/NEWS/302269953

147 http://www.washingtonpost.com/politics/health-co-ops-created-to-foster-competition-and-lower-insurance-costs-are-facing-danger/2013/10/22/e1c961fe-3809-11e3-ae46-e4248e75c8ea_story.html?hpid=z1

148 http://www.washingtonpost.com/local/md-politics/maryland-online-exchange-problems-cloud-doctors-vision-for-health-care/2014/03/07/5e856626-8e6c-11e3-b227-12a45d109e03_story.html

149 http://www.clintonlibrary.gov/assets/storage/Research%20%20Digital%20Library/formerlywithheld/batch5/2006-0885-F.pdf

150 http://www.nfib.com/research-foundation/cribsheets/individual-mandate

151 http://online.wsj.com/article/SB10001424127887324326504578467560106322692.html

152 http://www.quinnipiac.edu/images/polling/us/us07022014_U73jabn.pdf

153 http://www.iop.harvard.edu/sites/default/files_new/fall%20poll%2014%20-%20topline.pdf

154 http://www.naic.org/documents/index_health_reform_comments_121219_market_reform.pdf

155 http://www.washingtonpost.com/blogs/wonkblog/wp/2014/06/05/just-13-percent-of-uninsured-people-will-pay-the-obamacare-penalty-report-says/?tid=hpModule_79c38dfc-8691-11e2-9d71-f0feafdd1394

156 Sean Lowry & Jane Gravelle, "The Affordable Care Act and Small Business: Economic Issues," Congressional Research Service (April 2, 2014), pg. 21.

157 http://www.nytimes.com/2013/10/24/business/health-law-fails-to-keep-prices-low-in-rural-areas.html?pagewanted=3&_r=1&hp

158 http://www.wahbexchange.org/files/2713/9888/1218/WAHBE_End_of_Open_Enrollment_Data_Report_FINAL.pdf

159 http://www.finance.senate.gov/hearings/hearing/?id=d8c677d4-fa54-11f2-1c31-64fbd9076f32

160 http://report.heritage.org/bg2534

161 http://www.washingtonpost.com/blogs/wonkblog/wp/2013/07/17/obamas-last-campaign-inside-the-white-house-plan-to-sell-obamacare/?hpid=z1

162 http://www.whitehouse.gov/sites/default/files/docs/competition_memo_5-30-13.pdf

163 http://www.washingtonpost.com/business/economy/blue-cross-blue-shield-bets-big-on-health-care-exchanges/2013/06/21/d4d82db6-da87-11e2-a9f2-42ee3912ae0e_story.html

164 http://www.nytimes.com/2013/06/17/health/choice-of-health-plans-to-vary-sharply-from-state-to-state.html?src=rechp

165 http://blog.gulflive.com/mississippi-press-news/2013/06/mississippi_house_votes_to_ren_1.html

166 http://www.politico.com/story/2013/07/obamacare-mississippi-health-care-exchange-94842.html

167 http://www.politico.com/magazine/story/2014/10/mississippi-burned-obamacare-112181_Page4.html#ixzz3HYvl1Lcf

168 http://www.nytimes.com/2013/10/24/business/health-law-fails-to-keep-prices-low-in-rural-areas.html?hp&_r=1&

169 http://www.freep.com/article/20140624/OPINION05/306180016/obamacare-michigan

170 http://www.coveredca.com/news/PDFs/regional-stats-march/march-regionals-graphics.pdf

171 http://www.charlotteobserver.com/2014/10/22/5259998/blue-cross-ncs-affordable-care.html#.VFmqLN08KK0

172 http://m.bizjournals.com/seattle/print-edition/2014/04/04/premeras-power-politics.html?page=all&r=full

173 http://www.washingtonpost.com/blogs/wonkblog/wp/2013/05/30/wonkbook-as-obamacare-starts-health-insurers-are-just-guessing/

174 http://www.washingtonpost.com/blogs/wonkblog/wp/2013/09/25/how-much-will-obamacare-premiums-cost-depends-on-where-you-live/?hpid=z3

175 http://www.avalerehealth.net/news/spotlight/Exchange_Benefit_Design_Release.pdf

176 http://seattletimes.com/html/localnews/2022371201_exchangenetworksxml.html

177 http://news.yahoo.com/health-law-concerns-cancer-centers070542928.html;_
ylt=AwrBEiEjnClTm08AizTQtDMD

178 http://www.dol.gov/ebsa/faqs/faq-aca18.html

179 http://www.whitehouse.gov/the-press-office/2013/10/21/remarks-president-affordable-
care-act

180 http://www.irs.gov/pub/irs-pdf/p1854.pdf

181 http://www.federalreserve.gov/econresdata/2013-report-economic-well-being-us-
households-201407.pdf

182 http://www.usatoday.com/story/news/nation/2015/01/01/middle-class-workers-strug-
gle-to-pay-for-care-despite-insurance/19841235/

183 http://www.rollingstone.com/politics/news/in-defense-of-obama-
20141008#ixzz3Fm08GkTh

184 http://www.floir.com/siteDocuments/IndiviSmallGrpMarketMonthlyPremsbyGAPSil-
verPlanAnalyses9613.pdf

185 http://www.floir.com/PressReleases/viewmediarelease.aspx?id=2070

186 http://www.startribune.com/business/279332032.html

187 Id.

188 http://www.washingtonpost.com/blogs/fact-checker/wp/2013/10/30/obamas-pledge-
that-no-one-will-take-away-your-health-plan/?hpid=z2

189 http://www.politico.com/story/2013/11/bill-maher-debbie-wasserman-schultz-spar-
over-obama-lie-99253.html?hp=r1

190 http://www.washingtonpost.com/politics/transcript-president-obamas-nov-14-state-
ment-on-health-care/2013/11/14/6233e352-4d48-11e3-ac54-aa84301ced81_story.html

191 http://www.nytimes.com/2013/12/03/us/politics/insurers-are-offered-assistance-for-
losses.html?hpw&rref=politics&_r=1&

192 http://www.nytimes.com/2014/03/06/us/politics/obama-extends-renewal-period-for-
noncompliant-insurance-policies.html?_r=0

193 http://chis.georgetown.edu/pdfs/Active%20Purchaser%206%203%2011.pdf

194 http://www.hbe.arkansas.gov/FFE/Plan/AP/PMACActivePurchaserIssueBriefJune2012.
pdf

195 http://www.washingtonpost.com/blogs/wonkblog/wp/2013/06/09/chart-heres-how-
obamacares-markets-are-shaping-up/

196 http://chis.georgetown.edu/pdfs/Active%20Purchaser%206%203%2011.pdf

197 http://www.npr.org/blogs/health/2013/05/24/186430860/health-insurance-at-good-
prices-coming-to-calif-exchange

198 http://www.washingtonpost.com/blogs/wonkblog/wp/2013/05/28/california-didnt-have-rate-shock-but-california-isnt-like-most-other-states/

199 http://www.contracostatimes.com/news/ci_21205540/subsidized-health-insurance-marketplace-takes-shape?source=rss

200 http://www.insurance.ca.gov/0400-news/0100-press-releases/2013/release043-13.cfm

201 http://www.latimes.com/business/money/la-fi-mo-aetna-california-health-insurance-20130618,0,3414612.story

202 http://www.finance.senate.gov/imo/media/doc/04152013%20Tavenner%20QFRs1.pdf

203 http://seattletimes.com/html/localnews/2021661375_acaplanvotexml.html

204 http://seattletimes.com/html/localnews/2021968776_acachildrenssuitxml.html

205 http://www.thenewstribune.com/welcome_page/?shf=/2014/11/14/3488082_state-is-paying-former-insurance.html

206 http://www.spokesman.com/stories/2013/nov/24/providence-facilities-doctors-excluded-by-two/

207 http://www.politico.com/story/2013/12/doctors-the-new-gop-weapon-in-obamacare-fight-100617.html#ixzz2mTdMuPLX

208 http://www.washingtonpost.com/blogs/govbeat/wp/2014/07/28/health-care-ballot-measure-divides-south-dakota-republicans/

209 http://www.argusleader.com/story/news/politics/2014/07/28/questions-cost-choice-frame-sd-medical-debate/13258281/

210 http://www.argusleader.com/story/news/politics/2014/11/04/ballot-measures-support-minimum-wage-gambling-options-changes-health-insurance/18507001/

7) THE ACHILLES HEEL OF STATE REGULATION

211 http://www.kaiserhealthnews.org/stories/2013/april/18/actuaries-ties-to-insurance-rate-shock.aspx

212 Gar Alperovitz, *What Then Must We Do? Straight Talk About the Next American Revolution* (Chelsea Green Publishing, 2013), 84.

213 http://robertreich.org/post/119767465905#

214 http://www.reuters.com/article/2015/07/02/us-cigna-m-a-anthem-idUSKC-N0PC1XJ20150702

215 http://www.cms.gov/CCIIO/Resources/Fact-Sheets-and-FAQs/rate_review_fact_sheet.html

216 http://www.naic.org/documents/hhs_rate_review_reg.pdf

217 http://www.feinstein.senate.gov/public/index.cfm/press-releases?ID=41c2658b-a565-44ca-a525-ec9078ac4672

218 http://www.insurancejournal.com/news/southeast/2013/06/04/294130.htm?print

219 http://www.flsenate.gov/Session/Bill/2013/1842/BillText/er/PDF

220 http://www.billnelson.senate.gov/news/details.cfm?id=342868&

221 http://www.tdi.texas.gov/pubs/consumer/cb005.html#

222 http://www.npr.org/blogs/health/2012/07/20/157117573/texas-slow-to-review-health-insurance-rate-hikes

223 http://www.washingtonpost.com/blogs/wonkblog/wp/2013/11/19/white-house-republican-governors-finally-find-obamacare-agreement/?hpid=z1

224 http://www.insurance.ca.gov/0400-news/0100-press-releases/2013/release043-13.cfm

225 https://myportal.dfs.ny.gov/c/document_library/get_file?uuid=b4803066-2164-4621-ba31-4a32c39f5335&groupId=538523

226 http://www.dfs.ny.gov/about/press2014/pr1409041.htm

227 http://www.naic.org/documents/index_health_reform_rate_review_comments_nprm_110228.pdf

228 http://www.urban.org/UploadedPDF/412649-Monitoring-State-Implementation-of-the-Affordable-Care-Act-in-10-States.pdf

229 http://www.insurance.state.pa.us/dsf/ppaca_related_filings.html

230 http://health.wusf.usf.edu/post/no-rate-increase-can-it-be#.U6miaadwweR.twitter

231 http://oci.wi.gov/pressrel/0111comm.htm

232 http://doi.sc.gov/750/Meet-the-Director

233 http://www.texastribune.org/2012/09/07/insurance-commissioner-answers-industry-bias-charg/

234 http://www.dallasnews.com/opinion/editorials/20120824-editorial-regulator-should-be-protecting-consumers.ece

235 http://www.insurance.ohio.gov/Newsroom/Pages/06062013ACAProposedRates.aspx

236 http://www.insurance.ohio.gov/Newsroom/Documents/ACAProposedRatesFactSheet.pdf

237 http://codes.ohio.gov/orc/3923.021

238 http://www.insurance.ohio.gov/pages/2015%20Exchange%20Premiums.aspx

239 http://www.insurance.ohio.gov/Newsroom/Pages/05292014FederalExchangePremiums.aspx

240 http://www.oci.ga.gov/PublicInformation/Bio.aspx

241 http://www.ok.gov/oid/Public_Information/About_OID/About_Commissioner_Doak.html

242　http://usatoday30.usatoday.com/money/industries/insurance/2008-03-30-nocommish_N.htm

243　http://www.leg.state.vt.us/statutes/fullsection.cfm?Title=08&Chapter=107&Section=04062

244　http://gmcboard.vermont.gov/sites/gmcboard/files/12%2012%2013%20Rate%20Review%20Rule.pdf

245　http://www.cms.gov/CCIIO/Resources/Data-Resources/Downloads/2012-mlr-rebates-by-state-08-01-2013.pdf

246　http://m.bizjournals.com/seattle/print-edition/2014/04/04/premeras-power-politics.html?page=all&r=full

247　http://www.insurance.wa.gov/health-rates/Search.aspx

248　http://www.insurance.wa.gov/about-oic/news-media/news-releases/2014/documents/rate-changes-as-of-2013.pdf

249　http://www.bea.gov/newsreleases/regional/spi/spi_newsrelease.htm

250　http://seattletimes.com/html/localnews/2023644322_premerasettlementxml.html

251　http://www.idahostatesman.com/2013/03/03/2474785/idaho-health-insurers-pile-up.html#storylink=cpy

252　http://consumersunion.org/news/nonprofit-health-insurers-hoard-billions-in-surpluses/

253　http://seattletimes.com/html/editorials/2023067177_editmedicalinsurancetransparencybillxml.html

254　http://premeranews.com/2014/09/05/statement-on-premeras-individual-market-plans-in-alaska-under-the-aca/

8)　THE BATTLE AGAINST STATE EXCHANGES

255　*See* Nat'l Fed'n of Indep. Bus. v. Sebelius, 132 S. Ct. 2566 (2012).

256　http://www.texaswatchdog.org/2011/01/state-rep-john-zerwas-says-his-plan-for-texas-insurance-exchange/1294958898.column.

257　http://www.dallasnews.com/opinion/editorials/20120720-editorial-health-exchange-would-benefit-texans.ece

258　http://governor.state.tx.us/files/press-office/O-SebeliusKathleen201211150621.pdf

259　http://www.nytimes.com/2013/07/19/us/promoting-health-insurance-exchange-with-no-help-from-state.html?src=rechp&_r=0

260　http://www.issues2000.org/Archive/2012_State_Health_Care.htm

261　http://www.ajc.com/news/news/local-govt-politics/governor-pulls-health-exchange-bill-after-tea-part/nQrf8/

262 *Id.*

263 http://missoulian.com/news/state-and-regional/federal-officials-left-to-set-up-montana-health-insurance-exchange/article_5527e210-ae6e-11e0-a447-001cc4c002e0.html.

264 http://watchdog.org/49186/montana-insurance-exchange-on-the-agenda-for-interim-committee/

265 Ariz. Const. art. XXVII, § 2.

266 http://www.oudaily.com/news/2010/nov/03/state-question-results/; *see* Okla. Const. art. 2, § 37.

267 http://www.stltoday.com/news/local/govt-and-politics/prop-c-passes-overwhelmingly/article_c847dc7c-564c-5c70-8d90-dfd25ae6de56.html; *see* Mo. Rev. Stat. § 1.330 (2000 & Supp. 2010).

268 Ibid.

269 http://www.cleveland.com/politics/index.ssf/2011/11/early_results_in_on_ohio_issue.html.

270 Ohio Const. art. 1, § 21.

271 http://www.bizjournals.com/birmingham/blog/2012/11/alabama-amendment-results-what-do.html?page=all

272 http://www.cnn.com/election/2012/results/state/WY/ballot/01; *see* Wyo. Const. art. 1, § 38.

273 S.B. 464, 96th Gen. Asemb., 2d Reg. Sess. (Mo. 2012) (to be codified at Mo. Rev. Stat. § 376.1186), http://www.senate.mo.gov/12info/BTS_Web/Bill.aspx?SessionType=R&BillID=43.

274 Ibid.

275 Mont. Code Ann. § 50-4-902 (2011).

276 §2-1-501 (2011).

277 http://electionresults.sos.mt.gov/resultsSW.aspx?type=BQ&map=CTY.

278 http://www.politico.com/story/2012/12/christie-nixes-state-run-insurance-exchange-84718.html.

279 Ibid.

280 http://www.kansas.com/2012/11/08/2561344/brownback-kansas-wont-partner.html

281 http://www.kansascity.com/opinion/editorials/article2667821.html

282 http://houston.cbslocal.com/2012/11/16/perry-tells-feds-texas-will-not-set-up-health-care-exchange/

283 http://www.governing.com/government-quotes/I-was-invited-to-the-picnic-and-I-was-the-main-course.html

284 http://www.governorbryant.com/governor-bryant-issues-statement-on-health-care-exchange/

285 http://www.politico.com/magazine/story/2014/10/mississippi-burned-obamacare-112181_Page2.html#ixzz3HYt5XUFN

286 http://www.politico.com/magazine/story/2014/10/mississippi-burned-obamacare-112181_Page4.html#ixzz3HYvD4XRX

287 http://theadvocate.com/home/3307312-125/jindal-move-causes-stir

288 http://www.nytimes.com/2013/09/22/us/politics/reignited-battle-over-health-law.html?pagewanted=2&_r=0&hpw

289 http://www.nytimes.com/2013/10/11/us/in-florida-opposition-by-the-state-and-snags-in-signing-up-on-the-web.html?hpw&_r=0

290 https://www.youtube.com/watch?v=GtnEmPXEpr0&feature=youtu.be&t=31m25s

291 *Halbig vs. Burwell*, Slip. Op. at 35-36 n. 11 (D.C. Cir. 2014).

292 http://www.ca4.uscourts.gov/Opinions/Published/141158.P.pdf

293 http://www.supremecourt.gov/orders/courtorders/110714zr_n75o.pdf

294 http://www.supremecourt.gov/opinions/14pdf/14-114_qol1.pdf

9) WASHINGTON STATE: WHAT A STATE EXCHANGE LOOKS LIKE

295 http://www.commonwealthfund.org/Newsletters/Washington-Health-Policy-in-Review/2011/Jan/January-24-2011/Dozen-Pace-Car-States.aspx.

296 45 C.F.R. § 155.160(b) (2013).

297 http://www.washingtonpost.com/blogs/govbeat/wp/2013/09/21/the-state-that-taxes-the-poor-the-most-is-a-blue-one/?hpid=z10

298 http://articles.washingtonpost.com/2012-06-16/national/35461636_1_individual-mandate-health-insurance-insurance-reforms

299 *See* Wash. Rev. Code § 43.71.020 (2012).

300 Ibid.

301 *See* § 43.71.020(b).

302 *See* § 43.71.020(c).

303 *See* Nev. Rev. Stat. § 695I.300(2)(a)-(c) (2011).

304 *See* Wash. Rev. Code § 43.71.020(c) (2012).

305 *See* Wash. Rev. Code § 43.71.020(1)(a)(iv) (2012).

306 *See* § 43.71.020(1)(d)(4).

307 http://www.lifehealthpro.com/2012/03/26/state-ppaca-reform-news-wash-state-penn-advance-re.

308 *See* Wash. Rev. Code § 42.71.30(2) (2012).

309 *See* Wash. Rev. Code § 48.43.700 (2012).

310 http://www.healthcare.gov/law/resources/regulations/guidance-to-states-on-exchanges.html.

311 Wash. Rev. Code § 48.43.700 (2012).

312 http://health.usnews.com/health-news/health-insurance/articles/2012/10/03/many-insurance-plans-heap-healthcare-costs-on-consumers.

313 http://washingtonstatewire.com/blog/staggering-health-insurance-premiums-right-around-the-corner-predicts-premera-vice-president/.

314 http://www.spokesman.com/stories/2013/mar/22/premera-moderates-warning-about-rates/

315 *See* Wash. Rev. Code § 48.43.700(2) (2012).

316 *See* The Patient Protection and Affordable Care Act, Pub. L. No. 111-148, § 1302(e), 124 Stat. 119, 168 (2010) (codified as amended at 42 U.S.C. § 18022(e)(1), (2)).

317 http://seattletimes.com/html/localnews/2021176345_collegeinsurancexml.html

318 http://wahbexchange.org/wp-content/uploads/HBE_EB_120516_Financial_Report.pdf.

319 http://seattletimes.com/html/localnews/2014226748_statebuilding15m.html.

320 http://seattletimes.nwsource.com/html/healthcare/2022125947_acaexchangeerrorxml.html

321 http://video.foxnews.com/v/2849438177001/obamacare-fan-finds-out-she-cant-afford-it-after-all/

322 http://blogs.seattletimes.com/healthcarecheckup/2014/01/23/premera-dominates-in-new-insurance-exchange/

323 http://seattletimes.com/html/localnews/2023747538_acaexchangecomplaintsxml.html

324 http://www.washingtonpost.com/blogs/wonkblog/wp/2014/06/16/obamacare-strug-gles-even-where-its-succeeding/

325 http://m.bizjournals.com/seattle/blog/health-care-inc/2013/11/ceo-of-washington-health-exchange.html?ana=e_ptl_hc&r=full

326 http://seattletimes.com/html/localnews/2015916470_regence16m.html

327 http://avalere.com/expertise/managed-care/insights/state-based-exchanges-saw-higher-attrition-from-2014-to-2015-than-federally

328 http://wahbexchange.org/files/4514/2189/0185/EB_Budget_Impact_01222015.pdf

329 Letter from 103 health care stakeholders, to Christine Gregoire, Governor, Mary Anne Lindeblad, Dir., Wash. State Health Care Auth., Richard Onizuka, CEO, Wash. Health

Benefits Exch., Mike Kriedler, Comm'r, Office of the Ins. Comm'r, Robin Arnold-Williams, Sec'y, Dep't of Soc. & Health Servs. (Sept. 26, 2012) (on file with author).

330 http://www.insurance.wa.gov/about-oic/commissioner-reports/documents/2011-uninsured-report.pdf.

10) OTHER STATES MOVING FORWARD ON EXCHANGES

331 http://www.cbpp.org/files/CBPP-Analysis-on-the-Status-of-State-Exchange-Implementation.pdf

332 Mass. Gen. Laws ch. 118H § 2 (2012).

333 *See*

334 http://www.avenueh.com/images/PDFs/health%20reform%20history/The_Utah_Health_Exchange_-_A_Brief_Overview.pdf. (last visited Feb. 22, 2013).

335 Utah Code Ann. § 31A-42-201 (West 2012).

336 Ibid.

337 Ibid.

338 m.sltrib.com/sltrib/mobile2/55691666-218/health-utah-exchange-avenue.html.csp.

339 45 C.F.R. § 155.110(c)(3) (2012).

340 http://www.naic.org/documents/index_health_reform_111005_naic_letter_centers_medicare_medicaid_services2.pdf

341 Bernadette Fernandez & Annie L. Mach, Cong. Research Serv., R42663, Health Insurance Exchanges Under the Patient Protection and Affordable Care Act (ACA) (Jan. 31, 2013).

342 45 C.F.R. § 155.150(a) (2013).

343 http://www.governing.com/topics/health-human-services/closer-look-utah-health-insurance-exchange.html

344 *See* Health Insurance—Patient Protection and Affordable Care Act, ch. 655, Cal. Sess. Laws (2009-10); Health Insurance—California Health Benefit Exchange—Requirements, ch. 659, Cal. Sess. Laws (2009-10).

345 Ibid.

346 Ibid.

347 http://www.ltgovernor.ct.gov/wyman/cwp/view.asp?A=4029&Q=485090.

348 http://www.governor.maryland.gov/ltgovernor/pressreleases/130903.asp

349 *See* Colo. Rev. Stat. § 10-22-105(1)(a) (2012).

350 *See* Conn. Gen. Stat. § 38a-1081 (2012).

351 *See* Nev. Rev. Stat. § 695I.300 (2011).

352 *See* Haw. Rev. Stat. § 435H-4(a)-(b) (2005, Supp. 2011).

353 *See* Or. Rev. Stat. § 741.025(5) (2012); http://www.blueoregon.com/2011/04/consumers-deserve-better-health-insurance-exchange/.

354 *See* Conn. Gen. Stat. § 38a-1081(b)(2)(A)-(C) (2012).

355 *See* Md. Code Ann. § 31-104(d)(2)(i)-(iii) (West 2012).

356 *See* Conn. Gen. Stat. § 38a-1081(c)(9) (2012).

357 *See* D.C. Code § 31-3171.10(b) (2012).

358 www.ctmirror.org/node/14654.

359 *See* D.C. Code § 31-3171.10(a)-(b) (2012).

360 *See* Vt. Stat. Ann. tit. 33, § 1801(a) (LexisNexis Supp. 2012); *id.* at § 1821.

361 *See* Vt. Stat. Ann. tit. 18, § 9374 (2012).

362 Exec. Order No. 2012-587, Office of Ky. Governor Steven L. Beshear (July 17, 2012), *available at* http://apps.sos.ky.gov/Executive/Journal/execjournalimages/2012-MISC-2012-0587-222943.pdf; Press Release, Office of N.Y. Governor Andrew Cuomo, Governor Cuomo Issues Executive Order Establishing Statewide Health Exch. (Apr. 12, 2012) (contains text of order), *available at* http://www.governor.ny.gov/press/04122012-EO-42; Exec. Order No. 11-09, Office of R.I. Governor Lincoln D. Chafee (Sept. 19, 2011), *available at* http://www.governor.ri.gov/documents/executiveorders/2011/Executive_Order_11-09.pdf.

363 *See* Miss. Ins. Dept., Bulletin 2011-9, Oct. 18, 2011 (as amended Jan. 25, 2012), http://www.mid.ms.gov/bulletins/20119bul.pdf.

364 http://voices.idahostatesman.com/2012/12/12/idahopolitics/foes_otterbacked_idaho_health_exchange_protest_capitol_steps_thu#storylink=cpy

365 http://www.minnpost.com/politics-policy/2012/12/minnesota-s-health-exchange-process-gets-conditional-approval-feds.

366 http://www.liveinsurancenews.com/health-insurance-exchange-moves-a-step-forward-in-new-mexico/8521073/.

367 http://thehill.com/blogs/healthwatch/health-reform-implementation/193735-oregon-insurance-commissioner-to-advise-hhs-on-exchanges.

368 http://www.cbo.gov/sites/default/files/cbofiles/attachments/43907-BudgetOutlook.pdf.

369 http://www.politico.com/story/2013/12/obamacare-turnover-healthcaregov-101386.html?hp=l9

370 http://blogs.wsj.com/cio/2014/05/01/xerox-cio-fixing-nevada-health-exchange-as-tough-decisions-loom/

371 http://www.katu.com/news/investigators/Oregon-health-official-resigns-over-Cover-Oregon-236625111.html?mobile=y

372 http://www.katu.com/news/investigators/Cover-Oregon-invites-public-to-once-secret-Legislative-Oversight-meeting-253483611.html

373 http://blogs.seattletimes.com/healthcarecheckup/2014/08/08/oracle-sues-oregon-over-health-exchange-fiasco/

374 http://www.politico.com/story/2014/05/nevada-end-obamacare-exchange-healthcare-brian-sandoval-106897.html?hp=l5

375 http://www.washingtonpost.com/local/md-politics/md-health-secretary-to-attend-house-hearing-on-troubled-state-insurance-exchanges/2014/04/03/89419d94-bb26-11e3-9a05-c739f29ccb08_story.html

376 http://www.washingtonpost.com/local/md-politics/md-health-exchange-board-violated-law-on-private-meetings-compliance-board-says/2014/05/21/78bdb6d6-e0f8-11e3-810f-764fe508b82d_story.html?hpid=z4

377 http://www.washingtonpost.com/local/ganslers-fall-from-early-favorite-to-a-distant-second-in-marylands-gubernatorial-primary/2014/06/25/3b5b6c9e-fbb4-11e3-b1f4-8e77c632c07b_story.html?hpid=z5

378 http://bostonherald.com/news_opinion/local_coverage/herald_bulldog/2014/05/state_taps_new_company_to_fix_obamacare_site

379 http://www.bostonglobe.com/metro/2014/10/09/official-connector-website-will-work-when-open-enrollment-starts-nov/dmKF4SZ2nHgzk2uq6CTchP/story.html

380 http://www.bostonglobe.com/metro/2014/10/09/official-connector-website-will-work-when-open-enrollment-starts-nov/dmKF4SZ2nHgzk2uq6CTchP/story.html

381 http://www.politico.com/story/2014/03/kathleen-sebelius-obamacare-premiums-104580.html

382 http://avalere.com/expertise/managed-care/insights/state-based-exchanges-saw-higher-attrition-from-2014-to-2015-than-federally

11) THE FAILED PROMISE OF MEDICAID EXPANSION

383 http://www.governorbryant.com/gov-bryant-column-the-truths-about-obamacare-in-mississippi/

384 http://www.omaha.com/article/20130415/NEWS/704159914

385 http://www.cnn.com/2013/03/21/us/mississippi-anti-bloomberg-bill

386 http://www.washingtonpost.com/blogs/wonkblog/wp/2014/09/04/the-states-where-americans-are-the-most-and-least-obese/?hpid=z6

387 http://www.nytimes.com/2013/10/03/health/millions-of-poor-are-left-uncovered-by-health-law.html?pagewanted=all

388 http://www.cbo.gov/sites/default/files/cbofiles/attachments/43472-07-24-2012-CoverageEstimates.pdf

389 http://www.thestate.com/2013/01/16/2592664/full-text-sc-gov-nikki-haley-state.html

390 http://www.washingtonpost.com/local/md-politics/major-flaw-in-md-health-site-may-mean-30-million-in-unnecessary-medicaid-payments/2014/02/27/4092eb06-9f2f-11e3-a050-dc3322a94fa7_story.html

391 http://content.healthaffairs.org/content/32/6/1030.abstract

392 http://www.businessreport.com/article/20130422/BUSINESSREPORT02/130429997

393 http://www.washingtonpost.com/blogs/govbeat/wp/2014/02/08/the-koch-brothers-group-is-getting-involved-in-louisianas-obamacare-fight/?tid=hpModule_ba0d4c2a-86a2-11e2-9d71-f0feafdd1394&hpid=z12

394 http://theadvocate.com/news/opinion/8915688-123/our-views-take-money-for

395 http://m.therepublic.com/view/story/cdbadae09de2458882d1b97f0f7428ee/LA--Vitter-Press-Club

396 http://www.post-gazette.com/stories/local/state/gop-governor-trio-rips-affordable-care-act-685632/

397 http://www.keystonepolitics.com/2013/05/tom-corbett-still-doesnt-understand-obamacare/

398 http://www.flgov.com/wp-content/uploads/2013/02/2-20-13-REMARKSFORDELIVERY.pdf

399 http://www.miamiherald.com/2013/05/13/3395771/for-florida-lawmakers-healthcare.html

400 http://www.usatoday.com/story/opinion/2013/06/02/ohio-governor-reagans-compassionate-medicaid-expansion/2382737/

401 http://www.politico.com/story/2013/10/ohio-moving-toward-obamacare-medicaid-expansion-98609.html?hp=l3

402 http://azgovernor.gov/dms/upload/GS_010912_2012SoSAddress.pdf

403 http://www.azgovernor.gov/Medicaid.asp

404 http://www.washingtonpost.com/national/health-science/gop-governors-endorsements-of-medicaid-expansion-deepen-rifts-within-party/2013/06/02/b4a42eb8-c7b9-11e2-9245-773c0123c027_story_1.html

405 http://www.westernfreepress.com/2013/06/12/governor-brewer-flailing-colluding-with-democrats-on-arizona-medicaid-expansion/

406 http://azcapitoltimes.com/news/2013/06/11/az-gov-jan-brewer-calls-special-session-on-budget-medicaid/

407 http://www.nytimes.com/2013/07/22/us/arizona-republicans-are-at-odds-on-medicaid.html?pagewanted=1&_r=0&hp

408 http://www.freep.com/article/20130613/NEWS06/306130138/medicaid-expansion-michigan-house-approval

409 http://detroit.cbslocal.com/2013/06/15/michigan-house-approves-medicaid-expansion/

410 http://www.indystar.com/story/news/politics/2014/05/15/gov-pence-optimistic-feds-will-accept-medicaid-alternative/9115699/

411 http://www.washingtonpost.com/opinions/dana-milbank-indiana-gov-mike-pence-is-taking-obamacare-money-and-running-with-it/2014/05/19/7ae33bbe-dfa1-11e3-8dcc-d6b7fede081a_story.html?hpid=z5

412 http://www.npr.org/blogs/health/2013/11/19/246003602/wisconsin-chooses-its-own-path-to-overhaul-medicaid

413 https://law.marquette.edu/poll/2014/10/29/final-pre-election-marquette-law-school-poll-finds-walker-leading-burke-in-wisconsin-governors-race/

414 http://www.pewstates.org/projects/stateline/headlines/obama-administration-poised-to-approve-arkansas-style-medicaid-expansions-85899473677

415 http://www.finance.senate.gov/library/transcripts/index.cfm?PageNum_rs=2 (Oct. 1, 2009).

416 http://www.dhs.state.ia.us/uploads/Iowa%20Health%20and%20Wellness%20Plan%20Overview1.pdf

417 http://www.modernhealthcare.com/article/20130528/NEWS/305289966#

418 http://www.deseretnews.com/article/865597533/Gov-Gary-Herbert-offers-Utah-solution-to-Medicaid-expansion.html?pg=all

419 http://missoulian.com/news/local/vote-that-killed-medicaid-bill-was-a-mistake-lawmaker-says/article_28deaa2e-a92e-11e2-903e-001a4bcf887a.html

420 http://www.washingtonpost.com/local/virginia-politics/virginia-democratic-senator-to-resign-possibly-dooming-push-to-expand-medicaid/2014/06/08/901edf8e-ef54-11e3-914c-1fbd0614e2d4_story.html?hpid=z1

421 http://www.washingtonpost.com/local/virginia-politics/gov-terry-mcauliffe-vetoes-portions-of-virginia-budget-prolonging-medicaid-standoff/2014/06/20/960d98a8-f879-11e3-a3a5-42be35962a52_story.html

422 https://governor.virginia.gov/news/newsarticle?articleId=6347

423 http://www.washingtonpost.com/local/virginia-politics/va-legislators-approve-budget-deal-reject-medicaid-expansion/2014/09/18/f8abde32-3dfe-11e4-b0ea-8141703bbf6f_story.html

424 http://www.washingtonpost.com/local/dc-politics/dcs-medicaid-upheaval-puts-health-care-providers-in-a-tight-spot/2013/05/25/e546e456-c3b9-11e2-8c3b-0b5e9247e8ca_story.html?hpid=z9

425 http://www.washingtonpost.com/opinions/colbert-king-dc-taxpayers-on-the-hook-for-unpaid-health-bills/2013/06/07/07bb5952-cf79-11e2-8845-d970ccb04497_story.html

426 http://m.cjonline.com/news/2014-05-06/brownback-would-welcome-fbi-probe-kancare-contracts

427 http://www.kansas.com/2014/04/18/3411724/brownback-signs-bill-saying-medicaid. html

428 http://www.nytimes.com/2014/11/18/us/politics/health-law-turns-obama-and-insurers-into-allies.html

429 *Id.*

430 http://www.supremecourt.gov/opinions/11pdf/09-958.pdf

431 http://cdn.ca9.uscourts.gov/datastore/opinions/2013/05/24/12-55067.pdf

432 http://blog.thenewstribune.com/politicsblog/2013/05/14/supreme-court-hears-arguments-over-legitimacy-of-95m-court-award-to-care-workers-for-the-severely-disabled/

433 http://news.yahoo.com/supreme-court-sides-idaho-medicaid-pay-dispute-141017798--politics.html;_ylt=A0LEVy0XshpVB9MAjINXNyoA;_ylu=X3oDMTByMj B0aG5zBGNvbG8DYmYxBHBvcwMxBHZ0aWQDBHNlYwNzYw--

434 http://www.rollcall.com/news/the_hidden_failure_of_obamas_health_care_overhaul-233506-1.html?pos=hftxt

435 http://www.aafp.org/online/etc/medialib/aafp_org/documents/policy/fed/endorse-letters/act032910.Par.0001.File.tmp/HouseVoteHCR032910.pdf

436 http://www.washingtonpost.com/national/health-science/increase-in-doctors-pay-for-medicaid-services-off-to-a-slow-start/2013/05/18/79745d88-bfce-11e2-9b09-1638ac-c3942e_story.html?hpid=z8

437 http://www.washingtonpost.com/national/health-science/shortage-of-primary-care-doctors-in-dc-new-report-finds/2013/09/25/2c05ccba-2592-11e3-b3e9-d97fb087acd6_story.html

438 http://www.usatoday.com/story/news/nation/2015/01/04/kaiser-health-news-docs-face-big-cuts-in-medicaid-pay/21227683/

439 http://www.seattletimes.com/seattle-news/politics/lawmakers-may-redirect-some-pot-tax-money-meant-for-health-clinics/

12) THE ACA AND THE ANTI-CHOICE CRUSADE

440 http://www.ncsl.org/issues-research/health/health-reform-and-abortion-coverage.aspx

441 http://www.guttmacher.org/statecenter/spibs/spib_RICA.pdf

442 http://voices.washingtonpost.com/ezra-klein/2009/11/is_stupaks_amendment_a_trojan.html

443 http://www.huffingtonpost.com/2013/09/03/obamacare-abortion-coverage_n_3839720. html

444 http://www.aclupa.org/pressroom/pasenatepassesabortioninsu.htm

445 http://www.naralva.org/in-our-state/coveragebanvotes.shtml

446 http://www.naralva.org/in-our-state/abortioncoverageban.shtml

447 http://www.huffingtonpost.com/2013/12/11/michigan-rape-insurance_n_4428432.html

448 http://iga.in.gov/legislative/2014/bills/house/1123/#

449 http://nirhealth.org/sections/publications/documents/Sept2012-quicksheet-on-abortion-coverage.pdf

450 http://www.politico.com/politico44/2013/07/obama-aides-supporters-huddle-to-agree-on-obamacare-169264.html?hp=r20

451 http://www.washingtonpost.com/blogs/the-fix/wp/2014/10/13/mark-udall-has-been-dubbed-mark-uterus-on-the-campaign-trail-thats-a-problem/?tid=hpModule_ba0d-4c2a-86a2-11e2-9d71-f0feafdd1394&hpid=z10

452 http://www.denverpost.com/ci_26701817/cory-gardner-u-s-senate

453 http://www.nytimes.com/2014/11/02/opinion/sunday/frank-bruni-the-pitiful-whimper-of-2014.html?emc=eta1

13) ACT IMPOSSIBLE TO IMPROVE

454 http://douthat.blogs.nytimes.com/2014/11/05/republicans-fought-the-future-and-the-future-lost/?hp&action=click&pgtype=Homepage&module=span-abc-region&region=span-abc-region&WT.nav=span-abc-region

455 http://www.washingtonpost.com/wp-dyn/content/article/2010/03/24/AR2010032402262.html

456 http://www.nytimes.com/2013/05/27/us/politics/polarized-congress-thwarts-changes-to-health-care-law.html

457 Id.

458 http://www.nytimes.com/2013/05/01/us/politics/transcript-of-obamas-news-conference.html?pagewanted=all&_r=0

459 http://stream.wsj.com/story/latest-headlines/SS-2-63399/SS-2-343420/

460 http://www.politico.com/story/2013/10/5-obamacare-questions-kathleen-sebelius-wont-answer-98636_Page2.html

461 http://www.politico.com/story/2013/11/obamacare-enrollment-website-glitches-99213.html?hp=l4

462 http://www.governing.com/topics/health-human-services/closer-look-utah-health-insurance-exchange.html

463 http://www.politico.com/story/2013/10/obamacare-woes-move-beyond-web-site-99044_Page2.html

464 http://www.politico.com/story/2013/10/obamacare-affordable-care-act-barack-obama-99131.html?hp=t1_3

465 http://www.nytimes.com/2014/04/12/us/politics/sebeliuss-slow-motion-resignation-from-the-cabinet.html?hpw&rref=politics&_r=0

466 http://www.politico.com/story/2013/12/healthcaregov-rollout-official-steps-down-101607.html?hp=t3_3

467 http://www.nytimes.com/2014/04/12/us/politics/sebeliuss-slow-motion-resignation-from-the-cabinet.html?hpw&rref=politics&_r=0

468 http://www.gao.gov/assets/670/665179.pdf

469 Id.

470 http://about.bgov.com/health-reforms-cost-73-billion-counting/?thx

471 Id.

472 http://www.usatoday.com/story/opinion/2014/10/12/obamacare-health-care-enrollment-transparency-lacking-column/16933173/

473 http://www.politico.com/story/2014/06/2014-election-bowe-bergdahl-democrats-barack-obama-107497_Page2.html

474 http://www.nytimes.com/2013/05/15/us/politics/house-republicans-to-vote-again-on-repealing-health-care.html

475 http://www.politico.com/story/2013/06/house-gops-new-anti-obamacare-group-92377.html

476 http://www.washingtonpost.com/national/health-science/nfl-says-no-to-promoting-obamacare/2013/06/28/1d02af1e-e026-11e2-b2d4-ea6d8f477a01_story.html

477 http://mobile.nytimes.com/2014/06/02/opinion/the-vanishing-cry-of-repeal-it.html?ref=opinion&_r=1&referrer=

478 http://www.washingtonpost.com/blogs/the-switch/wp/2014/10/15/why-the-debate-over-kentuckys-healthcare-gov-site-matters/?hpid=z16

479 http://www.manhattan-institute.org/html/mpr_17.htm

480 Id. at 25.

481 Id. at 26.

482 Id. at 27.

483 http://www.nytimes.com/2014/11/01/us/politics/repeal-of-health-law-once-central-to-gop-is-side-issue-in-campaigns.html?hp&action=click&pgtype=Homepage&module=first-column-region&region=top-news&WT.nav=top-news&_r=0

484 http://www.coburn.senate.gov/public/index.cfm?a=Files.Serve&File_id=871b0ef8-7705-4f72-aef2-e81d01b9c009

485 Id.

486 http://americanxt.org/wp-content/uploads/2014/04/The-Freedom-and-Empowerment-Plan.pdf

487 Id. at 12.

488 Id. at 13.

489 Mike Huckabee, *A Simple Government: Twelve Things We Really Need from Washington (and a Trillion That We Don't)* (Sentinel Trade, 2012), 83.

490 Glen Beck, *Arguing With Idiots: How to Stop Small Minds and Big Government* (Threshold Editions, 2010), 242.

491 Id. at 240.

492 http://www.washingtonpost.com/sf/national/2013/09/25/transcript-sen-ted-cruzs-filibuster-against-obamacare/?hpid=z2

493 http://www.rwjf.org/content/dam/farm/reports/issue_briefs/2012/rwjf401409

494 http://healthpolicyandmarket.blogspot.com/2014/03/silly-republican-insurance-reform.html

495 http://healthpolicyandmarket.blogspot.com/2014/03/silly-republican-insurance-reform.html

496 http://apps.leg.wa.gov/billinfo/summary.aspx?year=2013&bill=5540

497 http://www.nbcnews.com/politics/hillary-clinton/hillary-clinton-talks-health-care-policy-small-business-owners-iowa-n342201

14) The Self-Defeating Democratic Party

498 Chris Hedges, *Death of the Liberal Class* (Nation Books, 2010), 6.

499 Chris Lehmann, *Rich People Things: Real Life Secrets of the Predator Class* (Haymarket Books, 2011), 138.

500 http://www.seattlepi.com/local/connelly/article/Chopp-s-House-holds-up-homeowners-rights-1278795.php; http://www.komonews.com/news/local/16370001.html

501 http://archive.adl.org/PresRele/HolNa_52/5308_52.htm

502 http://blog.seattletimes.nwsource.com/politicsnorthwest/2009/03/18/the_e-mail_saga_continues.html

503 http://online.wsj.com/article/SB121755649066303381.html

504 Frank, *Pity the Billionaire*, 173.

505 http://www.politico.com/story/2014/11/jonathan-gruber-obamacare-voters-112812.html#ixzz3KBb1Qu5v

506 http://online.wsj.com/article/SB10001424052748703808904575025030384695158.html?mod=WSJ_latestheadlines#printMode

507 http://www.washingtonpost.com/opinions/ej-dionne-the-obama-riddle/2013/05/26/add4e0aa-c4c6-11e2-8c3b-0b5e9247e8ca_story.html?hpid=z2

508 http://www.treasury.gov/press-center/press-releases/Pages/ls241.aspx

509 http://www.washingtonpost.com/blogs/post-politics/wp/2013/05/19/mcconnell-predicts-obamacare-will-be-biggest-issue-of-2014-election/?hpid=z1

510 http://www.politico.com/story/2014/08/2014-elections-anti-obamacare-democrats-110237.html?ml=tb

511 http://votesmart.org/public-statement/125657/statement-of-senator-patrick-leahy-on-the-nomination-of-john-g-roberts-jr-to-be-chief-justice-of-the-united-states#.UZfNP6Tn_IU

512 http://www.senate.gov/legislative/LIS/roll_call_lists/roll_call_vote_cfm.cfm?congress=109&session=2&vote=00001

513 http://www.politico.com/story/2013/06/democratic-super-pacs-seek-135-million-93161.html

514 http://thehill.com/opinion/op-ed/218525-2014-election-and-progressive-populism

515 http://www.nytimes.com/2014/09/25/us/republicans-corporate-donors-governors.html?hpw&rref=politics&action=click&pgtype=Homepage&version=HpHedThumbWell&module=well-region&region=bottom-well&WT.nav=bottom-well

516 http://www.washingtonpost.com/opinions/dana-milbank-where-money-talks/2013/05/24/d6d64afe-c47e-11e2-8c3b-0b5e9247e8ca_story.html

517 https://forms.house.gov/israel/issues/taxrelief.htm

518 http://thehill.com/blogs/ballot-box/house-races/274291-top-dem-to-obama-leave-tax-threshold-at-400000

519 http://www.nypost.com/p/news/local/dem_is_owe_so_lucky_AL5ZOizCFer5BIMpyLl92O

520 http://www.politico.com/story/2014/09/democrats-debbie-wasserman-schultz-111077.html

521 Cullen Murphy, *Are We Rome? The Fall of an Empire and the Fate of America* (Mariner Books, 2008), 49.

522 http://dingell.house.gov/press-release/dingell-statement-republican-faa-gimmick

523 http://www.nationaljournal.com/congress/congress-quietly-deletes-a-key-disclosure-of-free-trips-lawmakers-take-20140630

524 http://www.politico.com/story/2013/06/obamacare-lawmakers-health-insurance-92691.html?ml=po_r

525 http://www.politico.com/story/2013/11/older-capitol-hill-aides-obamacare-affordable-care-act-prices-health-insurance-100226.html#ixzz2lL3mRCiP

526 http://www.nytimes.com/2013/11/20/us/politics/for-lawmakers-a-gold-plated-insurance-exchange.html?hp&_r=0

527 http://blogs.rollcall.com/hill-blotter/health-insurance-for-congress-and-staff-its-complicated/?dcz=

528 http://www.washingtonpost.com/blogs/federal-eye/wp/2014/10/07/federal-workers-to-see-another-rate-increase-for-health-coverage/?hpid=z4

529 Hedges, *Death of the Liberal* Class, 25.

530 Ibid., 27.

531 http://www.vox.com/2014/7/8/5878293/lets-stop-using-the-word-moderate

532 Mark Halperin & John Heileman, *Double Down: Game Change 2012* (Penguin Books: 2013), 415.

533 Lehmann, *Rich People Things*, 215.

15) THE LURE OF LUCRE

534 http://www.nasdaq.com/article/ex-wellpoint-ceos-pay-up-55-in-2012-20130402-01155

535 http://www.startribune.com/business/204595621.html?refer=y

536 http://www.startribune.com/business/298924971.html

537 *Id.*

538 http://www.propertycasualty360.com/2011/08/03/joel-ario-leaving-hhs-health-ex-change-job

539 http://wainsurance.blogspot.com/2012/12/aetna-fined-1-million-for-insurance.html

540 http://www.opensecrets.org/politicians/summary.php?cycle=2012&type=I&cid=n00004643&newMem=N

541 http://bigstory.ap.org/article/fewer-health-applicants-expected-illinois

542 http://www.bna.com/cciio-director-steve-n12884910135/

543 http://www.opensecrets.org/orgs/summary.php?id=D000000348&cycle=2012

544 http://www.pciplan.com/forms/pdfs/2012Brochure.pdf

545 http://www.washingtonpost.com/blogs/the-switch/wp/2013/10/09/heres-everything-you-need-to-know-about-obamacares-error-plagued-web-sites/

546 http://www.nytimes.com/2013/10/21/us/insurance-site-seen-needing-weeks-to-fix.html?hpw&_r=0

547 http://www.nytimes.com/2013/10/26/us/politics/general-contractor-named-to-fix-health-web-site.html?hpw&_r=0

548 http://www.baltimoresun.com/news/maryland/sun-investigates/bs-md-sun-investi-gates-qssi-20131227,0,7266301.story

NOTES

549 http://www.nytimes.com/2014/06/21/us/health-site-is-changing-supervision.html?_r=0

550 http://mobile.nytimes.com/2014/07/01/business/unitedhealth-an-insurer-switching-roles-helps-hospitals-on-medicare-billing.html

551 http://www.politico.com/story/2013/08/robert-gibbs-ben-labolt-eli-lilly-95148.html?hp=l15

552 http://www.politico.com/story/2014/06/robert-gibbs-ben-labolt-legal-fight-teachers-union-incite-agency-108243.html

553 http://www.nytimes.com/2014/05/28/us/politics/obama-crowd-blanches-as-ex-aide-jim-messina-helps-british-conservatives.html?hp

554 http://www.nytimes.com/2013/09/18/us/politics/reaping-profit-after-assisting-on-health-law.html?hp&_r=0

555 http://www.washingtonpost.com/politics/political-intelligence-firms-set-up-investor-meetings-at-white-house/2013/05/26/73b06528-bccb-11e2-9b09-1638acc3942e_story.html?hpid=z1

556 http://potomacresearch.com/site/

557 http://www.washingtonpost.com/blogs/wonkblog/wp/2013/05/10/budget-request-denied-sebelius-turns-to-health-executives-to-finance-obamacare/

558 http://www.nytimes.com/2013/05/13/us/politics/health-secretary-raises-funds-for-health-care-law.html?_r=0

559 http://thehill.com/blogs/regwatch/business/302961-wall-street-lobbyists-rout-groups-pressing-for-new-tight-regulations#ixzz2V9jpdMce

560 http://thehill.com/business-a-lobbying/318577-architects-of-obamacare-reap-windfall-as-washington-lobbyists

561 http://www.politico.com/story/2013/11/johnson-and-johnson-drug-settlement-99326.html?hp=r8

562 http://kaiserhealthnews.org/news/obamacare-creates-boom-for-federal-contractors/

563 http://connectforhealthco.com/2014/07/connect-health-colorado-ceo-patty-fontneau-take-national-position-cigna/

16) MEDICARE ADVANTAGE AND THE BIRTH OF GOVERNMENT SUBSIDIZATION OF INSURERS

564 http://www.newyorker.com/reporting/2011/06/06/110606fa_fact_lizza

565 http://www.nbcnews.com/id/48959273/ns/meet_the_press-transcripts/t/september-mitt-romney-ann-romney-julian-castro-peggy-noonan-ej-dionne-bill-bennett-chuck-todd/

566 http://online.wsj.com/article/SB10001424127887324492604579087342347257028.html

COMPROMISED

567 http://www.commonwealthfund.org/Publications/Issue-Briefs/2008/Sep/The-Continu-
ing-Cost-of-Privatization--Extra-Payments-to-Medicare-Advantage.aspx

568 http://www.medpac.gov/chapters/Mar13_Ch13.pdf

569 http://www.medpac.gov/chapters/Mar13_Ch13.pdf

570 http://www.nber.org/digest/sep11/w16977.html

571 http://www.nbcnews.com/id/48959273/ns/meet_the_press-transcripts/t/september-
mitt-romney-ann-romney-julian-castro-peggy-noonan-ej-dionne-bill-bennett-chuck-
todd/

572 http://www.finance.senate.gov/hearings/hearing/?id=d8c677d4-fa54-11f2-1c31-
64fbd9076f32

573 http://www.finance.senate.gov/download/?id=efac4ac5-1a6e-4ca9-886e-9553d58cd822

574 http://www.politico.com/story/2013/09/mitch-mcconnell-humana-founder-96509.html

575 http://www.cbo.gov/publication/43471

576 http://www.cbo.gov/sites/default/files/cbofiles/ftpdocs/107xx/doc10731/effects_of_ppa-
ca_on_ma_enrollment_and_extra_benefits_not_covered_by_medicare.pdf

577 http://www.debates.org/index.php?page=october-3-2012-debate-transcript

578 http://www.politico.com/story/2013/04/insurance-medicare-advantage-cuts-health-
care-89569.html

579 http://www.washingtonpost.com/blogs/wonkblog/wp/2013/04/02/how-insurers-
flipped-a-medicare-pay-cut-into-a-pay-raise/

580 http://www.washingtonpost.com/business/economy/sec-issues-subpoenas-to-political-
intelligence-firms-connected-to-leaked-information/2013/05/01/43121794-b290-11e2-
bbf2-a6f9e9d79e19_story.html

581 http://www.nytimes.com/2014/11/15/business/tip-on-medicare-spurs-insider-trading-
investigation.html?module=Search&mabReward=relbias%3Ar%2C%7B%221%22%3A
%22RI%3A5%22%7D

582 Id.

583 http://www.ahipcoverage.com/2013/03/15/senators-baucus-and-hatch-send-letter-to-
cms-raising-concerns-about-proposed-medicare-advantage-cut/

584 http://www.ahipcoverage.com/wp-content/uploads/2013/03/Scan001.pdf

585 http://online.wsj.com/article/SB10001424127887323501004578388980625858300.html

586 http://online.wsj.com/article/SB10001424127887323296504578397201792485508.html

587 http://www.usatoday.com/story/opinion/2014/04/02/medicare-advantage-obamacare-
cuts-editorials-debates/7222695/

588 http://docs.house.gov/meetings/IF/IF02/20130520/100868/HHRG-113-IF02-Wstate-
DurhamD-20130520.pdf

589 http://www.nytimes.com/2014/10/13/us/us-finds-many-failures-in-medicare-health-plans-.html?action=click&contentCollection=Politics&region=Footer&module=MoreInSection&pgtype=article

590 Id.

591 Id.

592 Id.

593 http://articles.washingtonpost.com/2013-05-11/national/39187506_1_patients-appropriate-drugs-medicare-and-medicaid-services

17) EMPLOYMENT AND THE ACA

594 http://www.washingtonpost.com/blogs/wonkblog/wp/2013/07/03/wonkbook-big-business-continues-its-unbroken-winning-streak-in-health-reform/?tid=pm_business_pop

595 http://www.politico.com/story/2013/07/obamacare-provisions-timely-delay-94361.html?hp=r8

596 http://clerk.house.gov/evs/2013/roll361.xml

597 http://www.washingtonpost.com/page/2010-2019/WashingtonPost/2013/11/19/National-Politics/Polling/question_12488.xml?uuid=o67oYlDXEeOe5iWACG2CVA

598 http://www.urban.org/UploadedPDF/413117-Why-Not-Just-Eliminate-the-Employer-Mandate.pdf

599 http://www.rwjf.org/en/research-publications/find-rwjf-research/2013/04/state-level-trends-in-employer-sponsored-health-insurance.html

600 http://online.wsj.com/article/SB10001424052970204707104578094941709047834.html

601 http://laborcenter.berkeley.edu/healthcare/reduced_work_hours13.pdf

602 http://www.washingtonpost.com/national/health-science/as-health-care-laws-employer-mandate-nears-firms-cut-worker-hours-struggle-with-logistics/2014/06/23/720e197c-f249-11e3-914c-1fbd0614e2d4_story.html

603 http://thehill.com/blogs/healthwatch/health-reform-implementation/321663-report-trader-joes-to-drop-health-coverage-for-some-workers-under-obamacare

604 http://www.politico.com/story/2014/01/target-health-care-plans-102471.html?hp=fl

605 http://mobile.nytimes.com/2014/05/26/us/irs-bars-employers-from-dumping-workers-into-health-exchanges.html?from=homepage

606 http://www.washingtonpost.com/sf/national/2013/09/25/transcript-sen-ted-cruzs-filibuster-against-obamacare/?hpid=z2

607 http://kff.org/private-insurance/report/2013-employer-health-benefits/

608 http://seattletimes.com/html/nationworld/2021065979_employeehealthxml.html

609 http://www.nytimes.com/2013/08/05/nyregion/health-care-law-raises-pressure-on-public-employees-unions.html?hpw&_r=0

610 http://www.nea.org/home/62495.htm

611 http://www.nea.org/assets/docs/Actuarial_Study_on_Excise_Tax--In_Brief--March_13_2015.pdf

612 http://seattletimes.com/html/politics/2021046211_apushealthcareunions.html?fb_action_ids=10201466639731928&fb_action_types=og.recommends&fb_source=aggregation&fb_aggregation_id=288381481237582

613 http://thehill.com/opinion/op-ed/300823-treat-nonprofit-healthcare-fairly

614 http://nwlaborpress.org/2013/06/obamacare-insurance-exchanges-near-launch/?utm_source=Northwest+Labor+Press&utm_campaign=cd10db5216-6%2F21%2F13&utm_medium=email&utm_term=0_a098a455a3-cd10db5216-270642953

615 http://blogs.wsj.com/corporate-intelligence/2013/07/12/union-letter-obamacare-will-destroy-the-very-health-and-wellbeing-of-workers/

616 http://www.aflcio.org/About/Exec-Council/Conventions/2013/Resolutions-and-Amendments/Resolution-54-AFL-CIO-Convention-Resolution-on-the-Affordable-Care-Act

617 http://www.nytimes.com/2013/09/12/business/unions-misgivings-on-health-law-burst-into-view.html?hp&_r=0

618 http://www.politico.com/story/2013/09/white-house-labor-obamacare-exemp-tion-96793.html?hp=f2

619 http://www.nytimes.com/2014/01/19/us/rules-for-equal-coverage-by-employers-re-main-elusive-under-health-law.html?hp&_r=0

620 http://online.wsj.com/news/articles/SB10001424052702303749904579580604081967202#printMode

621 https://www.federalregister.gov/articles/2013/03/11/2013-04902/patient-protection-and-affordable-care-act-hhs-notice-of-benefit-and-payment-parameters-for-2014

622 http://www.washingtonpost.com/blogs/wonkblog/wp/2013/11/27/obamacares-online-exchange-for-small-businesses-is-delayed-by-one-year/?hpid=z1

623 http://www.rollcall.com/news/triage_for_healthcaregov_administration_punts_on_small_business_exchange-229355-1.html?pos=hftxt

624 http://www.federalwaymirror.com/business/203839001.html

625 http://seattletimes.com/html/businesstechnology/2022479459_acasmallbizfoloxml.html

626 http://seattletimes.com/html/localnews/2024992999_acaexchangexml.html

627 http://www.seattletimes.com/business/more-small-employers-using-states-health-insurance-exchange/

628 https://www.sba.gov/sites/default/files/advocacy/wa12.pdf

629 *Id.*

630 http://www.seattletimes.com/seattle-news/small-businesses-hail-ruling-that-protects-association-health-plans/

631 http://voiceofsandiego.org/2014/05/05/californias-still-struggling-to-set-up-shop/

632 http://www.gao.gov/products/GAO-15-58

633 http://www.politico.com/story/2013/12/next-obamacare-crisis-small-business-costs-101212.html

634 Kentucky's Market Report on Health Insurance, Kentucky Department of Insurance (April 1997), pg. viii.

635 http://www.coburn.senate.gov/public/index.cfm?a=Files.Serve&File_id=871b0ef8-7705-4f72-aef2-e81d01b9c009

636 http://ebn.benefitnews.com/news/ebn_hc_health_reform/california-delays-aca-for-small-employers-2742608-1.html?utm_campaign=ebn%20in%20briefjul%209%20 2014&utm_medium=email&utm_source=newsletter&ET=ebnbenefitnews%3Ae280896 2%3A4237886a%3A&st=email

637 http://www.aei-ideas.org/2013/06/jason-furman-would-serve-with-distinction-as-chair-of-the-council-of-economic-advisers/

638 http://www.mackinac.org/archives/2006/walmart.pdf

639 Suskind, *Confidence Men*, at 82-85.

640 http://www.nytimes.com/2014/10/08/business/30000-lose-health-care-coverage-at-walmart.html?hp&action=click&pgtype=Homepage&version=HpHeadline&module=s econd-column-region°ion=top-news&WT.nav=top-news

641 http://www.nytimes.com/2014/11/05/business/small-businesses-health-insurance-ACA.html?hp&action=click&pgtype=Homepage&module=second-column-region&region=top-news&WT.nav=top-news

642 http://www.cbo.gov/sites/default/files/cbofiles/attachments/43900_ACAInsuranceCov-erageEffects.pdf

643 http://www.nytimes.com/2013/06/23/business/why-a-health-insurance-penalty-may-look-tempting.html?_r=0

644 http://www.nytimes.com/2013/07/03/us/politics/obama-administration-to-delay-health-law-requirement-until-2015.html?hpw&_r=0

18) UNAFFORDABLE CARE

645 http://www.commonwealthfund.org/~/media/Files/Publications/Issue%20Brief/2012/ Dec/premiums/1648_Schoen_state_trends_premiums_deductibles_2003_2011_1210. pdf

646 http://www.hsph.harvard.edu/news/press-releases/patients-with-surgical-complications-provide-greater-hospital-profit-margins/

647 http://www.nytimes.com/2013/06/09/opinion/sunday/the-weird-world-of-colonoscopy-costs.html?src=rechp&_r=0

648 Often a single hospital dominates an area, giving insurers little leverage when negotiating reimbursement rates.

649 http://www.nytimes.com/2013/11/17/us/politics/in-fracas-on-health-coverage-some-democrats-feel-exposed.html?hpw&rref=politics&_r=0

650 http://www.dol.gov/ebsa/faqs/faq-aca18.html

651 http://www.hhs.gov/news/press/2013pres/05/20130508a.html

652 http://www.ncsl.org/issues-research/health/con-certificate-of-need-state-laws.aspx

653 http://seattletimes.com/html/businesstechnology/2021297310_hospitalceopayxml.html

654 http://seattletimes.com/html/localnews/2018631542_robot08m.html

655 http://www.tha.org/HealthCareProviders/Advocacy/Key%20Issues%20TX%20Hosp_012813indd.pdf; http://texas.construction.com/features/archive/2009/0809_F2_MedicalCenter.asp

656 http://www.washingtonpost.com/business/economy/maryland-pressing-for-expanded-powers-over-hospitals/2013/05/24/8adf92fe-b8c1-11e2-b94c-b684dda07add_story.html?hpid=z1

657 http://www.kaiserhealthnews.org/Stories/2014/January/10/maryland-hospitals-radical-plan-limit-spending-change-payment.aspx?utm_campaign=KHN%3A%20First%20Edition&utm_source=hs_email&utm_medium=email&utm_content=11609206&_hsenc=p2ANqtz-8WYZUYdJtiqTswhMf9Nr9

658 http://www.ahipcoverage.com/2013/03/11/the-bitter-pill-of-health-care-costs/

659 http://www.rwjf.org/content/dam/farm/reports/issue_briefs/2012/rwjf73261

660 http://www.nber.org/papers/w12244.pdf?new_window=1

661 http://www.kellogg.northwestern.edu/faculty/dafny/Personal/Documents/Publications/2_Dafny_Identification%20and%20Estimation%20of%20Merger%20Effects_2009.pdf

662 http://mobile.nytimes.com/2013/06/12/business/examinations-of-health-costs-overlook-mergers.html

663 http://www.pwc.com/us/en/health-industries/behind-the-numbers/health-cost-inflators-hospital-consolidation.jhtml

664 http://www.nytimes.com/2014/11/24/health/private-oncologists-being-forced-out-leaving-patients-to-face-higher-bills.html?_r=0

665 http://www.nytimes.com/2014/06/03/business/Medicare-Hospital-Billing-Data-Is-Released.html?hp&_r=0

666 Id.

667 http://www.manhattan-institute.org/html/mpr_17.htm at 25-26.

668 Id. at 26.

669 http://www.nytimes.com/2015/07/01/upshot/how-jeb-bush-made-a-profit-on-obamacare.html?hp&action=click&pgtype=Homepage&module=first-column-region&region=top-news&WT.nav=top-news

670 http://seattletimes.com/html/localnews/2021029685_westneat22xml.html

671 http://www.latimes.com/business/la-fi-hiltzik-20130623,0,3635519, full.column

672 http://www.bostonglobe.com/metro/2014/05/20/gubernatorial-candidates-react-coakley-deal-with-partners/2jsal851gmzFde1woArZmI/story.html

673 http://mobile.nytimes.com/2014/07/07/opinion/the-risks-of-hospital-mergers.html?ref=opinion&_r=2&referrer=

674 http://www.ontheissues.org/Governor/Charlie_Baker_Health_Care.htm

675 http://www.bostonglobe.com/business/2015/01/29/partners/s9TxpYCBakjPN6pDbBF-HGL/story.html

676 http://blog.thenewstribune.com/business/2013/06/10/tacomas-franciscan-health-system-expands-its-reach-to-bonney-lake-with-new-medical-pavilion/

677 http://www.library.ca.gov/crb/06/09/06-009.pdf

678 http://kff.org/other/state-indicator/beds/

679 http://econ.msu.edu/seminars/docs/freedman_nicubeds_1011.pdf

680 http://jama.jamanetwork.com/article.aspx?articleid=644551

681 http://www.washingtonpost.com/business/economy/spinal-fusions-serve-as-case-study-for-debate-over-when-certain-surgeries-are-necessary/2013/10/27/5f015efa-25ff-11e3-b3e9-d97fb087acd6_story.html?hpid=z1

682 http://www.nytimes.com/2013/06/02/health/colonoscopies-explain-why-us-leads-the-world-in-health-expenditures.html?hp&_r=0

683 http://www.nytimes.com/2014/01/19/health/patients-costs-skyrocket-specialists-incomes-soar.html?hp&_r=0

684 http://www.nytimes.com/2014/07/06/sunday-review/long-waits-for-doctors-appointments-have-become-the-norm.html?mabReward=RI%3A7&action=click&pgtype=Homepage&region=CColumn&module=Recommendation&src=rechp&WT.nav=RecEngine

685 http://www.newyorker.com/magazine/2015/05/11/overkill-atul-gawande

686 http://www.washingtonpost.com/business/economy/how-a-secretive-panel-uses-data-that-distorts-doctors-pay/2013/07/20/ee134e3a-eda8-11e2-9008-61e94a7ea20d_story.html

687 http://www.chron.com/news/texas/article/Feds-ban-some-Medicare-providers-in-crackdown-4689437.php

688 http://www.opensecrets.org/orgs/summary.php?id=D000000109

689 http://www.opensecrets.org/orgs/summary.php?id=D000021819

690 http://www.opensecrets.org/orgs/summary.php?id=D000000116

691 http://www.healthcostinstitute.org/files/HCCI_HCCUR2011.pdf

692 http://www.nytimes.com/1991/05/24/business/why-drugs-cost-more-in-us.html?pagewanted=all&src=pm

693 http://economix.blogs.nytimes.com/2013/11/19/medicare-part-d-republican-budget-busting/?src=rechp&_r=0

694 http://usatoday30.usatoday.com/news/washington/2007-05-10-senators-drug-bill_N.htm

695 http://www.gpo.gov/fdsys/pkg/CREC-2009-12-09/pdf/CREC-2009-12-09-pt1-PgS12745-2.pdf#page=45

696 http://www.gpo.gov/fdsys/pkg/CREC-2009-12-09/pdf/CREC-2009-12-09-pt1-PgS12745-2.pdf#page=45

697 http://www.nytimes.com/2015/04/15/us/doctor-in-menendez-case-is-indicted-on-medicare-fraud-charges.html?_r=0

698 http://www.nytimes.com/interactive/2014/10/28/us/politics/money-going-to-state-attorneys-general.html?_r=0

699 http://www.commonwealthfund.org/~/media/Files/Publications/In%20the%20Literature/2013/Apr/1685_Kanavos_higher_US_branded_drug_prices_HA_04_2013_ITL.pdf

700 http://www.aarp.org/content/dam/aarp/research/public_policy_institute/health/2013/lipitor-final-report-AARP-ppi-health.pdf

701 http://www.washingtonpost.com/business/economy/an-effective-eye-drug-is-available-for-50-but-many-doctors-choose-a-2000-alternative/2013/12/07/1a96628e-55e7-11e3-8304-caf30787c0a9_story.html?hpid=z1

702 http://www.thefiscaltimes.com/Articles/2013/06/27/Health-Care-CEOs-159-M-Pension-Is-a-Bitter-Pill.aspx#page1

703 http://www.justice.gov/opa/pr/2012/April/12-civ-539.html

704 http://www.opensecrets.org/politicians/contrib.php?cycle=2014&cid=N00007360

705 http://www.jsonline.com/watchdog/watchdogreports/charitys-investment-a-prescription-for-profits-for-drug-maker-p79tfc9-208027961.html

706 http://www.washingtonpost.com/business/economy/pharmaceutical-firms-paid-to-attend-meetings-of-panel-that-advises-fda-e-mails-show/2013/10/06/a02a2548-2b80-11e3-b139-029811dbb57f_story.html

707 http://mobile.nytimes.com/2014/06/25/opinion/refusals-to-pay-high-drug-prices.
     html?_r=0

708 http://seattletimes.com/text/2018396749.html

709 http://www.nytimes.com/2014/07/09/health/some-generic-drug-prices-are-soaring.
     html?ref=us

710 http://www.wsj.com/articles/pharmaceutical-companies-buy-rivals-drugs-then-jack-
     up-the-prices-1430096431

711 Id.

712 Id.

713 http://www.rollingstone.com/politics/news/in-defense-of-obama-
     20141008#ixzz3Fm1qk6Xi

714 http://www.washingtonpost.com/page/2010-2019/WashingtonPost/2014/04/29/Nation-
     al-Politics/Polling/question_13961.xml?uuid=tnco4s9TEeOnFL5-fxQghQ

715 http://www.nejm.org/doi/full/10.1056/NEJMp1305298

716 http://www.nytimes.com/interactive/2014/10/27/us/is-the-affordable-care-act-working.
     html?_r=0#/

717 Id.

718 http://content.healthaffairs.org/content/early/2014/08/27/hlthaff.2014.0560.full.
     pdf+html

719 http://www.pwc.com/us/en/health-industries/behind-the-numbers/key-findings.jhtml

720 http://www.pwc.com/us/en/health-industries/behind-the-numbers/key-findings.jhtml

721 http://www.pwc.com/us/en/health-industries/behind-the-numbers/health-cost-defla-
     tors-high-deductible-plans.jhtml

722 http://kff.org/private-insurance/report/2013-employer-health-benefits/

723 http://us.milliman.com/MMI/

724 http://economics.mit.edu/files/7870

725 http://content.healthaffairs.org/content/early/2014/08/27/hlthaff.2014.0560.full.
     pdf+html

726 http://www.politico.com/story/2015/05/how-affordable-is-the-affordable-care-
     act-118428.html

727 https://www.whitehouse.gov/the-press-office/2015/07/02/remarks-president-discus-
     sion-affordable-care-act-nashville-tn

728 http://www.nytimes.com/2015/07/04/us/health-insurance-companies-seek-big-rate-
     increases-for-2016.html?hp&action=click&pgtype=Homepage&module=first-column-
     region&region=top-news&WT.nav=top-news&_r=0

729 http://thehill.com/blogs/congress-blog/healthcare/247288-the-aca-and-insurance-rate-hikes

19) MOVING FORWARD

730 http://www.pbs.org/moyers/journal/07312009/ahip1.pdf

731 http://www.pbs.org/moyers/journal/07312009/ahip2.pdf

732 http://www.bloombergview.com/articles/2014-10-22/sorry-obamacare-is-still-unfixable

733 http://mobile.nytimes.com/2014/05/26/us/irs-bars-employers-from-dumping-workers-into-health-exchanges.html?from=homepage

734 http://www.nytimes.com/2014/07/26/us/politics/insurer-backed-health-care-ad-illustrates-opaque-finance-system.html?hpw&action=click&pgtype=Homepage&version=HpHedThumbWell&module=well-region&region=bottom-well&WT.nav=bottom-well&_r=0

735 http://democrats.energycommerce.house.gov/index.php?q=news/democratic-leaders-introduce-legislation-to-save-taxpayers-more-than-140-billion-in-medicare-dr

736 http://www.cdc.gov/nchs/fastats/life-expectancy.htm

737 http://seattletimes.com/html/localnews/2023709134_safetynetxml.html

738 Id.

739 http://www.washingtonpost.com/politics/blogsandcolumns/healthcaregov-doesnt-help-obamas-argument-for-greater-government/2013/10/26/6259aafa-3e44-11e3-b0e7-716179a2c2c7_story.html?hpid=z10

740 http://m.washingtonpost.com/opinions/restore-balancing-among-the-branches-of-government-in-washington/2014/06/27/81440022-f49d-11e3-b633-0de077c9f768_story.html

741 http://www.nejm.org/doi/full/10.1056/NEJMp1212974

742 http://vtdigger.org/2012/02/07/shumlin-bends-on-health-benefits-exchange/

743 http://www.burlingtonfreepress.com/story/news/politics/2014/11/05/two-term-incumbent-governor-nearly-lost/18563053/

744 http://www.nejm.org/doi/full/10.1056/NEJMp1501050?query=TOC&utm_campaign=KHN%3A+Daily+Health+Policy+Report&utm_source=hs_email&utm_medium=email&utm_content=17254971&_hsenc=p2ANqtz--hC-SV5xWnbS12zKBh-6WxT4cvwWmnIPzz1sEfv_eYvDKifDWu514AjG_ZiBsQrCGK11crxQ8byykFH46X-Mi2XVMN4Hbg&_hsmi=17254971&

745 http://www.mass.gov/governor/agenda/healthcare/cost-containment/summary-health-care-payment-reform-conference-committee-report.pdf

746 http://www.washingtonpost.com/blogs/wonkblog/
wp/2014/01/10/%253Fp%253D74854/

747 http://www.washingtonpost.com/blogs/wonkblog/wp/2013/02/25/oregon-gov-john-
kitzhaber-no-one-thinks-fee-for-service-is-working/

748 http://www.thenation.com/article/174473/john-kitzhabers-oregon-dream?page=0,2

749 http://www.oregon.gov/oha/OHPB/Pages/members.aspx

750 http://www.oregon.gov/oha/OHPB/Pages/health-reform/certification/CCO-Govern-
ing-Boards.aspx

751 http://www.governing.com/topics/health-human-services/Nations-Only-Health-Insur-
ance-Commissioner-Takes-Health-Care-System.html

752 http://www.ohic.ri.gov/documents/Press/PressReleases/2010%20Lifespan%20BCB-
SRI%20Press%20Release/1_Press%20Release%20Lifespan%20BCBSRI.pdf

753 http://www.providencejournal.com/breaking-news/content/20130703-r.i.-senate-oks-
hittner-as-health-insurance-chief.ece

754 http://online.wsj.com/public/resources/documents/WSJNBCpoll04232014.pdf

755 http://www.thenation.com/blog/174830/health-insurance-lobby-gears-defeat-effort-
strengthen-obamacare-california

756 http://www.latimes.com/local/political/la-me-health-insurance-20141103-story.html

757 http://online.wsj.com/news/articles/SB10001424052702303468704579572724216799330

758 http://www.stophighercosts.com/wp-content/uploads/2014/05/Kingsdale-Report-
May-2014.pdf

759 http://www.latimes.com/business/la-fi-health-rates-ballot-20140703-story.html

760 http://www.sacbee.com/2014/08/21/6645891/california-health-exchange-weighs.html

761 http://www.latimes.com/local/politics/la-me-cap-proposition45-20141016-column.
html

762 http://m.sfgate.com/bayarea/matier-ross/article/Dignity-Health-spends-big-at-Levi-s-
Stadium-5753830.php

763 http://blog.sfgate.com/nov05election/2014/11/06/nancy-pelosi-turned-tide-on-
prop-45/

764 http://kff.org/private-insurance/report/survey-of-non-group-health-insurance-enroll-
ees/

765 http://www.floir.com/PressReleases/viewmediarelease.aspx?id=2070

766 http://publiccorruption.moreland.ny.gov/sites/default/files/moreland_report_final.pdf

767 http://seattletimes.com/html/opinion/2024345477_seancorryeleanorhamburgeroped-
mentalhealthparity20xml.html

768 http://seattletimes.com/html/editorialsopinionpages/2024321014_whatstroublingmentalhealthcare.html

769 http://www.courts.wa.gov/opinions/pdf/889406.pdf

770 http://www.courts.wa.gov/opinions/pdf/889406.pdf

771 http://seattletimes.com/html/editorials/2024779477_editmentalhealthparity15xml.html

772 https://dchealthlink.com/node/1788

773 http://online.wsj.com/article/SB10001424127887323475304578501820197828966.html?mod=WSJ_hp_LEFTWhatsNewsCollection

774 http://www.cbpp.org/cms/index.cfm?fa=view&id=2223

775 http://www.nytimes.com/2013/06/08/your-money/fine-print-and-red-tape-in-long-term-care-policies.html?pagewanted=all&_r=0

776 http://m.washingtonpost.com/local/dc-politics/broad-new-tax-to-fund-dc-health-exchange-challenged-in-court/2014/07/03/5b4bdfd8-02d1-11e4-8572-4b1b969b6322_story.html?tid=HP_local

777 http://www.cms.gov/Research-Statistics-Data-and-Systems/Statistics-Trends-and-Reports/ReportsTrustFunds/Downloads/2014TRAlternativeScenario.pdf

778 http://www.nytimes.com/2012/09/07/health/policy/long-term-care-looms-as-rising-medicaid-cost.html?pagewanted=all&_r=0

779 http://www.nytimes.com/2013/06/24/nyregion/reinventing-long-term-care-and-endorsing-firms-accused-of-fraud.html?src=rechp&_r=0

780 http://mobile.nytimes.com/2014/05/09/nyregion/medicaid-shift-fuels-rush-for-profitable-clients.html?from=homepage

781 Gar Alperovitz, *What Then Must We Do?*, 84.

782 https://www.cbo.gov/sites/default/files/cbofiles/attachments/49892-breakout-AppendixB.pdf

CPSIA information can be obtained at www.ICGtesting.com
Printed in the USA
LVOW06s0921090815

449425LV00017B/686/P